Sovereignty of Death

Rob Weatherill

REBUS PRESS

© Rob Weatherill

First edition 1998

Printed in Great Britain

All rights reserved

No part of this book may be reprinted or reproduced or utilised in any form or by any electronic, mechanical or other means, now known or hereafter invented, including photocopying and recording, or in any information storage or retrieval system, without permission in writing from the publishers.

Rebus Press
76 Haverstock Hill
LONDON
NW3 2BE

ISBN 1 900877 11 2

For Margaret, Ben and John

ACKNOWLEDGMENTS...

This book has evolved through a number of metamorphoses in recent years, through lectures and discussion with students of psychotherapy and psychoanalysis, through debate and work with many colleagues in the Irish Forum for Psychoanalytic Psychotherapy and the Association for Psychoanalytic Psychotherapy of Ireland, and indeed friends and colleagues outside the psychoanalytic milieu. Their feedback and criticism has been crucial. Not least, I should like to thank my immediate family for their tolerance and patience in my long hours of seclusion and oftentimes bad humour and bouts of anxiety that accompany a project such as this.

I should like to thank Dr. Cormac Gallagher for permission to quote from his privately circulated translations of the works of Jacques Lacan, in particular, Lacan's article in *Encyclopédie Française*, *La Famille*, also, *Seminar V, The Formation of the Unconscious*, and *Seminar X, On Anxiety*. My thanks also to Tavistock publications for permission to quote from the English Translation of Lacan's *Ecrits*. My thanks to Sage Publications Ltd. for permission to quote from Jean Baudrillard's *Symbolic Exchange and Death* (1993).

I am most grateful also to the staff of Rebus Press, in particular, Kirsty Hall for her interest in this work, for her careful reading of the manuscript, her support and encouragement throughout.

Finally, the many hours I have spend with my analysands and supervisees have grounded my speculations and sharpened my perceptions in psychoanalytic theory and practice. However, what I write here and the inevitable mixture of clarity, bias and prejudice, etc. is entirely my responsibility.

Rob Weatherill, Dublin, 1997

CONTENTS

	PREFACE	1
1	FREUD ON THE DEATH DRIVE	7
2	KLEIN ON ENVY AND PERSECUTION	29
3	BION: UNLINKING, UNTHINKING	53
4	LACAN: SPEAKING AROUND DEATH	73
5	ENTROPY, HELPLESSNESS AND APOPTOSIS	103
6	ENJOY DEATH: INITIATORY PROCESSES?	119
7	BAUDRILLARD: FREUD AGAINST FREUD	149
8	CONCLUSION: CLINICAL IMPERATIVES	175
	NOTES	187
	BIBLIOGRAPHY	197
	INDEX	208

PREFACE

This book puts together some ideas that have been developed around Freud's controversial second reference point - namely the death drive (*Todestrieb*). Formulated in 1920, the death drive problematizes and subverts the whole productivity of psychoanalysis as a therapy and a system of meaning. Consequently, death drive theory has been rejected by many analysts, and completely rejected outside of psychoanalysis itself. The very negativity of the concept, as we shall see, runs totally against the cultural grain. This book, however, takes a different viewpoint, namely, believing, firstly that psychoanalysis can claim some credit for still holding to and keeping faith with this controversial ground of human suffering, and secondly that exploring this curse, this malediction, may itself may be redemptive.

If Freud, as I shall argue, was to undermine his own brilliant theoretical superstructure, he wrote at a time of widespread cultural change and ferment. Freud had already proudly included psychoanalysis in the modern tradition of the decentring of man from his narcissistic belief in being at the centre of the universe. Firstly, he claimed he was following Copernicus, who in 1543 introduced the heliocentric theory of planetary motion over and against the Ptolemaic geocentric view. Secondly, the 1859 Darwinian theory of evolution removed *Homo sapiens* from his privileged position in creation. Then, at the end of Lecture XVIII of *The Introductory Lectures* in 1916-17, Freud states: '... human megalomania will have suffered its third and most wounding blow from the psychological research of the present time which it seeks to prove to the ego that it is not even master in its own house...'(Freud 1916-17 p.285)

Close to the time of the death drive formulation itself, science was busy abolishing stable absolutes. In 1911, Rutherford proposed that the atom was mostly *empty space*, with an immensely dense nucleus orbited by electrons. The new physics was fast destroying cherished certainties. Heisenberg's 'uncertainty principle', formulated in 1927, established *indeterminacy* as an inherent property of sub-atomic matter. The speed and position of an electron cannot be established simultaneously: if you establish its speed you cannot establish its accurate position, and vice-versa. Here the energy required to observe the particle's position accurately, inescapably alters its speed. The act of observation can no longer be independent of the object being observed, at least at this infinitesimal level, at the level of quantum mechanics.

The reality perspective of the observer has from now on to be taken into account. This was part of an older problem of whether or not light consists of particles or waves. Depending upon the perspective of the observer, light can be seen as continuous electromagnetic waves, or conversely, as streams of packets of energy, photons. In 1916, Einstein published his *General Theory of Relativity* which followed the earlier papers on the Special theory of Relativity. Here, the defining absolutes of time and space were abandoned. Similarly, with the publication of the famous formula, $E=mc^2$, matter and energy become equivalent and interchangeable. In the field of linguistics, Ferdinand de Saussaure's treatise, *Cours de Linguistique Generale*, produced in 1915, ended any *natural* equivalence between words (signifiers) and what they signify in reality (signifieds). Here begins the autonomy of language, and the radical break with the notion that language simply *reflects* reality.

In August 1914, Kafka began writing *The Trial*, the same month that the Great War started. According to George Steiner, 'Kafka prophesied the actual forms of the disaster of Western humanism which Nietzsche and Kierkegaard had seen like an uncertain blackness on the horizon' (In Bradbury, 1988, p260). This work followed on other prophetic works: for instance, Dostoevsky's *Crime and Punishment* (1866), *The Possessed* (1892), Conrad's, *The Heart of Darkness* (1902), *The Secret Agent* (1907). And in 1922, T. S. Eliot published *The Waste Land*.

Freud warns us ominously, at the end of that same lecture XVIII referred to above: 'beyond all this we have yet to disturb the peace of the world in still another way'. We may presume this to be the death drive theory which is a convulsion within the revolutionary nature of psychoanalysis itself. Freud was asserting that Eros, life and the Good are *not* primary, but that death is. Here, Freud is breaking profoundly with a whole tradition of Christian and Western metaphysics, by resurrecting a notion of radical evil, a heretical notion of a terrifying autonomy of malice. The domain of the repressed unconscious was revolutionary enough, but the death drive is yet more and beyond. A simple formula: the unconscious decentres; the death drive decentres absolutely.

Thus, the foregoing will be an exploration of this demon that haunts psychoanalysis. At the outset, this contribution will not be setting out to prove the truth or otherwise of any of these hypotheses, and this must especially be the case with the death drive theory. Instead, these ideas are interesting *in themselves*, as a way of working with, structuring and organising thought about mental life, culture and human subjectivity. Freud himself took a similar view in 'Why War', his address to Einstein: 'It may perhaps seem to you as though our theories are a kind of mythology and, in the present case, not even an agreeable one. But does not every science come in the end to be a kind of mythology like this? Cannot the same be said today of your own Physics?'. (1933b, p. 211). Even science itself undermines its own verities. All its hard experiential findings must be regarded as provisional, as refracted from the real of the universe of possible meanings. These also are myths in the true sense - narratives set up to explain other narratives. Psychoanalytic myths, like those of the natural sciences, are not therefore untrue, but fascinating stories whose veiled meanings are waiting to be discovered afresh. At their best, they are elegant, enigmatic, compelling and challenging.

The term psychoanalysis has become something of a catch-all phrase with boundaries that have become stretched, blurred and fractured. Allegiances have become strong, disparate and fought over, so that few practitioners can span the whole discipline. The foregoing is work in progress and is unashamedly eclectic. The author subscribes to the view of the British Independent tradition, which takes from all orthodoxies as it sees fit (see Rayner, 1991). No attempt here has been made to limit different perspectives, although tentative syntheses have been made on occasion. However, the reader must be prepared for discontinuity for two reasons: (1) it is not really possible or desirable to integrate, for instance, the Lacanian and the non-Lacanian psychoanalytic perspectives (most writers limit themselves to one or other position) and (2) the subject matter of the book, the death drive itself, is *disintegrative*, in that structure, language, the code of human discourse inevitably opens upon an ecstatic void. Both the content and the style of the book reflect this disintegrative effect. I constantly reiterate this point of failure. However, against this fragmentation, I believe that psychoanalysis must maintain some centre of gravity in order to avoid what would otherwise be a fatal dispersal into holistic psychotherapy and counselling on the one side, or medicine, or religion on the other. Psychoanalysis must maintain a difference or lose its identity altogether. This work, therefore, lies somewhere between dispersal and integration. If the death drive theory decentres and destabilizes psychoanalysis itself, at least the discipline will have been undermined from its *own* rigour, rather than being led away and domesticated by social need.

The book asks a number of questions. Is the death drive just another word for human destructiveness? Is any accommodation possible between Eros and Thanatos, or does one trend have the upper hand? Undoubtedly, religion and modern psychotherapy seem to favour Eros. Or is the death drive beyond any dialectical relationship between good and evil? Is the death drive a biological drive as such, in spite of the fact that the science of biology will have nothing to do with it because it is anti-evolutionist? Or, rather than being some mysterious biological given underlying life, is the death drive theory constructed - not discovered - by Freud in a *particular* human and historical context? In other words, is the theory simply an *effect* of twentieth century culture? Thinking clinically, how does the death drive manifest itself, and if one takes the theory seriously, how will this affect one's clinical practice? Is the theory a fatally reductive one, making all human suffering inevitable, distancing attention perhaps from the importance of *external* sources of aggression in infancy, childhood and the wider culture? Freud himself was concerned that his theory might be used to justify war and stressed the need to strengthen Eros by encouraging emotional ties between people. If there is a connection between the death drive and aggression, there is the question of forms of aggression that are life promoting - might these get lost in a one-sided preoccupation with destructiveness? What is the connection between the death drive, madness and psychosis?

The first four chapters of the book attempt an overall theoretical understanding of the death drive theory as elaborated and developed by four leading psychoanalytic pioneers, namely Freud, Klein, Bion and Lacan. Chapter one briefly traces the history of Freud's drive theory before focusing on his final duality of the life and death drives. Here we try to situate the death drive, as Freud does himself, clinically, topographically, and from an evolutionary point of view, before considering some of the important arguments raised against this theory since its inception.

In chapter two, we follow Klein's exposition of the fate of the death drive in the primitive splitting of the infantile ego, the early development of the super-ego, greed, envy and the anguished sense of loss that accompanies these intense affects. Klein's unique contribution to human thought is briefly and critically examined, and consideration is given as to how her ideas may, to some degree, have been influenced by her own turbulent life.

In chapter three, Bion's theory of the psychotic process, which further develops Kleinian thought, is discussed. Briefly, the psychotic process attacks the structure of thought and the fundamental links that make thinking possible. Also considered is Bion's influential concept of the container/ contained and his paradoxical and quasi-mystical notion of the analyst as container, 'without memory, desire or understanding'.

In chapter four, we cross the divide, as it were, to review Lacanian psychoanalysis. Here, it is the human *subject* that is subjected to death from the three Lacanian registers, namely, the Symbolic, the Imaginary and the Real. Death haunts the subject while he speaks and tries to fill that appalling gap that opens as soon as the subject is torn away from the (maternal) world and obliged to accede to human language. Much attention is given to Lacan's register of the Real, the impossible real of sex and death, and in this context consideration is given to Laplanche's theory of primal seduction. The objet *a* - the object that must be lost, must interminably be searched for, yet which must never be entirely rediscovered - is discussed with examples of the radical destabilization that can occur when this object (of death) reappears in the life of the subject. Finally, what happens when repression which ultimately stands guard over life, begins to fail?

Chapter five, in a very different vein, takes Freud's *biological* speculations a little further. Biology illustrates very clearly the interweaving of life and death and it also shows that life must be seen as an antientropic process. All this is well known. What is less well known are recent findings in cell biology which indicate that cells need to signal to each other continuously in order to save themselves from dying. This phenomenon is known as apoptosis and it carries interesting parallels with Freud's death drive theory.

Moving from the biological back towards the psychological, chapter six enters upon an extended and persuasive discussion of the *redemptive* value of death and suffering, as delineated by humanistic, integrative and spiritual psychotherapies. Towards the end of this chapter, however, such notions of healing and transcendentalism are criticized as inadequate and illusory.

Chapter seven looks at the stimulating, interesting and provocative work of Baudrillard, by way of complicating the picture further. Here death is linked with 'symbolic exchange' which Baudrillard believes haunts the subject in modernity in its (fatal) pursuit of the one-sided accumulation of life capital. The exorcism of death in modernity condemns us to an *equivalent* death in life, a deferred death as banal and interminable survival. This is one meaning of the death drive. For

Baudrillard, the primordial principle of reversibility or seduction precedes, undermines and subverts the whole modern world's erection of 'phallic' production, which he claims is everywhere collapsing into indifference and impotence. As classical psychoanalysis itself is part of this elaborate production of meaning, it too has been seduced by its own theorizations. Furthermore, as the psychoanalytic project was based largely on its denial of seduction at its origin, seduction has now returned in virulent forms. However, Baudrillard's critical notion is that when *everything is real* and transparent under what he regards as the obscene glare of media-technology, which allows for *no* secret, *no* enigma, *no* shadow. This is 'cool seduction', which no longer plays, allures, challenges, but instead exposes us without protection or charm to the *pure operation* of sex and death.

Finally, by way of conclusion, some assessment is made of the clinical imperatives that follow from the complex and conflicted discussion of earlier chapters. What must now be the fate of the discourse of truth with which psychoanalysis has always been entangled, when every truth is subverted in an endless de-centring process? What now must be at the heart of the psychoanalytic encounter and outcome?

This book attempts to put together psychoanalytic concepts in a new and invigorating way. Therefore, it may prove of interest to students and practitioners of psychotherapy alike. Using the single vehicle of the death drive, we are attempting to remain precariously amidst the conflicts, suffering and contradictions of human subjectivity. Consequently my aim is that this book might make interesting and provocative reading well beyond psychoanalysis . It raises issues that go to the heart of human hope itself.

One problem remains, namely the term 'death drive' itself. Firstly, the notion has an archaic and reductive ring to it, as if it is the final explanation for everything emerging out of the arrogance of modern scientific positivism. It is a totalising, consummate term that closes down meaning in an absolute determinacy. Ironically, at the same time it connotes the entropic capacity to fragment and disperse meaning to infinity - radical *in*-determinacy. Either way it signifies inordinate inhuman power. There might be very good reasons, therefore, for leaving it to one side. In the clinical situation it can either be avoided or disbelieved, or it can be encountered.

1. FREUD ON THE DEATH DRIVE

Vicissitudes of theory

In Freud's early formulations on the nature of instinct[1] he had assumed that there were *two* major instincts governing human behaviour. On the one hand there was the sexual instinct, connected with the drive for pleasure, and on the other there was the ego instinct, which strove for self-preservation. Using these conceptualisations, Freud was able to account for many of the psychological phenomena that he had been studying. They were explained as the conflicts and compromises produced between the demands of the sexual instincts over and against the demands of the self preservative ego instincts. In this way he could explain that the sexual instincts created the wishes or desires latently present in dreams, jokes, slips of the tongue, pathogenic ideas, and so on, whereas the ego instincts, realizing that the acting-out of these wishes would spell disaster, institute a process of suppression or repression into the unconscious. A compromise would be reached between these two conflicting instinctual tendencies, so that what would emerge would be the *manifest* dream, the joke, the bungled action or the neurotic symptom.

However, in 1914 Freud's observations on narcissism led him to revise his instinctual theory. Narcissism involves an excessive self-regard, or self-love and aggrandizement. It clearly should form part of the ego instincts: but narcissism also involves a *diminution* of sexual energy. The more narcissistic a person is the less they can love, and vice versa. The inverse relationship between sexuality and narcissism is well illustrated by the person who is ill. He tends to become withdrawn and self-centred and not interested in sexuality. On the other hand the person who is in love tends to undervalue himself and is the opposite of narcissistic. So it seemed that the sexual instincts and the ego instincts were not independent of one another, as Freud had thought, but instead were manifestations of one basic instinct. Love of self and love of others are part of the ebb and flow of what Freud referred to as 'libido'.

In his paper 'On Narcissism' (1914a), he suggested that sexual libido should be understood as object libido or ego libido, depending upon whether it is invested in external objects or the self. Its energy is the same, the major difference deriving from the memories and ideas it invests. Ego instinct functions are now taken over by ego libido; the sexual instinct is now referred to as object libido. Thus ego libido and object libido are interchangeable manifestations of one basic instinct.

This view of human behaviour as being moved by a *single* and highly generalised sexual instinct was maintained by Freud for the next six years[2]. But it was his observations on the *compulsion to repeat* that led him to his final formulation of the life and death instincts. The so-called 'repetition compulsion' (*Wiederholungzwang*) seems to deny one of the basic tenets of psychoanalysis, namely the striving for pleasure. Moreover, the repetition compulsion seemed to be a troubling and fundamental force in human experience. We will look at it more closely before seeing how Freud derived his final instinctual duality from these considerations.

Repetition in life of pleasant or happy situations can be readily accepted since these accord with the pleasure principle and commonsense. But Freud had uncovered abundant evidence of the compulsion to repeat painful and unpleasant experiences. For instance, in the Dora case (1905), Dora had unconsciously re-created her painful relationship to Herr K in her transference to Freud, who now became the new focus of her ambivalent feelings. She was repeating with her doctor the same constellation of complex feelings that she had felt for Herr K. This indeed led her to break off the treatment with Freud prematurely.

Freud was clear that what cannot be remembered in words, is expressed in action. He gives some examples in his paper 'Remembering, Repeating and Working-Through' (1914b): firstly there is the patient, who as a boy was critical and defiant towards his father, now repeating that attitude towards his doctor who is trying to help him. In a second case, instead of remembering being ashamed of sexual activities as a child, the patient repeats this sense of shame, but now in relation to the process of his analysis. In another, the patient does not remember the feelings of helpless deadlock he reached as a child in searching for the truth about sexual matters, but now feels confused and blocked, and complains that he can never carry anything through to completion in his adult life.

Freud noted that the play of children also illustrated this compulsion to repeat. He cited the *fort-da* game of his grandson. He also suggested that a child who has undergone an unpleasant experience, such as a medical procedure, will re-enact in his subsequent play the earlier experiences. But this time the playmate may be on the receiving end. Freud came to realize that this type of repetition was done in the hope of mastering a potentially traumatic situation. By repeating the act over and over, the child gains a sense of retrospective control.

The best examples of all are the so-called traumatic neuroses, that Freud observed in the casualties of World War 1, when very stressful events often caused by 'close calls' rather than actual physical injury, are repeated in anxiety attacks and nightmares in which they re-live the terrible moment. But how could such repetitions of clearly very painful experiences be understood in terms of the pleasure and reality principles, and the striving for tension reduction? Clearly, the compulsion to repeat involves an increase in tension and unpleasure, and therefore should be totally avoided. Altogether, Freud noted repetition of painful experiences operating in four broad areas: the painful repetitions of transference; the tragic life histories of people; the traumatic neuroses and aspects of children's play.

The vesicle in danger

In 1920 Freud tried to deal with these anomalies in his speculative and controversial work, *Beyond the Pleasure Principle*. Here he asks the reader to consider the psychical apparatus as a 'vesicle' capable of being stimulated. Its existence in the external world, exposes it to a constant bombardment by external stimuli. The outermost layer therefore forms a crust that becomes ideally suited to perceive external reality, and also to protect the internal parts of the vesicle. The outside layer dies, and 'by its death, the outermost layer has saved the deeper one from a similar fate ... *Protection against* stimuli is an almost more important function for the living organism than the *reception* of stimuli.' (1920, pp. 298-9). So the receptive layer has been withdrawn from the surface and all that remains are the special sense organs which sample the external world in small quantities. At this point, Freud speculates on Kant's notion that 'time and space are necessary forms of [conscious] thought.' (ibid. p. 299) However, earlier Freud has pointed out that the unconscious is timeless. (1915a) Freud concludes that perhaps our abstract notion of time and space also works as a shield against excessive stimuli - by *spreading them out*, as it were, along the axis of time. Hence, we can take energies, from the drives, in *small* doses, small enough to *bind* them and preserve them from destruction.

Such a vesicle also receives stimulation from *within* against which there is no equivalent protective shield, and these stimuli give rise to the pleasure-unpleasure series. But these endogenous energies may be much less than the external ones, or, Freud suggests, 'the excitations coming from within are, however, in their intensity ... more commensurate with the system's method of working than the stimuli which stream in from the external world.' (1920, p. 300) The crust has the function therefore of reducing external stimuli to roughly the same magnitude as those arising from endogenous sources. Therefore the normal state of affairs in the psyche is one of relatively low energy levels. Also, too great an increase of *inner* stimulus can be treated as if it were coming from the *outside*. This is the origin of projection, to which we will return again and again.

When this normal quiet state of affairs in the psyche obtains, mental functioning operates according to the pleasure and reality principles. It is only when the psyche receives a traumatic amount of stimulation, which *breaks through* the protective crust, that normal functioning is suspended. The breech in the crust leads to the deployment of the 'second line of defence', a so-called 'quiescent cathexis' which attempts to 'bind' the energy surging in. This is accompanied by anxiety - a necessary phenomenon if this second line of defence is going to hold.

Physical injury involves a massive 'narcissistic cathexis' in which libido is invested in the injured part of the self. Since the injured parts are associated closely with the trauma itself, the narcissistic cathexis serves the same function as the quiescent cathexis in dealing with the traumatic breech.

The person who is in some way prepared for the trauma, and the person who is actually physically injured by it, fare better than the person who is neither prepared nor injured. For this group, the second line of defence is not established, the crust is unprotected, and the psyche is traumatically flooded with masses of external stimulation. Now in order to try and deal with this devastation, *after* the event, the organism initiates a process in which it becomes 'retrospectively anxious' about the trauma. It has to go over it again and again in order to relive it sufficiently, to cathect it enough, to form that second line of defence behind the breech. This involves the reliving again and again of the unpleasant memories and feelings of the events with great intensity and pain. This clearly contradicts the pleasure principle. It is this painful re-living with all its distressing consequences which is the organism's attempt to bind and understand what has happened. This is the *function* of the compulsion to repeat, which requires the suspension of the pleasure principle. It is indeed the *beyond* of the pleasure principle. The needs of the organism when traumatized in this way seem to go far beyond the pursuit of pleasure. There is much more at stake, involving survival itself.

It was therefore his understanding of the compulsion to repeat that led Freud to the death instinct. He felt that there was something uncanny and irresistible about this compulsion, it had an almost instinctual flavour. ('instinctual' is not a good translation of the German *Triebhaft*, which has more urgency than the English equivalent). He went on to suggest that there must be an instinct to repeat, and that perhaps repetition is a property of *all* instincts: '*It seems, then, that an instinct is an urge inherent in all organic life to restore an earlier state of things* which the living entity has been obliged to abandon under the pressure of external disturbing forces...' (1920, p. 36)

This is the conservative trend of all instincts, and it is part of a trend that is inherent in life, namely to return to its origins in the inorganic state. He is asserting what seems on the face of it a rather perverse theory, namely that '*the aim of all life is death.*' (1920, p. 38) Not only death in general but a particular kind of death which might be different for different species. He cites the example of the salmon that undergo terrible ordeals to return to the place of their own conception, to spawn and then to die. This is not just any death, but a particular kind of death that regressively recreates earlier stages of existence.

However, *external* reality demands of the instincts that they should *not* be conservative and regressive, but progressive and life enhancing. This external reality creates obstacles to the organism's unique path towards death, so these obstacles must be fought off by the instinct. Here the instincts can actually take on life enhancing properties, as they deal with these obstacles that stand in the way of the pursuit of death. There is a temporary *diversion* of the drives into the circuit of life.

Whatever one may think about an organism desiring its own particular death (an issue that we will take up in chapter five), Freud had theorized about a pool of destructive energy, a destructive instinct, with which he was able to explain many puzzling clinical phenomena. The death instinct, like the sexual instincts or libido (now called the life instincts), can be directed *outwards* towards others, or inwards towards the self. In the former it becomes aggressive acts and behaviour; in the latter it becomes self-destructive. The libido, or the life instinct, has the task of deflecting the death instinct outwards, with the help of the musculature, where it becomes the instinct for mastery or the will to power. Some of the instinct joins or fuses with the libido and thus becomes sadism. Some of the instinct remains within the organism where it is bound by libido into masochism.

By 1920, we have a new instinctual duality: the life instincts (also the libido, the sexual instincts, also in some sense at least, the instincts of self preservation and the ego instincts) versus the death instincts. But Freud asks: 'Is it really the case that there are no instincts that... aim at a state of things which has never yet been attained?' (1920, p. 41) Is there an instinct for evolution and progressivity? He goes on to answer emphatically:

> I know of no certain example from the organic world that would contradict the characterization I have thus proposed. There is unquestionably no universal instinct towards higher development observable in the animal or plant world... It may be difficult, too, for many of us, to abandon the belief that there is an instinct towards perfection at work in human beings, which has brought them to their present level of intellectual achievement and ethical sublimation ... I cannot see how this benevolent illusion is to be preserved' (ibid. pp. 41-2)

But, Freud continues, 'What appears in a minority of human individuals as an untiring impulsion towards further perfection can easily be understood as a result of instinctual *repression* upon which is based all that is most precious in human civilization... The backward path that leads to *complete* satisfaction [death] is as a rule obstructed by the resistances which maintain the repressions (ibid. p. 42 my italics). Consequently, it is only when instinctuality is repressed, blocked from full satisfaction that there is civilization - striving after the barely attainable, the highest forms of human achievement. Eros, the capacity to produce higher and higher unities and syntheses, works *only because repression works.*

At this point, it might well be asked, why Freud should have developed and maintained for the next 20 years against considerable opposition such a malign view of life, viz, that it aims towards its own particular death. Apart from the clinical material, referred to above and below, which need explanation, there are undoubtedly personal factors at work. Firstly, Freud had been shocked as had many others by the terrible slaughter and carnage of the World War 1. This trauma had shattered the pre-war optimistic vision of unfettered scientific progress, and the vision of human goodness. Freud, commenting on the death instinct in the *New Introductory Lectures*, observed that the 'belief in the 'goodness' of human nature is one of those evil illusions by which mankind expect their lives to be beautified and made easier while in reality they only cause damage.' (1933, p. 104) Secondly, it is clear from Jones's (1957) biography that Freud was a man obsessed with death. He thought about dying every day after he was forty. The first signs of his cancer did not appear until early 1923, but it is possible that when he wrote *Beyond the Pleasure Principle* his well known preoccupation with death was intensifying, and the death instinct theory was a way of structuring and assimilating this great anxiety about his own death. It was also during this last phase of his life that his own mother died. Thirdly, Freud had always thought in dualistic terms, in terms of opposing forces and conflict. With his new ideas on narcissism, and the notion of one basic instinct, the libido, the old dualism between the sexual and the self-preservative instincts had broken down. A new dualism was sought, not least because Freud was coming dangerously close to Jung's idea of libido as an all embracing psychic energy. A new force was required to oppose the libido. This was to be the death instinct.

Clinically

In his work, *Civilization and its Discontents*, Freud states that 'man's natural aggressive instinct, the hostility of each against all and all against each, opposes this programme of civilization. The aggressive instinct, is the derivative and the main representative of the death instinct, which we have found alongside of Eros...' (1930, p. 122) In the *New Introductory Lectures*, he discusses the fusion of Eros and the death instinct, and encourages analysts to make use of the theory *clinically*. He goes on to say, 'we may regard the self-destructiveness as the expression of a 'death instinct' which cannot fail to be present in every vital process ....some portion of the death instinct remains operative within the organism and we have sought to trace quite a number of normal and pathological processes and phenomena to this internalization of the destructive instinct.' (1933, p. 107)

We will briefly turn our attention to those clinical phenomena for which the death instinct may hold the key. As has been noted, the widespread compulsion to repeat is part and parcel of any neurotic or psychotic process, and Freud now speculates this compulsion represents a regressive propensity inherent in life itself. Psychoanalysts had been finding ambivalence, aggressiveness, sadism, masochism, particularly in illnesses like obsessional neurosis and melancholia. As early as 1915, Freud had introduced the idea of *primary* masochism. This is no secondary reaction to frustration from an external object, but a destructiveness that is inherent in life itself. In *The Ego and The Id* (1923), Freud points out that the death instinct can be seen in almost a pure form when it tends to become *defused* from the life instinct. This happens in the case of severe depression, or melancholia when the sadism of the super-ego becomes 'a pure culture of the death instinct'. (1923, p. 53) In *An Outline of Psychoanalysis* (1937), Freud observes the operation of the death instinct in masochism, the unconscious sense of guilt and the negative therapeutic reaction.

In 'The Economic Problem of Masochism' Freud identifies three kinds of masochism - erotogenic, feminine and moral. He cites moral masochism as a good example of the fusion of instinct. 'Its danger lies in the fact that it originates from the death instinct and corresponds to the part of that instinct which has escaped being turned outwards as an instinct of destruction.' (1924, p. 170) However, moral masochism assumes a different structure. According to Freud:

> All other masochistic sufferings carry with them the condition that they shall emanate from the loved person and shall be endured at his command. This restriction has been dropped in moral masochism. The suffering itself is what matters; whether it is decreed by someone who is loved or by someone who is indifferent is of no importance. It may even be caused by impersonal powers or circumstances; the true masochist always turns his cheek whenever he has a chance of receiving a blow.' (ibid. p. 165)

All that matters is 'that it should be possible to maintain a certain amount of suffering'. (ibid. p. 166)

In the so-called negative therapeutic reaction, patients get worse during treatment because of an unconscious sense of guilt, which, Freud suggests, is always silent. Freud speaks of the patient finding satisfaction in illness and refusing to give up the suffering. '... as far as the patient is concerned this sense of guilt is dumb; it does not tell him he is guilty; he does not feel guilty he feels ill. This guilt expresses itself only as a resistance to recovery which is extremely difficult to overcome.' (1923, pp. 49-50). In the Masochism paper referred to above, Freud explains the difficulty in making patients aware of this unconscious sense of guilt. He points out that the sadism of the super-ego and the masochism of the ego complement one another resulting in a severe sense of guilt derived from the death instinct. And much later, in 'Analysis Terminable and Interminable', Freud speaks of 'a force which is defending itself by every possible means against recovery and which is absolutely resolved to hold on to illness and suffering.' (1937, p. 242)

For Freud, the death instinct makes its appearance during the dissolution of the Oedipus complex, in association with penis envy or castration anxiety. This is in contrast to Klein, who, as we will discuss at length in the next chapter, sees death instinct anxiety from birth, the process of which is thought to engender strong persecutory anxiety. Ultimately this oppressive and all pervading sense of Oedipal guilt derives from, Freud tells us, 'the two great criminal intentions [phantasies] of killing the father and having sexual relations with the mother.' (1916, p. 332) This criminal sensibility resides in the super-ego, and creates a torturous tension between the super-ego and the ego. In the final analysis for Freud, what he called 'the dark power of Destiny' (1924, p. 168) resides in the super-ego, and it is from this agency that the ego's fear of death resides.

Freud did not explicitly relate the resistances of narcissistic conditions, as expressions of the death instinct. Perhaps the reason for this is that Freud's original theory of narcissism was based on the notion of primary narcissism, in which the individual directs his *libido* (Life instinct) towards the self, and a secondary narcissism in which he withdraws libido from objects back towards the self. Indeed, it was in 'Instincts and Their Vicissitudes' that he wrote about a pleasurable narcissistic stage. The external object, when it appears, is the target of the infant's destructiveness. 'Hate, as a relation to objects, is older than love. It derives from the narcissistic ego's primordial repudiation of the external world with its outpouring of stimuli.' (1915b p. 139) This thought finds its logical extension in Freud's notion of the Nirvana principle, which expresses the ultimate trend of the death instinct, going beyond the law of constancy or homeostasis in its aim to reduce all excitation to zero.

It is important to emphasise here, for discussion in later chapters, that the life instinct or Eros has eventually become for Freud not the disruptive force that sexuality once was, but that force which now aims to *bind elements together* into greater and greater unities. After all manifest sexuality is the union in coitus or of the gametes at fertilization. The death instinct, at the opposite pole, is now designated as the disruptive force in Freud's new formulation. It undoes connections and destroys things. In 1920 Freud wrote that normally, 'the erotic [life] instincts and the death instincts would be present in living beings in regular mixtures or fusions, but 'defusions' would also be liable to occur.' (1920, pp. 258-9) In 1933 he adds 'For fusions may also come apart and we may expect that functioning will be most gravely affected by defusions of such a kind.' (1933, p. 105) We shall see in later chapters how many analysts have explored and used effectively these tentative ideas of Freud's in seeking to explain psychopathology.

Where is the death instinct to be located?

Although the death instinct is a *biological* concept, the question arises - how is it manifested in mental life? Where, if anywhere, is the death instinct located in the new topography? Only the ego is capable of *experiencing* anxiety, it is 'the actual seat of anxiety', (1923, p. 57) and therefore only the ego is capable of experiencing the anxiety due to death, because 'death is an abstract concept with a negative content for which no unconscious correlative can be found.' (ibid. p. 58) There is no negation in the unconscious. Therefore there can be no *unconscious* fear of death, there is no representative of the death instinct in the unconscious. Only the ego can imagine its non-being. However, with his new tripartite structure in place in 1923, Freud makes little effort to map the new instinctual antithesis onto these agencies, preferring to state: 'There can be no question of restricting one or the other of the basic instincts to one of the provinces of the mind. They must necessarily be met with everywhere.' (1938 [1940], p. 149). However, according to Laplanche and Pontalis, it is the id that preferentially comes to represent *all* the instinctual demands in opposition to the ego. (1973 p. 100). The ego can find itself in great danger. In extreme regression, the ego can give itself up, abandon itself, as it were. As Freud suggests, 'The fear of death in melancholia only admits of one explanation: that the ego gives itself up because it feels itself hated and persecuted by the super-ego, instead of loved... It sees itself deserted by all protecting forces and lets itself die.' (Freud 1923, p. 58)

Further, Freud says: 'The fear of death, like the fear of conscience [is] a development of the fear of castration.' (ibid. p. 58) However, while 'the unconscious seems to contain nothing that could give any content to our concept of the annihilation of life. Castration can be pictured on the basis of the daily experience of the faeces being separated from the body, or on the basis of losing the mother's breast at weaning. But nothing resembling death can ever have been experienced; or, if it has, as in fainting, it has left no observable traces behind. I am therefore inclined to adhere to the view that the fear of death should be regarded as analogous to the fear of castration...' (Freud 1926, pp. 129-30) Freud is emphasizing here that there are no traces of death in the mind. We will need the Lacanian concept of the Real to further understand this failure to represent death. (see chapter four).

Primary repression

At this point, we are close to a preoccupation that runs throughout Freud's work, namely the existence of a trauma, which in its essence is psychically inaccessible. From the beginning, in *The Studies on Hysteria* (1893-5), there is the traumatic sexual incident (the pathogenic idea), against which the hysteric defends herself. The incident is repressed. In places, Freud hypothesized about the *primary* stage in this general process of repression or defence - the so-called primary or primal repression (*Urverdrängung*). The origin of primal repression is the extreme pleasurable intensity of archaic experiences. Freud says, 'It is highly probable that the immediate precipitating causes of primal repressions are quantitative factors, such as an excessive degree of excitation, and the breaking through of the protective shield against stimuli.' (1926 p. 94) After all, as has been noted, this breaking through is precisely what happens in the traumatic neurosis.

It is *primary* repression that holds out against this excessive degree of excitation, and therefore it must be primary repression that puts the limit on instinctuality in its most deathly aspects, leaving the excess outside. Laplanche argues that the death drive is an extension of the original concept of sexuality - 'it is nothing other than the extreme of sexuality, in its least civilized aspect.' (1981 p. 86) Primary repression cuts this extremism, and represents a fundamental turning away, a fundamental leaving behind.

At the beginning of the subject's history, there is an inevitable and tragic rupture, which founds the unconscious, as a sort of repository for archaic, intensely pleasurable (therefore traumatic) memories, which must be more or less abandoned. Primal repression is, therefore, this hypothetical *first phase* of repression, in which a number of unconscious ideas - the primal repressed - constitute the unconscious nuclei, which, in turn, attract the contents of consciousness, joining forces with the repulsion or (secondary) repression operating from the superior agencies (after pressure).

There is a close connection between primal repression and fixation, in the narrow genetic sense, which is not fixation at a libidinal stage, but the (primary) fixation of an instinct to an idea, and the 'registration' (*Niederschrift*) of this idea in the unconscious. This instinctual representative (psychical or ideational representative) persists unaltered, and the instinct remains attached to it, in the unconscious - kept there by an anticathexis, which is a permanent expenditure of energy which guarantees the permanence of the repression. 'Anticathexis is the sole mechanism of primal repression.' (Freud 1915c, p. 181)

The subject is marked by and attached to the earliest archaic experiences of satisfaction and types of object relationship. Freud postulated the idea of 'a fixation to a trauma' in *Introductory Lectures on Psychoanalysis* (1916-17, p. 282) and in 'Five Lectures on Psychoanalysis', he connected 'fixation of mental life to pathogenic traumas with the compulsion to repeat.' (1910, p. 17) Fixation, therefore, is the basis of repression, and the first stage of the process. In Section III of the Schreber case Freud speaks of fixation as 'the precursor and necessary [pre]condition of every "repression"'... 'the second phase then emanates from the more highly developed systems of the ego... "after-pressure".' (1911, p. 67) There is then the third phase, the so-called 'return of the repressed'. (ibid. p. 67) Interestingly here, Freud speaks of many fixation points, and 'we must be prepared to find a similar multiplicity of the mechanisms of repression proper.' (ibid. p. 68)

He envisaged an actual inscription or registration of traces. According to Laplanche and Pontalis, '[there are] primal moments at which certain privileged ideas are indelibly inscribed in the unconscious, and at which the instinct itself becomes fixated to its psychical representative - perhaps by this very process constituting itself *qua* instinct.' (1973 p. 164).

These are therefore, if I may take an analogy from physics, the first crystallization's of the somatic excitations into a psychic registration, around which all further crystalline accretions of unconscious ideas will arrange themselves, both attractively and problematically. These are the nuclei which will fundamentally influence the rest of the structure and its expression in the subject's life, although the subject will always try to remain unaware of them directly, due to the omnipresence of the anticathexis. Of course, as we shall see, sometimes this crystallization fails or can be badly disrupted, and there is indeed the return of the repressed...

According to Smith primal repression is the original turning away from danger (because of too much excitation), towards an image of the object - i.e. away from the Lacanian Real and towards an image. This is a repression in primary process functioning. He says: 'The turning away from danger or "too much excitation", structures an ongoing tendency to anticipate and avoid danger [trauma].' (1991 p. 25) Smith postulates a whole organization in the primary process, a whole structuring, and 'grammar of being', or a 'proto-language' prior to a acquisition of language proper. But the term, 'primal repression...is reserved for that never-to-be-witnessed-or-known first turning. There it can only be assumed that the drive drives towards the image of the object.' (ibid. p. 114) We will return to this aspect in chapter four.

The place of the pleasure principle

Where does the primacy of the trauma and its attendant repetitions, leave the pleasure principle? Is the pleasure principle on the side of Eros or Thanatos? By the time Freud wrote the masochism paper, he was prepared to assert that 'The *Nirvana* principle expresses the trend of the death instinct; the *pleasure* principle represents the demands of the libido [Eros]; and the modification of the latter principle, the *reality* principle, represents the demands of the external world.' (1924c, p. 160) But this is in opposition to Freud's statement four years earlier that, 'The pleasure principle seems actually to serve the death instincts.' (1920, p. 63) To be sure, if *one* meaning of the pleasure principle is reduce tensions to zero and minimize unpleasure, then the pleasure principle and the Nirvana principle *are the same*. This notion harks back to the *Project*, where the pleasure principle was linked to the 'principle of neuronal inertia'. So where does this leave the related 'principle of constancy', or the maintenance of energy at a constant level suitable for living, and where does it leave Eros? And how can we talk of a *beyond* of the pleasure principle, if Thanatos and the pleasure principle are thus connected?

After 1920 Freud seems to have changed his position. Perhaps Laplanche and Pontalis can help us. They claim that, '[the] two principles of mental functioning... correspond to the two great classes of instincts: The Nirvana principle, which corresponds to the death instincts, is clearly defined, but the pleasure principle (and its modified form the reality principle), which is *supposed to represent the demands of the life instincts* is hard to understand in any economic sense, and Freud reformulates it in "qualitative terms"' (1973, p. 242, my italics). We could subsume here the principle of constancy within the pleasure-reality principle, both of which operate to serve the demands of the libido, Eros and the problems of everyday living.

Finally in the *Outline* in 1940, Freud states clearly:

> ... we have decided to assume the existence of only two basic instincts, *Eros* and the *destructive instinct*. (The contrast between the instincts of self-preservation and the preservation of the species, as well as the contrast between ego-love and object-love, fall within Eros). The aim of the first of these basic instincts is to establish ever greater unities and to preserve them thus - in short, to bind together; the aim of the second is, on the contrary, to undo connections and so to destroy things... to lead what is living into an inorganic state...' (1940 p. 148)

However there are still problems which need to be addressed. There is the question of the apparent contradiction between the pleasure principle and the compulsion to repeat. Freud summarizes the position, 'But how is the compulsion to repeat - the manifestation of the power of the repressed - related to the pleasure principle? It is clear that the greater part of what is re-experienced under the compulsion to repeat must cause the ego unpleasure, since it brings to light activities of repressed instinctual impulses. That, however, is unpleasure of a kind we have already considered and does not contradict the pleasure principle: unpleasure for one system [ego] and simultaneously satisfaction for the other [id].' (1920, p. 20) However, a little further on, Freud acknowledges, that the compulsion to repeat, 'seems more primitive, more elementary, more instinctual than the pleasure principle which it over-rides.' (ibid. p. 23)

Furthermore, Laplanche and Pontalis make the central point: recognizing in the death instinct, 'a new conceptual departure: the death instinct makes the destructive tendency, as revealed for example in sadomasochism, into an *irreducible datum*; it is furthermore the chosen expression of the most fundamental principle of psychical functioning;

and, lastly, in so far as it is 'the essence of the instinctual', it binds every wish, whether aggressive or sexual, to the wish for death.' (1973, p. 103)

Sex and death

Freud following Weismann, again recalls biological theory. Weismann had noted that 'unicellular organisms are potentially immortal, and that death only makes its appearance with the multicellular metazoa.' (1920 p. 46) But Weismann felt, contra Freud, that death was not a 'primal characteristic of living substance.' (ibid. p. 46) Freud noted biological experiments that conclude that single celled organisms never die. They reproduce asexually and in a sense their bodies, although fragmenting, *continue for ever*. However, conjugation amongst these cells leads to rejuvenation (Lipschutz). And, against this, 'An infusorian... if it is left to itself, dies a natural death owing to its incomplete voidance of the products of its own metabolism.' (ibid. p. 48) Freud contents himself with the idea that the death instincts may be present in the protista as well as higher organisms, but in a latent state, masked by life processes. Freud agrees with Schopenhauer: 'For him death is the "true result and to that extent the purpose of life".' (ibid. p. 50) But Freud goes on to postulate not only that conjugation is rejuvenative, but that the general evolutionary tendency for cells to join together into multicellular organisms, is in their own narcissistic libidinal interests as part of Eros, the life instincts, which hold living things together. Freud considers the Darwinian argument that 'the chance conjugation of two protista, was retained and exploited in later development', (ibid. p. 56) because it offers evolutionary advantages, and he again cites Weismann who believed 'that an intermingling of this kind leads to an increase in the variability of the organism concerned.' (ibid. p. 56 note 2). However, Freud is still worried that life instincts are at work in the most primitive of unicellular organisms, since this would necessitate him abandoning the death instinct hypothesis: unless, he suggests, 'we must suppose them [the death instincts] to be associated from the very start with life instincts.' (ibid. p. 57)

In modern terms however, with the evolution of sexuality, the individual dies leaving only the single celled gametes to perpetuate the species. Therefore the introduction of sexuality also heralds the introduction of death, together with the possibilities for *difference* (genetic difference), genetic creativity, rejuvenation to stretch a point, since each individual of a sexually reproducing species is genetically unique. The price for diversity and evolution of the species is the *death* of the individual. Here then biology, creativity and desire are linked to death - a Freudian notion that is central to psychoanalysis. It is enshrined in the Oedipus complex, where the young child tragically encounters the separate and exclusive sexual relationship of his parents and is obliged to recognize his cut-offness, his lack and to enter the circuit of desire, forsaking omnipotence - the asexual perpetuation of sameness or the absence of desire. What Freud and others had noticed in the protista, their apparent immortality based on the life instincts, can perhaps better be seen as a kind of death in disguise, a silent operation of the death instincts (Freud always emphasizes the muteness or silence) hidden under their manifest lifelike proliferation. For this perpetuation of sameness is a kind of death. This idea will be returned to in later chapters.

Critique.

After this brief introduction, we will now turn to some of the criticisms, inconsistencies and reservations that other psychoanalysts have had about what was Freud's most controversial theory. Firstly, they object to the idea of a death drive itself. They suggest that there can be other ways of interpreting the clinical data without recourse to a death drive. There are many ways in which the new dualism of life and death drives is inconsistent with Freud's earlier theories. Freud's theory has its own internal inconsistencies. In his important work *The Anatomy of Human Destructiveness*, Fromm investigates the conditions of human existence which lead man to orgies of destruction and violence. He specifically discusses Freud's theory in the appendix. (1974, pp. 581-631) Space will permit only a listing of some contentious areas below.

How is the nirvana principle, the decrease in the life force towards zero, consistent with the *passion* for destruction, that we observe during war and violence of one sort or another? This begs a wider question - how does Freud's physiologically based psychology of homeostasis (constancy, stability) and tension reduction compare with the wealth of clinical data which would indicate that as often as not we seek tension *increase*, and excitement? This criticism has been in part accounted for above, and by Freud himself, when he acknowledges in the Masochism paper that the pleasure principle and tension reduction can be 'paralyzed' by pain and suffering. He concedes: 'It seems that in the series of feelings of tension we have a direct sense of the increase and decrease of amounts of stimulus, and it cannot be doubted that there are pleasurable tensions and unpleasurable relaxations of tension.' (1924, p. 160) He further notes that there may be a *rhythm* to these rises and falls of tension. At any rate, there *can* be pleasure in tension increase. However, in keeping with Freud, let us suggest the following: unmodified by Eros and the relative tranquillity of the pleasure/reality principles, the death drive, in its beyond and *on its way* to the final zero state, will develop terrifying increases of excitation - intense pleasure for the *un*conscious, and at the same time, terrifying unpleasure for the conscious.

How does the notion of the death 'instinct' fit with Freud's earlier contention that instincts are associated with special *somatic* zones? What erogenous zones are associated with the death instinct? The answer is simple - any zone, oral, anal, phallic, etc. - can be the vehicle for destructive urges as well as erotic ones. Similarly, Eros is not an instinct, and Freud never uses the term 'Eros instinct', preferring instead 'life instinct'. Eros refers to a Platonic tendency inherent in life itself to achieve greater unities, and it is not associated with specific bodily organs. So how can the former sexual instinct (of the earlier Freud) and Eros be the same? Freud (1940 [1938]) surmounts this difficulty by asserting that Eros is a primal instinct (the death instinct is the other), of which sexuality is only one component.

Furthermore, the catch-all term, the 'death instinct', tends to conflate sadism, aggressiveness, assertiveness, destructiveness, mastery and the will for power, which are qualitatively different phenomena. Freud did see the differences between these qualities of aggressiveness, but in his final duality he was forced to lump them all together. Finally, if the aim of life is to seek death, how can Eros hope to compete with such a powerful instinct? How can Eros hope to fend off the perverse desire of life to return to its origins?

Here we must consider the ontological status of human destructiveness. Having underestimated the role of human aggression in his early theorizing, it could be argued that in the last twenty years of his life, Freud overcompensated by giving it pride of place in his new dualism. Therefore, it will be of great importance to consider how destructiveness arises. Is it a component part of all the instincts, and therefore, primary? Or, does it arise as a result of frustration by an external object? If this is the case, aggression and destructiveness are *secondary* phenomena, even though they may appear right from the start of life. Others have noted the *de*-fused nature of some forms of aggression, but could not subscribe to the idea that the primary and initial focus of the aggression was the self. The main criticism centres around Freud's notion that the death instinct is *innate*. But beyond that, it is primordial, cosmic in its extension and in *all* life. Each of these critics sees aggression in all its clinical manifestations as being *reactive* to early environmental failure, such as separation, failure of the early feeding relationship, neglect, privation, abuse, etc. Aggression can be extreme, but it is construed by these writers to be the result of impingement or perhaps genetic endowment, local rather than cosmic.

Analysts who think this way cover a very large spectrum and indeed may have little else in common. For instance Storr (1968) sees all aggression as a reaction to the stifling of independent assertive urges. Hartmann (1958) and the ego-psychologists, who put adaptation at the centre of life's requirements, see aggression as a reaction to the conflicts inherent in the adaptation process. From a different orientation upon which we will concentrate, there are the British Independent object-relations theorists whose sense of the reactive nature of aggression goes right back to the earliest days of a child's life. Here frustration takes on another meaning. It is not just the curbing of impulses at the behest of external authorities, but something almost inherent in life itself - the potential deprivation inflicted by life itself, outside the womb, but still local.

For instance, Winnicott says that the death instinct seems to disappear simply through being unnecessary. Aggression is seen more as evidence of life. Under favourable conditions, fusion occurs between the erotic and motility drives. However, Winnicott acknowledges that, 'failure of fusion, or loss of fusion that has been achieved, produces a potential element of pure destructiveness (i.e. without guilt-sense) in the individual, but even this destructiveness remains a lifeline in the sense of its being the basis of object relationships that feel real to the patient.' (1965a, p. 127) Aggression or destructiveness is failed constructiveness. Winnicott refers to the 'antisocial tendency' and delinquent behaviour *as a sign of hope.* (1958) For these children, he says, *'things went well enough, and then they did not go well enough'* (1986, p. 91) There has been a de-privation (not a privation), in that 'there has been a loss of something good... that has been withdrawn,... which compels the environment to be important. The patient through unconscious drives compels someone to attend to management' (1958, p. 309). Winnicott himself notes the similarity between deprivation as used here and Bowlby's observations, during the 1950s, on two or three-year-olds who go to hospital and their intense responses to being on their own, as if abandoned. These fall into the well-known three phases over time: aggressive protest; increasing despair; final detachment.

Therefore the important question for these theorists, is whether or not the environment is well enough adapted to the infant's primary needs. Guntrip (1968) following Fairbairn's approach centres aggression in the vicissitudes of object relating, upon which he understands mental health or illness to be based. For him, the life and death instincts are a 'mythology'. Contra Freud and Klein, Guntrip argues: 'Fear, persecutory anxiety, arises in the first place as a result of an actually bad, persecutory environment, what Winnicott calls "impingement".' (1968, p. 146) Guntrip wanted to remove psychoanalysis from its direct association with biology and instinctualism (sexuality) and make the infant's requirement for object relations primary. Balint speaks of the '"lack of fit" between the child and *the people* who represent his environment' (1968 p. 22), which leads to the feeling that something is missing and represents a 'basic fault' in the personality to which the person must regress if he is to be healed. And, unlike Freud, who saw regression as an aim of the death instinct, Balint envisions a benign regression, and asks, 'are we allowed to infer from the fact that in a number of cases with regressed patients the analytic treatment can be successfully terminated, that the force of the death instinct is perhaps not so overwhelming after all?'. (ibid. pp. 122-3)

But the claim that all aggression is environmental and reactive does not seem to answer the obvious: namely, the unbelievable cruelty and destructiveness that erupts in human behaviour. Freud pinpoints the excessiveness that characterizes such violence. 'As a rule this cruel aggressiveness waits for... some other purpose, whose goal might have been reached by milder measures'. (1930, p. 111,) We know that excess is very common, and this calls into question the assumption that aggression is simply reactive. Heimann (1952) has shown how regularly human beings exceed the boundaries of necessary aggression by resorting to extremes of sadism without any inhibition arising from empathy, guilt or horror. Clearly this kind of violence is *anti*-life and reveals a kind of demonic lust for death. It is hard to explain such atrocities on the basis of a reactive theory of human aggression, unless one takes the reaction back to the earliest experiences of the infant which of course the British Independent School does. They postulate that infants are faced with 'unthinkable anxieties' and these are potentially violent acts are extreme reactions to them. *The further back one goes, the more extreme and totalizing these 'reactions' are likely to become.* So perhaps this is tantamount to saying here, that the reactive theory and the innate theory almost coincide in the earliest infant experiences, especially where these involve significant failures in adaptation.

Freud did not address himself to those examples of aggression which are a sign of life and vitality, a refusal, as it were, even a violent one, to acquiesce with deprivation. Here I have in mind, on the one hand the deprived infant, and on the other, the wider sense in which injustice should be fought against, with a sense of moral indignation. Freud did speak of externalizing the death instinct, but then he tended to see this as destructive of others. We either destroy others or ourselves. There is little in Freud's notion of the death drive that can be seen in a positive light, although his earlier emphasis on self-preservation comes closer to the reactive type of aggression.

Perhaps, the death drive theory fails to take account of the appalling human suffering that is manifestly inflicted *from without* - in families, in authoritarian regimes, in torture and war. In many cases these in themselves would be more than sufficient to account for gross psychic trauma and disturbance. Surely the environmental contribution must be crucial. It is hard to conceive of such trauma arising *endogenously*. I think very few analysts would entertain such an idea. Yet the theory implies that this is at least a possibility - violence does not *have* to be determined by an external cause. Violence is not ultimately to be explained by appealing to bad social conditions. However, for well known and very broadly influential analysts like Wilhelm Reich and Alice Miller, the explanation for *all* human violence is to be located purely and simply in *patriarchal* brutality, and sexual abuse.

In response to this, a psychoanalyst might legitimately answer that there has been an over-emphasis on the external genesis of aggression in psychology and social theory this century, and a dangerous evasion of *internal* psychical realities. Arguably, psychoanalysis (especially Kleinian and Lacanian) might be almost unique in this particular emphasis. If one sees oneself as a victim of a bad marriage, a bad family, of poverty, of gender, and so on, one can project all badness out there, without realizing one's own complicity in the situation. The analyst might further argue that the psychoanalytic emphasis on the primacy of internal phantasy has been radically ignored (See Chasseguet-Smirgel and Grunberger, 1976). The universal tendency to attribute *endogenous* excessive stimulation (violence) via projection (as we noted in Freud's account, above) to others has had disastrous consequences socially and politically. Clearly, these projections are increasing. In reality, the situation is always a complex one involving violent internal phantasies and external abuse or deprivation, and a mutual malign interaction of the internal and external.

The concept of an innate origin for human destructiveness, has two further important consequences. Firstly, it leads towards a bleak pessimism that sees suffering and illness as somehow inevitable and there is little that can alleviate it. Secondly, it fosters a social conservatism, both in the short term and the long term. If suffering is unavoidable, we have no need to change the structures of injustice within society. Even if we should want to change and reform culture there is little point in doing so, because injustice and cruelty are built into the individual, community and life itself, and therefore cannot be eradicated by social and political action.

Therefore, Freud's, and later Klein's, emphasis on the innateness of human destructivity, marked an *inescapable* ambivalence to life, an unavoidable human datum. And while external sources of aggression and suffering (from earliest infancy through to adult misfortune), should never be ignored an essential destructiveness throughout life with still have to be reckoned with. Paradoxically, it is Winnicott who says that, 'the difficult thing is for each individual to take full responsibility for the destructiveness that is personal, and that *inherently* belongs to a relationship to an object that is felt to be good.' (1986, p. 82) (my italics).

Finally, and perhaps most problematically, does not the concept of the death drive bring back into the foreground the *moral* category of evil? It is hard to escape the moral waste involved in such a concept. Up to this point psychoanalysis could take pride in its tolerance, its reliability, its acceptance of the unacceptable, and what the theologian Paul Tillich called its grace, which 'has gained a new meaning by the way in which the analyst deals with his patient.' (1959, p. 124) In what Tillich called the deepest insight of psychotherapy, he says: 'The law cannot break compulsions... Instead of encountering the law, the patient encounters acceptance on the part of the effective analyst. He is accepted in the state in which he is, and is not told to change his state before becoming acceptable ... In the analytic situation there is neither command nor permission, but acceptance and healing.' (1964, pp. 45-6) Does not a belief in the death drive compromise analytic neutrality?

Or is neutrality merely a dishonest avoidance of the ethical dimension? Consider Phillips, for instance: 'Only someone entranced by the possibilities of his own goodness could now find a use for the notion of evil.' (1994, p. 59) And he speaks of, 'the unconscious complicity of object-relations with Christianity', that attempts to make evil, 'soluble in the good-enough mothering of analytic treatment.' (ibid. p. 61) The evasion is complete when he says: 'The categories of good and evil are no longer viable objects of thought.' (ibid. p. 64)

It is true that simplistic oppositions like good/evil can lead to closure, but notions of morality haven't gone away. What was formerly called badness is now called sickness. The church has been replaced by the hospital or the psychotherapy clinic. Morality, as subtle condemnation, returns via the categorizing of patients (psychotic, neurotic, borderline, etc.) and the ethical debate about who is fit to practice. It is also possible that such a virulent term like the death drive intruded into the theory with a vengeance - the moral dimension having been barred for so long by Freud's striving for scientific credibility. The virulence of the term is too much for most analysts. However, any therapy that purports to involve an encounter that goes to the heart of things must surely encounter the moral dimension, but with grace[3].

In moving on to discuss Melanie Klein's unique contribution to our understanding of aggression and her amplification of Freud's death drive theory, the Independents' view of destructiveness as a reaction to environmental impingement must form an important counterbalance. Perhaps, destructiveness has to be seen as both innate and reactive, as part of nature and nurture, genetics and the environment. To err on one side is to miss the complex interweaving of the genetic predisposition, the earliest environmental provision, and later social circumstances and life events. Is it the specific focus and unique position of psychoanalysis to attempt to take account of all of these factors, internal and external? Or, is Freud's radical conception, the simple one that desire untrammeled will consume itself, the ultimate end point of psychoanalysis?

2. KLEIN: ON ENVY AND PERSECUTION

Annihilation anxiety

Melanie Klein, working with young children as well as adults, endorsed Freud's death drive theory without question and produced abundant clinical evidence to support her views. It was in her book, *The Psychoanalysis of Children* (1932) that she first took up Freud's ideas on the life and death drives. She saw the fundamental anxiety as originating from the presence and danger of the death drive within the self. This is termed annihilation anxiety. Untroubled by the controversy surrounding Freud's instinctual dualism, and ignorant of biology, Klein felt free to use the death drive theory to account for the various ways in which children feel afraid of being damaged, overwhelmed or annihilated. 'The threat of annihilation by the death instinct within is, in my view - which differs from Freud's on this point - the primordial anxiety, and it is the ego which, in the service of the life instinct - possibly even called into operation by the life instinct - deflects to some extent that threat outwards.' (1957, pp. 190-191)

According to a modern leading Kleinian analyst, we can observe in the human infant's survival-oriented behaviour, such as crying loudly when hungry, cold, or afraid or otherwise threatened, that there must be an instinctive taking into account the possibility of death. This behaviour can be observed from birth onwards and therefore must be innate. The danger of dying must also be felt instinctively by the human baby as the threat of a terrible annihilating force which at times will be an overwhelming anxiety, which might have its evolutionary history in predator/prey relationships or the fight/flight response. (Grotstein, 1981)

Klein's view of the mind is of a dynamic interplay of immensely powerful forces in which conflicting emotions and mental processes are operating simultaneously. There is love and hate, introjection and projection, splitting of good from bad, powerful unconscious phantasies, integrating and fragmenting processes, which imply that the child's mind is a seething mass of conflict, a cauldron, with anxiety the dominant feature. This annihilation anxiety must be urgently dealt with by the inchoate ego, and worked through in early childhood by repeated experiences of persecutory and depressive anxieties and their successful resolution.

Clearly such a turbulent and conflicted view of the child's emotional world seems a little crazy at first sight. After all, the majority of children and babies in normal settings are clearly not filled with traumatic anxieties, terror of persecution and going to pieces. Often we will think of them as thriving and full of vitality, heading towards integration and maturity. There can be no argument about this, but it must be born in mind that Klein is describing *unconscious* and therefore hidden processes which relate to the earliest stages of life, which live on underneath the ongoing processes of maturing. She is talking about a hidden recess in the mind which is tortured and mad, as well as the healthy vital side with which we are all familiar. She is also describing children and adults who have not been so fortunate, and that for one reason or another have become disturbed by the emergence of this hidden recess into ordinary life and reality. In the foregoing, therefore, it must be stressed that what is being referred to is this turbulent *underworld* of feelings, part of an intensely *affective* unconscious, which for some (psychotics and borderlines) is daily reality. There are problems with centring theory so primordially in early infancy and *extreme* affectivity, in that it seems to undermine the more classical psychoanalytic approach, which emphasizes the *repressed* unconscious and the genetic or developmental approach to human maturation. However, some of the criticisms of the Kleinian approach will be addressed at the end of this chapter.

In her paper on the development of mental functioning, Klein states that the ego reaches deep down into the id throughout life and is therefore under the constant influence of unconscious processes. She regarded Freud's discovery of the life and death instincts with their polarity and fusion from birth onwards as a tremendous advance in our understanding of mental processes:

> I recognized, in watching the constant struggle in the young infant's mental processes between an irrepressible urge to destroy as well as to save himself, to attack his objects and to preserve them, that primordial forces struggling with each other were at work. This gave me a deeper insight into the vital clinical importance of Freud's concept of life and death instincts. (1958, p. 236)

She goes on to say that 'the danger of being destroyed by the death instinct thus gives rise to primordial anxiety in the ego.' (ibid. p. 237) In order to deal with this anxiety the primitive ego uses two processes:

some of the death instinct is deflected outwards (projected) into the object, which is then felt to be a persecutor; while the part of the death instinct that is retained within the ego attacks the persecutory object.

The life instinct is also projected into external objects which are then felt to be loving, idealised and protecting. Also, introjection 'combats the death instinct because it leads to the ego taking in something lifegiving (first of all food) and thus binding the death instinct working within.' (ibid. p. 238)

Primitive splitting

According to Klein, from the beginning of life both instincts attach themselves to the mother's breast. Depending upon whether destructive or loving impulses predominate, the breast is felt to be at times good or at times bad. The introjection of gratifying experiences at the breast, together with projection of the life instincts, build up in the infant's mind repeated experiences of the 'primal good object', which is the *foundation of all mental health*. The projection into the breast of the death instinct on the other hand leads to the development within the infant's mind of the 'primal bad object'. Clearly, the ego, when supported primarily by the good internal object, is able eventually to master anxiety and preserve life, binding the destructive forces within.

It is a characteristic of early development that the good idealised objects and the bad persecuting ones are split and separated, as far as possible, implying a defusion of the life and death instincts. Similarly, the ego is split into good and bad parts. It is only the introjection of good experiences and the availability (perhaps in part constitutionally determined) of the life instincts for projection, that will enable the split to be lessened and integration to be achieved. '... integration is based on a strongly rooted good object that forms the core of the ego, a certain amount of splitting is essential for integration; for it preserves the good object and later enables the ego to synthesize the two aspects of it.' (1957, p. 192).

In the *New Introductory Lectures on Psycho-Analysis*, (1933) Freud had already suggested a split within the ego, with one part coming to stand over and against the other part. This part he suggested, performs many of the functions of the super-ego and contains introjected aspects of the parents. Where Klein disagreed with Freud was in the *timing* of this development. For Freud, the super-ego proper developed at the dissolution of the Oedipus complex, but for Klein it was much earlier, in the second quarter of the first year. She states: 'Thus the early introjection of the good and bad breast is the foundation of the super-ego and influences the development of the Oedipus complex. This conception of super-ego formation [which is dealt with in detail below] is in contrast to Freud's statements that the identifications with the parents are the heir of the Oedipus complex and only succeed if the Oedipus complex is successfully overcome.' (1958, p. 239) (See also Klein, 1928, 1932, 1945 and 1952). For years Klein had been producing unmistakable evidence for the very early development of the super-ego and of this structure's extreme severity. This early super-ego was the manifestation of the death drive acting against the individual, 'the pure culture of the death instinct', from Freud, already referred to.

The primitive super-ego

The Kleinian conception of the super-ego must now be looked at in more detail, and the closely related notion of the internal object. Klein was working with very young children, some as young as two, and she found unmistakable signs of guilt and remorse which she wanted to explain. At about this time Freud was developing his new topography, and in 1923, he describes the super-ego as being formed after the Oedipus complex, at around the age of four or five. There was clearly a confusing discrepancy here between Freud's orthodoxy on the origin of the super-ego, and Klein's new findings with her very young children. In 1926, she states that, 'in the cases which I have analysed the inhibitory effect of feelings of guilt was clear at a very early age.' (p. 133)

In 1924, Abraham, Klein's analyst, had already pointed to the harshness of the early super-ego by connecting it with the sadism of the pre-Oedipal stages of psychosexual development. Klein echoes these findings about the harsh super-ego when she considers criminal tendencies in children (1927), and the biting, devouring, cutting, poisoning super-ego under the dominance of oral and anal sadism (1928).

But it wasn't until 1932, and more clearly in 1933, that Klein felt confident enough of her position to assert the radical nature of her new discoveries, viz, that the excessive violence of the early super-ego, results from the deflection outwards of the death drive, the ultimate source of the oral and anal sadism already cited. Relying on Freud's speculations in *Beyond the Pleasure Principle* (1920), she suggested that the first function of the ego is to expel the death drive into an external object. This then, is the core of the super-ego which is intensely destructive. While there is still a link with Freud here, the implication of her new theory of the super-ego is a considerable departure from Freudian psychoanalysis. The super-ego is no longer connected to the Oedipus complex as theorized by Freud. However, it could be argued that Klein's description of the early super-ego amplifies and extends Freud's model in a way which is arguably one of the most valuable contributions to modern psychoanalytic theory. We are inhabited by others, who at the most primitive level, are no longer just prohibitors, but at worst, desire our death. The repercussions of this discovery clinically represent the central contribution to psychoanalysis of the Kleinian tradition. Nobody explains this brutal phenomenon as well as they do.

Therefore, in the Kleinian mode, it no longer makes sense to talk of an implied monolithic structure or agency, the super-ego. Kleinians prefer to talk in terms of multiple 'internal objects'. We must now move to consider this concept before returning to the operation of the death instinct in the internal world.

Part objects

The term 'object' in psychoanalysis is used to denote the aim of an instinctual impulse. The aim of the impulse is any thing or person that is of interest for the satisfaction of instinct. Freud's early work required a rather impersonal (scientific) terminology involving instinctual energies cathecting objects, even though these objects were often human beings in the shape of parents. However, the infant, *ab initio*, does not have a conception of a specifically *whole* human person, in his or her own right, so it remains accurate to talk in terms of an object even when that object is human in reality. For the baby, the mother is seen initially only *in parts* (part objects), the breast, for instance. This part object perception and usage is caused by the immaturity of the brain and the prematurity of birth making extreme and specifically focused instinctual demands imperative for survival. The baby literally cannot, and does not need to see the mother as a whole and separate person, until much later. At first he needs the breast *urgently* when he is hungry.

When the baby is hungry, he conjures up the phantasy of a good feed. When the breast is actually offered and he has the warm satisfying experience of being fed, he incorporates it, in phantasy. He takes it into himself in a very concrete kind of way, so that this good object, the so-called 'good breast' is actually felt to be located in his tummy. When, however, he is hungry but there is no feed, and he feels pain and discomfort in his tummy, he magically attributes his bodily discomfort to the motivation of a malevolent object, the so called 'bad breast', which he feels in his tummy and would like to expel violently. The difficult point here is that the baby's bodily sensations which are very intense are experienced mentally as simultaneously and automatically *connected* to an object. The baby inhabits an animistic world in which everything feels and has intentions which can be good or bad, sometimes in the extreme. So all his bodily feelings, such as eating, warmth, comfort, soothing, wetting, rage, messing, and so on, become inextricably linked to an object, or a part-object. Satisfied instinctual impulses become good objects and therefore comforting, frustrated impulses become bad objects and therefore dangerous.

Projection and the talion principle

The baby's first interpretation of the world relates to his bodily sensations. Good objects (appear to) want to cause good harmonious feelings of satisfaction and plenty. Bad objects want to cause painful feelings. There is the hungry greedy bad object that gnaws away in his tummy. There is the biting object that makes his gums hurt during teething, or the painful faeces that want to harm and poison his insides. There is a terrifyingly angry object, that is attacking his feeling of frustration. The primitive ego believes that the environment has the *same* instinctual aims as himself, only with much more power. The talion principle is at work. Wanting to bite means being bitten. Wanting to hurt means being hurt. Clearly the inchoate ego's first understanding of the world represents a radical *mis*-understanding[1]. The strength and intense demands of the infant's physiological needs, which he cannot satisfy himself, and yet requires to be satisfied urgently, leads to a world full of demanding, voracious, attacking persecutors (bad internal/external objects). Fortunately, there will be also some magically good objects who are believed to be the cause of all the good bodily sensations.

This is the internal world of the infant, which is a massive distortion of reality in its most primitive formations. The bad internal objects are the precursors of the super-ego. There are potentially many of them.

This earliest stage of development is referred to as the 'paranoid-schizoid' position (see Klein 1946), because of the predominance of splitting and projection and persecutory anxieties stemming from gross instinctuality of the internal world - ultimately the death drive.

During this stage the ego is in a relatively unintegrated state, and is struggling to maintain itself in the face of objects that threaten it with annihilation. Here is the death drive operating in the internal world, threatening to fragment the ego, and perhaps representing a failure or partial failure of the primary deflection of the death drive outwards. Here is the source of the most primary anxiety: the persecutory fear of an object that is about to overwhelm, fragment and destroy the ego. It can only ultimately be countered by the introjection of the good object which will hold the fragile ego together.

The trouble is that the ego is greatly weakened by the fragmentation process, and therefore relatively incapable of introjection of good objects, at just the point when it needs these desperately. The introjection can become so greedy and omnipotent that the good objects are likely to be damaged. The phantasies that bring about introjection are predominantly oral in nature. The baby wants to suck dry, scoop-out, devour, bite up, and rob the mother of the food she has inside her. The baby also wants to expel dangerous substances, faeces and urine, out of the self. This is the splitting process which is the crucial defence in the paranoid-schizoid position, together with introjection and idealization of good things and expulsion (projection) of bad things. Attempting to keep good and bad parts of the self and object well separated is paramount at this stage, lest the good, which is so precious and upon which life depends, be damaged by the bad.

Particular focus has been given to the projected bad parts of the self. Clearly there is relief at getting rid of them, but of course they do not go away. The excrements are expelled into the mother in what amounts to a vicious attack. 'These excrements and bad parts of the self are meant not only to injure but also to control and take possession of the object. In so far as the mother comes to contain the bad parts of the self, she is not felt to be a separate individual, but is felt to be *the* bad self... When projection is mainly derived from the infant's impulse to harm or to control the mother, he feels her to be a persecutor.' (1946 p.8) In a footnote Klein apologizes for describing these primitive procesess in these terms, such as 'projecting into another person'. She feels there is no other way to describe unconscious processes which take place in an infant who has no words. According to Klein, it is clearly the only way to explain the intensity of hatred experienced by the psychotic, directed against other persons. The person's own badness and the other's become totally confused. The other is accused of carrying the badness which has been projected, and simultaneously, the accused becomes a frightening accuser.

Projective processes appear in ordinary everyday language, for example, 'the shit hits the fan', there are 'smear campaigns', 'you're full of shit', someone is described as a 'piss-artist', or we hear of 'the dirty tricks department' of some undercover organization. Much cursing, swearing and the 'hurling' of obscenities can be understood in terms of the ongoing need to expel badness from within.

The process of the projection of badness (the death drive) with the aim of controlling the other, Klein calls 'projective identification', a topic which has become a key notion in Kleinian psychoanalysis since the fifties. We shall take this up more fully in the next chapter.

Primary envy

The clearest manifestation of the death drive appears in Klein's understanding of envy. She defines envy as 'an oral-sadistic and anal-sadistic expression of destructive impulses, operational from the *beginning* of life.' (1957 p. 176, my italics). Envy is primary and Klein believes it has a constitutional basis. 'Envy is the angry feeling that the other person possesses and enjoys something desirable - the envious impulse being to take it away or to spoil it.' (ibid. p. 181) Greed is not quite so destructive. She describes greed as an insatiable craving over and beyond what can be provided, a sucking dry and a devouring, 'whereas envy not only seeks to rob in this way, but also to put badness, primarily bad excrements and bad parts of the self, into the mother, and first of all into her breast, in order to spoil and destroy her. In the deepest sense this means destroying her creativeness.' (ibid. p. 181) Greed and envy are closely related and both are destructive; the former is allied to a destructive introjection (mainly oral, sometimes anal) and the latter to destructive projection (oral or anal).

For Freud the death drive makes its appearance during the dissolution of the Oedipus complex in association with either penis envy or castration anxiety. But for Klein, envy, constitutionally based, is present *ab initio*. This is primary envy. Therefore, it 'contributes to the infant's difficulties in building up his good object, for he feels that the gratification of which he was deprived has been kept for itself by the breast that frustrated him.' (1957, p. 180) The more the mother is envied the more envy persists. Paradoxically, the fundamental insatiability and the 'feeling of harm done by envy, the great anxiety that stems from this, and the resulting uncertainty about the goodness of the object, have the effect of increasing greed and destructive impulses.' (ibid. p. 187) Inordinate envy of the breast fosters severe ego-splitting, into the good excessively idealised and the bad excessively feared persecutory breast. This will hinder eventual integration because the good has to be continuously separated and protected from the powerful bad.

Some babies tolerate frustrations and deprivations poorly in that, from the start, they will begin to enviously attack and destroy the good object, the life-giving breast. This destruction of what is good interferes with the smooth introjection of the good breast, and this represents an attack and therefore a loss of that which could sustain life. The baby turns away from the breast in hate. This potential first hatred of the world is the same as Freud's observation that, as we have already noted, 'Hate, as a relation to objects, is older than love. It derives from the narcissistic ego's primordial repudiation of the external world with its outpouring of stimuli' (1915b, p. 139).

The situation can spiral downwards as attack is mounted on attack. Klein comments:

> From the contention that envy spoils the primal good object, and gives added impetus to sadistic attacks on the breast, further conclusions arise. The breast attacked in this way has lost its value, it has become bad by being bitten up and poisoned by urine and faeces. Excessive envy increases the *intensity* of such attacks and their *duration,* and thus makes it more difficult for the infant to regain the lost good object. (1957, p. 186)

Perhaps an extreme version of this process indicates how brutal paranoid violence can occur. The victim of the attack is perceived as a persecutor (a damaged, hence threatening and useless breast), requiring more brutal assaults to kill off the mounting sense of persecution. This in turn makes the victim more damaged and consequently more persecuting, requiring more attacks, and so on. The fatal loss of the good object inside makes the subject feel so endangered, greedy and enviously destructive that he suddenly lashes out to destroy everything (including himself) to end the nightmare. Consequently, it must be important to gauge the *degree* of malignancy that may be present, but hidden. To what extreme can this go? This is crucial clinically in order to ascertain the depth to which envy can go, although in practice it is very hard to do. In some instances, envy can proceed so far on its own, so far away from anything to do with Eros, that the subject feels destined for death at some point. This may be very far from the patient's consciousness, and it may be that only the analyst perceives this in his or her own countertransference - that is as a particular kind of fear, dread or apprehension in the presence of this patient.[2]

Envy must be distinguished from other forms of attack on objects. Envy spoils the good object *because it is good*. There has been a failure in the infant to split off successfully good from bad, a failure in primary discrimination. Primary splitting must be regarded in the first instance as healthy, in that the good objects are preserved from destructive attacks derived from the death drive, which are then reserved for bad frustrating objects. But envy's tendency to establish hostile relations with *good* objects, leads to a fundamental *confusion* in object relations, a failure to sort out what is good and bad in oneself and others, a tendency to destroy what is helpful and nourishing in others and in oneself, indiscriminately. These confusions are the precursors of schizophrenia, and a good example of the disintegrating effects of the death drive. This is not to say that envy is unmodifiable. In normal development the infant will be able to take on board sufficient memories of nourishment and goodness to render envious impulses less destructive, transforming them into less dangerous forms of aggression - jealousy, rivalry and competitiveness. He does this via the fundamental experience of introjection of the good breast which becomes a core of felt goodness and security with the self. It is only in the severe mental disorders, where modification has significantly failed, that destructiveness continuously threatens to fragment, torture and disorganize the higher ego functions. In such a situation we might say there has been an initial failure to deflect the death instinct outwards, which Klein believed was at least in part dependent upon an inherited predisposition. This confirms, in part at least, the psychiatric evidence in support of a constitutional basis for the severe mental disorders.

The awareness of not having sufficient goodness within arouses a greedy and envious attack on the good object, and a desire to invade and inhabit it, leading to a confusion between self and non-self. In such a situation, any separation from the good object becomes immediately intolerable. Envious phantasies may involve getting into the object for the purposes of taking it over, controlling and spoiling it.

The infant becomes confusingly identified with the object in a magically omnipotent way.

Defences against envy

Klein elaborates a number of defences against envy. The earliest, the primordial defences, such as splitting, denial, projection and omnipotence are all carried out at the behest of envy. In the same vein, Klein adds the defence of idealization:

> it not only serves as a defence against persecution but also against envy. In infants, if the normal splitting between the good and the bad object does not initially succeed, this failure, bound up with excessive envy, often results in splitting between an omnipotently idealised and a very bad primal object. Strongly exalting the object and its gifts is an attempt to diminish envy. However if envy is very strong, it is likely, sooner or later, to turn against the primal idealised object and against other people who, in the course of development, come to stand for it. 1957, p. 216)

Klein then cites confusion as another defence, *any* confusion. A failure of a normal and adequate splitting between good and bad leads to confusion. This leads to a failure in 'clear thinking' - a point that we will be taking up with Bion in the next chapter. But this confusion has the effect of mitigating envy. 'By becoming confused as to whether a substitute for the original figure is good or bad, persecution as well as the guilt about spoiling and attacking the primary object by envy is to some extent counteracted.' (ibid. p. 216) Not knowing what to think is the best defence against hate.

Perhaps linked to confusion, is the dispersal of envy, or the displacement of envy from the primal object to the father and the siblings and indeed to all others, but to the extent that this flight is based on envy and its avoidance, 'a flight from the hate of *her* [the mother], ... such defences are not a basis for stable object relations...' (1957, p. 217, my italics)

Devaluation is frequently resorted to. A devalued or spoiled object no longer arouses envy. Klein notes how quickly idealization can become devaluation. A good analytic interpretation can be destroyed in this way. A whole analysis can be destroyed. The envy of the analyst's health can lead her to be idealised by the analysand, only later for the analyst to be equally devalued by the breakthrough of envy. Similarly, denial of envy can lead to the devaluation of self. Klein points out a common theme: 'By devaluing their own gifts they both deny envy and punish themselves for it.' (ibid. p. 218) The deepest source of this devaluation is 'guilt and unhappiness about not having been able to preserve the good object because of envy.' (ibid. p. 218)

Linked to idealization is the phantasy of a massive and greedy possession of the good object to fend off envy. But like idealization this can quickly revert to its opposite, because, by the greed of the possession and its ruthlessness, 'the good object is felt to turn into a destroyed persecutor.' (ibid. p. 218)

The attempted ridding of envy, by stirring envy in *others*, by pointing to or flouting our own good fortune and success, is, like all the other defences, a brittle defence. Envious people, and as we will note in the next chapter, the envious internal object, are the worst persecutors. The desire to triumph over and beat others gives rise soon enough to renewed fears of persecution and isolation.

A crucial defence against envy is the paradoxical intensification of hate and the *'stifling of feeling of love'* (ibid. p. 219) Klein concurs with Rosenfeld's elaboration of this defence. Rosenfeld noted how the death drives (envy), can be split off and idealised for their powerful deadening effect on the libidinal self. This is what Rosenfeld terms 'destructive narcissism', where de-fused aggressiveness takes over the whole of the borderline or psychotic patient's personality. Rosenfeld comments: 'When considering narcissism from the destructive aspect, we find that self-idealization again plays a central role, but now it is the omnipotent destructive parts of the self that are idealised. They are directed against any positive libidinal object relationship and any libidinal part of the self which experiences the need for an object and the desire to depend on it.' (1987, p. 106) I have outlined the social consequences of this destructive narcissistic pathology in Weatherill, (1994), Ch. 6.

From the point of view of the Oedipus complex, excessive envy 'implies that the infant turns too early [defensively] towards genital gratification, with the consequence that the oral relation becomes genitalized and the genital trends become too much coloured by oral grievances and anxieties.' (Klein 1957, p. 195) This makes for a premature Oedipal experience and a resultant tendency to over-sexualize everything. The primitive phantasy that the mother contains the penis of the father or that they are locked in continuous exclusive intercourse (the so-called 'combined parent figure', (ibid. p. 199) is exacerbated by envy and precludes the development of the less severe Oedipal jealousy in the triangular situation.

For Klein unlike Freud, penis envy is *preceded* by primary envy: the mother's breast is the object of envy during the oral phase, whereas the father's penis becomes the object of envy during the Oedipus complex. For the little girl:

> The envious relation to the mother expresses itself in an excessive Oedipus rivalry. This rivalry is much less due to love of the father that to envy of the mother's possession of the father and his penis. The envy experienced towards the breast is then fully carried over into the Oedipus situation. The father (or his penis) has become an appendage to the mother and it is on these grounds that the girl wants to rob her mother of him. (1957, p. 200)

So it is to hurt the mother (and other women) and triumph over her, that the father (or other men) are wanted. *Both* parents seem to be wanted for the harm that the envious child might be able to be inflict upon them. If in the boy, envy is excessive, it may disturb the boy's later Oedipal love for his mother, leading to disturbances of potency later in life. Excessive envy of the breast is likely to extend to all feminine attributes, in particular to the woman's capacity to bear children.

In summary, for Klein the death drive gives rise to excessive envy, the inevitable compulsion to repeat remnants of archaic Oedipal and pre-Oedipal struggles, splitting of the object, omnipotence, denial, idealization, devaluation of other or self, confusion of thought, premature genitalization, and therefore too early ego activity - all as defences against excessive envy and the associated primordial anxieties.

The realization of loss

The above account of the phenomena of the paranoid-schizoid position, under the impact of envy, would be incomplete without a brief reference to Klein's other position, namely the depressive position (see Klein 1935, 1940). This position lies in a dialectical relationship to the paranoid-schizoid position. One cannot be considered without its relationship to the other. We will have much more to say about this dialectic in the next chapter. Whereas the paranoid-schizoid experience is all about more or less violent splitting attacks on the ego and its objects, the depressive position is tentatively achieved when these fragments of self can begin to be *integrated*, at around the end of the first six months (the timing is not ultimately important), when the infant can begin to perceive 'whole' objects.

Under the aegis of the smooth introjection of the good object and the infant's loving impulses towards it, the infant begins to experience a sense of mourning, a sense of depression, a anguished sense of pining for what is now felt to be a more or less lost or damaged object - lost or damaged, it is now realized, by the destructiveness that has gone on (in powerful unconscious phantasies) in the preceding phase of blind splitting. Depressive anxieties are now felt for the safety of this ultimately loved and needed object. Connections are made between expulsive violence and the object's integrity. And attempts will be made at reparation - a creative rebuilding of the object that has been destroyed in phantasy.

The goal of a Kleinian analysis is to bring about this new kind of awareness - this depressive realization of destructiveness, and to hold to it. There is always a danger where the depressive realization is too strong and the damaged object becomes *persecutory* again, that splitting processes will recur, and the new awareness will be lost in the fragments. Or if reparation begins to fail and repair becomes impossible, there may be a resort to a manic reparation (the manic defence), which in effect is a return to the blind unthinkingness of the paranoid-schizoid position, what Klein calls, 'a denial of psychic reality'. (1935, p. 262) Here, the reparation has a drivenness about it. It is too much, inappropriately helpful, a forcing of goodness.

However, even the normal early development of the child is seen by Klein as a very dramatic process, with a growing sense of and more accurate perception of the external world. She says:

> We may say that every step in emotional, intellectual and physical growth is used by the ego as a means of overcoming the depressive position. The child's growing skills, gifts and arts increase his belief in the psychic reality and of his constructive tendencies, in his capacity to master and control his hostile impulses as well as his "bad" internal objects ... The strengthened ego, with it greater trust in people, can then make still further steps toward unification of its imagoes - external, internal, loved and hated... (1940, p. 353)

There is a parallelism in Kleinian thinking between external and internal objects. The loss of the love of an external object endangers the internal economy, raising fears or memories of earlier losses. According to Klein, 'the poignancy of the actual [external] loss of a loved person is, in my view, greatly increased by the mourner's unconscious phantasies of having lost his *internal* 'good' objects as well'. .(1940, p. 353) Hence, with 'the strengthening of the subject's belief in goodness... the mourner is able to surrender fully to his feelings, and to cry out his sorrow about the actual loss. ...Through tears, the mourner not only expresses his feelings and thus eases tension, but since in the unconscious they are equated with excrements, he also expels his "bad" feelings and his "bad" objects'. This greater feeling of freedom in the inner world allows the internal objects more freedom to feel, and says Klein, 'in the mourner's state of mind, the feelings of his internal objects are also sorrowful. In his mind they share his grief, in the same way as actual kind parents would.' (1940, p. 359)

The depressive position offers the infant a chance to become *human*. Winnicott thought that for the infant to achieve this position, it had already gone a long way towards maturity. He preferred to call this stage of development, the 'stage of concern'. (Winnicott 1963) In this position the infant is able to respond and show concern for the object. The infant now has memories of many good experiences with the object, so much so that he acknowledges his dependency on that continued goodness, even if it is always in danger from his tendency to maltreat and enviously destroy it. It is important now, that he recognize and integrate these malign aspects of himself. As Hinshelwood succinctly puts it: 'The infant has to contend with the fact that he hates, with the most unrestrained and paranoid intensity, the mother whom he can now see is the same person he loved for feeding and caring for and loving him.' (1989, p. 141)

Klein here was following in the tradition of Freud and Abraham in believing that the fundamental basis of depression (melancholia) was the loss of a loved object. Klein says:

> It now becomes plain why, at this phase of development, the ego feels itself constantly menaced in its possession of internalized good objects. It is full of [depressive] anxiety lest such objects should die. Both in children and adults suffering from depression, I have discovered the dread of harbouring dying or dead objects (especially the parents) inside one and an identification

of the ego with objects in this condition. (1935, p. 266)

However, if the infant is fortunate enough to be able to work through the depressive position and to become more in touch with *external* reality, he is also likely to feel 'that the object's badness is largely due to his *own* aggressiveness and the ensuing projection. This insight ... brings about feelings of relief and hope, which in turn make it less difficult to reunite the two aspects of the object and of the self... [He has] the growing unconscious knowledge that the internal and external object is not as bad as it was felt to be in its split-off aspects... It is no longer so strongly felt to have been destroyed and the danger of its being destroyed in the future is lessened.' (1957, p.196 my italics)[3]

More *than a breast*

This is all very well, but if there is the element of beyondness in desire which Freud designated as the death drive, then it follows that the breast is, as Klein says, 'instinctively felt to be the source of nourishment and therefore, in a deeper sense, *of life itself*' (1957, p.178, my italics) It represents therefore *more* than just the simple need satisfying object of the pleasure principle. Herein lies our whole problematic, and the justification for making Klein central in the elucidation of the death drive theory. Because the breast lacks nothing, it creates anxiety, lust, the yearning to attempt to exhaust its inexhaustibility. This is the anxiety of Freud's 'excessive stimulation' to which the little primary vesicle is always prone and against which it pits a continuous anti-cathexis of primary repression (see last chapter). This is the primary anxiety of a helpless (*hilflos*) craving, or, 'a ubiquitous yearning for an unattainable perfect internal state.' (Klein, 1963, p. 300) Furthermore we must note, contra Winnicott and the Independent school, this envy arises not necessarily from some environmental deficiency, but indeed from a *superabundance* and its seductiveness! Envy exists because of this prodigality of the breast and it unattainability. Envy is the mental correlate of knowing that there is something very good out there. Segal emphasizes that the breast represents, 'an *inexhaustible* reservoir of food and warmth, love, understanding and wisdom. The blissful experience of satisfaction which this wonderful object can give will increase the infant's love and his desire to possess, preserve and protect it, but the same experience stirs in him also the wish to be himself the source of such perfection [hence]... he experienced the painful feelings of envy which carry with them the desire to spoil the qualities of the object which can give him such painful feelings.' (Segal 1973, pp. 40-41, my italics) Furthermore: 'Even when the environment is conductive to gratifying experiences, they may still be modified or even prevented by internal factors.' (ibid. p. 39) These 'internal factors', we are arguing are the existence of desire itself. Klein speaks of an *inevitable* loneliness: 'I am referring not to the objective situation of being deprived of external companionship.' (1963 p. 300) but, she suggests that this essential state of loneliness, 'derives from the depressive feeling of an irretrievable loss.' (p. 301)

There is, at some critical point, most often underplayed by object relations theorists, but insisted upon here, a desire that *no* object can satisfy. The death drive as envy has little or nothing to do with *biological* need, although it can be stimulated by deprivation; rather it has much more to do with a loss that is inherent in life itself. Ultimately, it is not an objective or a reasonable state which can be resolved. Envy is roused by glimpsing perfection and the abundance of life itself. The radical meaning of the depressive position is just this: a beloved object is lost *beyond recovery*.

Critique

My emphasis here has been that the whole of Kleinian psychoanalysis is predicated upon the potentially malign presence of the death drive within, and the subject's only *partial* success in overcoming and mitigating its influence in mental life. For many theorists, this is the return of 'original sin', and is therefore unacceptably pessimistic. Donald Meltzer (1978) suggests that, 'Melanie Klein constructed a quasi-theological system in which internal objects have the significance of deity.' (part 3, p. 2) This echoes the criticism raised in chapter one, that the death drive carries with it connotations of evil and reintroduces into psychoanalysis a moral dimension. How can an infant tell good from bad, a good object from a bad object? One answer might be that 'good' and 'bad' are words that are much later ascribed to primitive experiences *felt* to be either life-promoting and nourishing or disintegrative and threatening. To this extent, the Kleinians would understand there to be a phylogenetic basis to the infant's intuitions.

Klein's concept of 'positions' rather than 'phases' implies that, in a certain sense, we never grow out of or beyond these infantile structures. We return to them again and again in adult life, continuously reworking them in face of real and imagined losses. However, there has been much criticism of her approach - in particular, her concept of envy which is our main focus here. Space will only allow a summary of these criticisms:

1) Her dogmatic stance makes psychoanalysis into too much of a pedagogy or a new moralism, perhaps a terrorism, with its insistence on finding destructiveness, greed and envy and finally grief and suffering as a result. This may *reduce* the analytic project in advance, towards a negativity and depression. It can give the analyst too much power to be overly interpretive and can foster regression and the development of persecutory anxieties in the analysand.

2) Too early, too frequent and over-extensive interpretation by the analyst of the so-called 'total' situation also encourages regression to the possible exclusion or marginalisation of the wider aspects of personality functioning, at the various genetic levels described by classical psychoanalytic theory. It is as if all the phases of development - oral, anal, phallic, etc., are collapsed into just two central positions. This argument reached its crescendo during the 'Controversial Discussions' in the war years.

3) A tendency to deny the reality of the *external* world (of past and present) in favour of the single-minded uncovering of primitive and ruthless unconscious phantasies, carries the danger of a loss of discriminatory power in the analyst and the analysand. One patient who had undergone a long Kleinian analysis asked anxiously if her new analyst would understand and take cognizance of the fact that she could remember *real* deprivations in her life.

4) Little or no distinction seems to be made between various types of aggression if every aggressive impulse is deemed to be a derivative of the death drive. In chapter one, for instance, we discussed Winnicott's belief that aggression can be a sign of life.

5) Kleinian theory seems to emphasis the death instinct and envy, above and beyond the influence of the libido (love) in mental life. Creativity is reduced to *reparation* for past and present destructiveness. This is not so for the Independents where creativity exists in its own right.

6) The loss of the centrality of the classical *Oedipus*, and in particular the role of the father, and its replacement by the depressive position - Klein's version of the Oedipus complex now brought back to the first year of life - bears little relation to the classical model with the drama of the intervention of the father. The central role of castration in *sexu-*

al and generational differentiation seems to have been marginalized.

7) There has been a subtle shift in emphasis from *content to process.* The emphasis with Klein seems to demote the *contents* of the unconscious to be uncovered, in favour of *affective processes,*[4] biologically driven by primordial energies which by their very nature have less and less to do with the subject's history, but which unfold by means of a pre-structured plan inherent in instinctual life itself, which gives rise to unconscious phantasy. According to Susan Isaacs, 'There is no impulse, no instinctual urge or response which is not experienced as unconscious phantasy.' (Isaacs, 1952, p. 83)

8) Klein's emphasis on the talion principle, of good and bad internal objects, as they are tranferentially projected into the analyst, and perhaps back again, reduces the analytic process, according to the Lacanian critique, to an *Imaginary* transaction which sponsors progressive alienations, miscognitions and paranoia (see chapter four). Analysis becomes a dyadic process in which the *third* dimension of language, in the Lacanian sense, will be marginalized. However, this familiar Lacanian polemic conveniently leaves out the role and subtlety of the depressive position - the rarely glimpsed position of truth *beyond* the mirrors.

9) There is also the practical problem of investigating the alleged existence of phantasies in the first years of life *before* language acquisition. Does the Kleinian method of deep interpretation *create* a belief in these primitive infantile phantasies, or are they really there in the beginning? It has been argued that the phantasies of biting, devouring, drowning, etc. are too cognitively sophisticated for the infantile mind, and what is really involved is retrospective sophistication, namely, older children regressing under the impact of frustration and now able to talk about these feelings. But, what are they regressing to if not some primitive phantasy already there in the unconscious, waiting, as it were, to be put into words!

Isaacs argues strongly in favour of claiming the infant's phylogenetic inheritance of primitive phantasies, and that 'the earliest impulses of desire and aggressiveness, are expressed in and dealt with by mental processes far removed from words and conscious relational thinking, and determined by the logic of emotion... There is a wealth of evidence to show that phantasies are active in the mind long before language has developed... Meanings like feelings are far older than speech.' (1952, p. 89) She cites dancing, acting, drawing, painting, sculpture and music as meanings beyond words. She cites Freud's emphasis of the visual equating closely to the unconscious both ontogenetically and phylogenetically. She gives the clear example of a child's terror of her mother's shoe, from which the sole had become detached. This shoe caused the child such distress that the mother threw the shoes away. Much later, the child asked her mother where the shoes had gone. On being told that they have been thrown away, the child reported that they might have eaten her up. Here, phantasy can be *felt* as real, long before it can be put into words. Clearly, the capacity to use words changes things, but does not gainsay the impact of the very real reality of the primary affective experience.

10) Whatever reservations we may have about the Kleinian approach, Hinshelwood concludes:

> The problems therefore remain. For the Kleinians, the death instinct is not silent but active as an important factor that greatly disturbs and modifies the natural progression of the libidinal development through the early phases; whilst classical psychoanalysts minimize the clinical importance of the death instinct and emphasize the epigenetic development of the libido and ego. What critically decisive situations in clinical practice would lead to deciding these issues is yet to be given serious attention. (1989, p. 55)

I myself have tried to make an assessment of this apparent Kleinian departure from psychoanalysis towards biology in the context of Lacan's so-called 'return to Freud'. In this paper, I argued that what is crucially important is that 'Klein takes us further back into the structured past, to a point where structure almost ceases to be a meaningful concept, and where we witness the often extreme anxieties involved in the birth of a subject.' (Weatherill 1992, p.12) This hypothetical extreme point - the point of the so-called psychotic core - is the one *uniquely emphasized* by Kleinian psychoanalysis.

With all the attendant risks and reservations outlined above, it seems as if Klein has succeeded in delineating in a remarkably clear and excitingly dramatic way the poignant distress inherent in life itself and in attaining and maintaining human subjectivity. For the arguments that I am developing in this book, the Kleinian approach to emotional life is indispensable.

Finally, we might ponder on how these extreme formulations were caught by Klein, as it were, rescued from oblivion, and then maintained and deepened in the teeth of opposition?

Klein's personal losses

Klein's early experiences of irretrievable loss, it could be argued, predisposed her towards an awareness of the losses of her child patients. Her sister Sidonie died of scrofula in 1886, when she was 8 and Melanie was 4. This blow to her was especially poignant, since Sidonie had showed much kindness to her and would take her side against the teasing of the older siblings, Emilie and Emanuel, from whom Melanie felt excluded. Even when she was sick and dying, Sidonie taught her the fundamentals of arithmetic and reading. Melanie reflects, 'but my feeling is that, had she lived, we would have been the greatest friends.' (Klein quoted in Grosskurth 1985, p. 15) Apparently, Melanie never quite got over Sidonie's death.

The inner circle of the family, Melanie's mother Libussa and Emanuel her brother, was emotionally intense[5]. Her father was Moriz Reizes, a doctor, much older than her mother, indeed fifty when Melanie was born. By her own account he neglected her, and openly favoured her older sister. According to Grosskurth, there was a pattern of matriarchy in the family. Melanie was greatly attracted to the cultural ambiance and values of her mother's family, while being scornful of her father's. Grosskurth significantly points out that Emanuel's 'feeling for his mother and his sister was not simply affection, but *possession*.' (ibid. p.35, my italics) Emanuel wrote to his mother: 'My darling, I am longing for you immensely. We would spend a beautiful few weeks together...' (ibid. p. 27) Of Melanie, he declared she was 'a work of art I will never again be able to behold anywhere else, neither in nature nor in imitation.' (ibid. p. 27)

Emanuel was *the* major influence on Melanie's life. He himself was very gifted, and inspired Melanie. Emanuel fancied himself as a writer, artist and musician. He started out in medical studies but abandoned them in favour of the arts. He felt doomed to an early death, as his heart had been weakened by an attack of scarlet fever followed by rheumatic fever at the age of 12. He saw himself as the dying artist. He died in 1902 in a hotel in Genoa of heart failure, at the age of 25, as a result of malnutrition, alcohol, poverty, drugs and a will to self-destruction. Here again Melanie feels, as with Sidonie, a terrible loss. As Grosskurth says: 'He was her surrogate father, close companion, phantom lover - and no one in her life was ever able to replace him.'

(ibid. p. 39) Melanie carried a guilt about his death for the rest of her life.

In October 1933, Melanie's daughter, Melitta Schmideberg, was elected to membership of the British Institute where she was to embarrass her colleagues 'by the virulence of the vendetta she waged against her own mother.' (ibid. p. 213) Members recall Melitta as 'intense and humourless'. During meetings she made repeated untruthful accusations against her mother, who, in spite of inner pain and turmoil, would 'preserve a dignified silence' during these tirades.

Then, most tragically of all, in April 1934, Melanie's son, Hans, died tragically in a climbing accident. Melitta's immediate reaction to her brother's death was that it had been suicide, which Eric Clyne was able emphatically to deny. But, as Grosskurth remarks, Melanie, who may have felt that Hans' problems might have been exacerbated by her chronic depression when he was a child, was so affected by these events and her earlier bereavements, that 'for the rest of her life she was to turn her attention to the questions of loss, grief, and loneliness, experiences that formed the recurrent pattern of her life.' (ibid. pp. 215-216)

1934 had been a terrible year, Melitta's treachery, Hans' death. Her intense grief must have aroused past sorrows. As well as those we have mentioned, there was her unhappy and very ambivalent relationship with Arthur Klein, whom she divorced in 1926 after 23 years of marriage; her devastation after Abraham's early death in December 1925, after a very brief and unfinished analysis with him; and the uneasy course of her romantic affair with Chezkel Zvi Kleotzel (a journalist in Berlin, whom Klein had met during dancing classes), who painfully rejected her around the same time.

According to Grosskurth, the papers, 'Infantile Anxiety-Situations Reflected in a Work of Art and in the Creative Impulse' (1929), and 'A Contribution to the Psychogenesis of Manic-Depressive States' (1940), which follows on the 1935 paper, enabled Klein in some way to sublimate her grief and to understand it as a stepping stone towards maturity and development. Grosskurth likens this to Freud's dream book which arose out of his own self-analysis. Klein, like Freud, realized that she had made a major discovery which would only be preserved and disseminated by devoted, loyal and gifted students. Consequently, like Freud, she demanded unflinching loyalty and she could be ruthless in casting off those who expressed doubt or appeared to be pursuing independent lines of investigation.

In spite of all these difficulties, losses and real set-backs, Melanie Klein has provided us with a prophetic and brutal insight into the dynamics of human desire. Her analysis of the vicissitudes of the death drive is unique in the history of psychotherapy. Hinshelwood puts the Kleinian contribution succinctly: 'If ever an epitaph for Kleinian psychoanalysis has one day to be written, it will surely refer to the relentless hunting down of all the forms of destructiveness that so spoil the greatest human aspirations.' (1994, p. 235) Her work has inspired many, and it is now logical for us to turn to one of the greatest exponents of Kleinian theory, Wilfred Bion.

3. BION: UNLINKING, UNTHINKING

Wilfred Bion was arguably one of the most distinguished elaborators of Melanie Klein's work, and indeed the most highly influential. There can be few analysts working today who have not been affected by him in their thinking and practice. His contribution is vast and complex. He was born in India, sent off on his own to an English boarding school at the age of eight. He was a tank commander in the First World War (winning the DSO) before studying medicine and then psychoanalysis. Although Bion's training was in science, he had great ambitions to be a philosopher: he wanted to create an extensive psychoanalytic epistemology[1]. In the 1940s he made valuable discoveries relating to group psychology. After Klein's (1946) paper on schizoid mechanisms, schizophrenia became an important focus of psychoanalytic investigation and treatment. The nub of the problem in schizophrenia was seen to be understanding the origin and fate of excessive sadism (the death drive) within the personality. Klein, as we have seen, related this to the failure of the deflection of the death drive which manifests itself in primary envy and the spoiling of the good and helpful object upon which mental health ultimately rests. We must now examine how Bion takes up these issues and fleshes them out. We will concern ourselves only with those aspects of Bion's work which have a direct bearing on the substance of this book.

Reverie, containment and thinking

Bion describes a fraught analytic session with a patient:

> The analytic situation built up in my mind a sense of witnessing... in infancy a mother who dutifully responded to the infant's emotional displays. The dutiful response had in it an element of impatient: "I don't know what's the matter with the child". My deduction was that in order to understand what the child wanted the mother should have treated the infant's cry as more than a demand for her presence. From the infant's point of view, she should have taken into her, and thus experienced, *the fear that the child was dying*. It was this fear that the child could not contain. He strove to split it off together with the part of the personality in which it lay and project it into the mother. An understanding mother is able to experience the feeling of dread that this baby

was striving to deal with by projective identification, and yet retain a balanced outlook. This patient had to deal with a mother who could not tolerate experiencing such feelings and reacted either by denying them ingress, or alternatively by becoming prey to the anxiety which resulted from introjection of the infant's bad feelings. (1959, p. 104, my italics)

Bion formulated what amounts to a law of psychological functioning (Grotstein, 1979). He did not claim it was a law, but it perhaps has cause to be considered as such as its application goes well outside psychoanalysis. This is his theory of relationship called the 'container-contained'. It derives from Klein's original description of the establishment of the ego via projective and introjective processes. A person puts parts of himself (the contained) into another (the container), and takes parts of the other (the contained) into himself (the container). This is a way of describing affective and ideational introjections and projections between people. Bion was particularly concerned to build up a model of these processes in normality and abnormality.

The concept is best understood prototypically (as above) on the model of the infant mother relationship. Bion (1962a) described the mother's state of mind when she is available and receptive to the infant's needs and feelings, as being in a state of *reverie*. Primitive anxieties and terrors relating to the paranoid-schizoid position and the activity of the death drive within, delineated in the last chapter, are *too* much for the infant alone to contain. The infant finds them intolerable, and will insert them (by projection) into the mother's mind, which then becomes the container for his contained. Ideally, the mother receives the projected anxiety, she 'picks up' (introjects) the infant's anxiety or dread. The mother's reverie becomes a process of making sense of it for the infant. Various metaphors are often used in describing what the mother does with the contained projection. She processes it, gives it meaning, detoxifies it, metabolizes it, makes it digestible for the infant's re-assimilation. The infant is now able to introject the mother's containing function, her capacity for reflection and understanding, into himself. Repeated cycles of projective and introjective experiences like this build up within the infant a psyche or mind that is capable of containing its own contents because it has internalised the so-called good breast. The good breast is now seen by Bion as not only a provider of supplies, as a part object, but also as a *link* between infant and object. The function of the mother is to make links for the infant.

Therefore the good breast is good because it makes *meaning from non-sense* for the baby. The links are an embryonic form of learning, whereby incomprehensible bodily experience (contained) is connected to consciousness, meaning and understanding, as represented in the first instance by the mother (container).

The coupling of mouth and nipple is the prototype for Bion of the way mental objects are put together, one inside the other. Thus sense experience is assembled into embryonic thoughts, in the first instance. If this process of containing goes well, thoughts can be linked to other thoughts, thoughts linked to words, concepts, and so on, into ever widening forms of linking and sophistication. But the first and most important foundational moment for mental life is the containing of the infant's desperation and helplessness, of his fear that *he is dying*. The infant is seen as a contained (fear of annihilation) seeking a container (the wise and understanding breast/mother):

> Normal development follows if the relationship between the infant and the breast permits the infant to project a feeling, say, that it is dying into the mother and to reintroject it after its sojourn in the breast has made it tolerable to the infant psyche. If the projection is not accepted by the mother the infant feels that its feeling that it is dying is stripped of such meaning as it has. It therefore reintrojects, not a fear of dying made tolerable, but a nameless dread. (1962b, p. 116)

The normal maternal mind in this state of reverie for the infant performs a crucial function for the infant, which Bion (1962a) termed 'alpha-function'. How is the gap crossed between body and the mind? How do we get from raw biological sensation to an *experience* of that sensation? Susan Isaacs, to whom we have already referred, made the connection between instinct and unconscious phantasy, by stating that 'phantasies ... are the psychic representatives of a bodily aim', and *'phantasy is the link between id impulse and the ego mechanism'* (1952 p. 112). Alpha function for Bion is this conversion process whereby raw sense data can be digested, assimilated and transformed into what he termed 'alpha elements', which are the building blocks, the elementary particles, essential for manipulation in a process to be called 'thinking'. He further suggested that alpha-function enables the division between conscious and unconscious. By creating alpha-elements from raw chaotic sense data (later to be called beta-elements), the former can now be safely repressed into the unconscious for use in dream thoughts, unconscious phantasies, unconscious thinking, and so on. Here is a method of processing the vast and overwhelming inpouring of stimuli that would overwhelm the psychical apparatus were it not for the alpha-function's capacity to capture, fix and store them for later use in psychical activity and representation. There are now *experiences* that can be safely rendered unconscious (repressed), leaving consciousness free to pursue activities on the outside. The energy in these repressed elements is relatively contained and can be used in what Freud called primary process thinking for the production of dreams, phantasies, neurotic symptoms, parapraxes, jokes, etc.

Bion describes the 'developmental history' of a thought (1962a,b). In this model, an innate preconception (one that we are born with, like a Platonic form) meets with a realisation in the outer world, to form a conception. The preconception is an inherited expectation, an empty thought that cannot be known for itself by itself. The earliest example is the pre-conception of a mouth searching for the realisation of the nipple. When it meets with the realisation, the mouth finds and/or is given the nipple, a conception is born. Conceptions result from satisfying linkages. The conception itself can be used as a further preconception which requires further realisation to form new conceptions, and so on, in an ever widening series.

What happens when a preconception meets with no realisation? This is a crucial moment. The infant experiences the absence of the breast *as a concrete presence,* the presence of a 'no breast'. This is *potentially* a bad object. But if the immature ego can tolerate the frustration of the absence he may be able to experience it as a thought while accepting its absence. Here Bion echoes Freud who viewed the development of thought as arising from the *absence* of satisfaction. The thought occurs in the gap that opens between desire and its fulfilment. The ability to *distinguish* the thought from the object itself (the capacity known as symbolisation) or an hallucination of it, is a prerequisite for thinking. So conceptions can result from positive and negative realisations, or from links that satisfy, or from links which are wished for but in a tolerable way do not happen. Therefore, thinking is based on the experience of satisfaction or the tolerance of frustration which can act as a stimulus for thought, and the consequent shift from the pleasure principle to the reality principle. However, Bion like Klein, considers that infants vary in their toleration of the absence of satisfaction. Beyond a certain point for certain infants, frustration does not lead to negative realisations and the origins of creative thinking, but to pathological processes which we will come on to in the next section.

All this primitive thinking can only begin take place in the ambience of the mother's reverie. The infant cannot begin to think in a vacuum. In her over-arching containing function, she protects the fragile infantile psyche (the primary vesicle) from going to pieces, or being torn apart by excessive instinctual tension, and provides the means for integrative processes - containing, alpha-function, conceptions, realisations, unconscious thinking, psychical processing of experience, and so on.

Before going on to see how all this can go wrong, we will summarise the ideas so far. The maternal capacity for empathy and understanding of her infant's needs and terrors (preconceptions) enables him to introject the experience of being contained by a container. Raw unthinkable sense data arising in his body is projected into the mother for her modification, and then converted into alpha elements to be manipulated in an embryonic unconscious thinking process: a process which will provide for the necessary separation between conscious and unconscious, for waking life and dream life, in short for psychic life in general. This is the foundation for his mental health, his capacity to think thoughts, contain himself, learn from experience, in the presence and tolerable absence of satisfaction. In more Kleinian terms, the infant has introjected good objects, which will mitigate in large degree, the bad objects associated with violent phantasies arising from the death drive.

The above model represents the so-called normal use by the infant of projective identification (see Bion, 1959). Here it functions as a means of communication. The mother picks up the child's anxieties and modifies them for the child's reintrojection. It is the same in analysis. In the most general sense, the pain that the patient brings is projected into the analyst who through his or her commitment and training tries to feel, understand and put into words the core of an experience which has always eluded the patient's grasp. This takes place mainly through the medium of speech and within the total transference, countertransference dialectic.

Violent projective identification

We must now look at the *abnormal* use of projective identification. In this situation, the infant/adult *violently expels a painful state of mind* into the other for the purpose of immediate relief, and of controlling the other. The other person in receipt of the projection, in some degree, feels manipulated, set-up and coerced into behaving in a certain way. A refusal to do so (a refusal of the projection) will provoke a more violent attack. Thus we can see that pathological projective identification is the natural corollary of the failure of normal projective identification. So when the normal use of the mechanism fails, a violent form ensues, which is highly likely to sponsor a more violent retaliation, on the principle of the talion referred to in the previous chapter.

Bion (1957) distinguished the psychotic from the non-psychotic aspects of the personality. His work with schizophrenics enabled him to clearly elucidate the psychotic process, and demarcate it from normal and neurotic functioning. In the psychotic process, varying degrees of violent projective identification are likely to be common.

Summarising schizophrenic psychopathology, Bion notes four basic features: (1) a preponderance of destructive impulses, relating to envy and greed (the death drive); (2) a hatred of reality and the reality principle; (3) dread of annihilation; (4) thin but tenacious object relations. Here the death drive has not been successfully deflected and contained by another. The psychotic is, as it were, stuck at that stage of trying to get his nameless (death) dread *felt*, by the massive use of projective identification, as a brutal means of communication with the other. The breast is attacked and even the perceptual apparatus itself. Destructiveness is such that even the basic mental processes of thinking, perceiving external reality, and communicating through language, are disturbed, interfered with and degraded. The linkages described above, which give rise to realisations and thinking are to some degree disrupted and broken. In short, (sexual) intercourse, and all the creative generativity that it symbolises, are prevented by destructive attacks.

Bion describes a patient, who thus splits up words and meanings. As Bion put it, this patient had defective hearing and a mouth that destroyed language. The account Bion gives of this patient, he says, is of necessity compressed. Here is the extract:

Patient: I picked a tiny piece of skin from my face and feel quite empty.
Analyst: The tiny piece of skin is your penis, which you have torn out, and all your insides have come with it.

Patient: I do not understand...penis...only syllables.
Analyst: You have split my word "penis" into syllables and it now has no meaning.
Patient: I don't know what it means, but I want to say, "If I can't spell I cannot think".
Analyst: The syllables have been split into letters; you cannot spell - that is to say you cannot put the letters together again to make words. So now you cannot think.
The patient started the next day's session with disjointed associations and complained that he could not think. I reminded him of the session I have described, whereupon, he resumed correct speech; thus:
Patient: I cannot find any interesting food.
Analyst: You feel it has all been eaten up.
Patient: I do not feel able to buy any new clothes and my socks are a mass of holes.
Analyst: By picking out the tiny piece of skin yesterday you injured yourself so badly you cannot even buy clothes; you are empty and have nothing to buy them with.
Patient: Although they are full of holes they constrict my foot.
Analyst: Not only did you tear out your own penis but also mine. So today there is no interesting food - only a hole, a sock. But even this sock is made of a mass of holes, all of which you made and which have joined together to constrict, or swallow and injure, your foot.

This and subsequent sessions confirmed that he felt he had eaten the penis and that therefore there was no interesting food left, only a hole. But this hole was now so persecutory that he had to split it up. As a result of the splitting, the hole became a mass of holes which all came together in a persecutory way to constrict his foot. (1953 p. 28)

Bion suggested that 'despite his wishes and mine, we could not, or felt we could not communicate. I suggested that he felt he had a very bad and hostile object inside him which was treating our verbal intercourse to much the same kind of destructive attack which he had once felt he had launched against parental intercourse whether sexual or verbal'. (ibid. p. 30)

Such patients feel imprisoned with these destructive internal objects. These internal objects contain the infant's own violent envy, whose function is to strip the ego of any goodness and meaning. The normal processes of thinking, behaving and communicating are all disrupted by these destructive objects.

Beta-elements and bizarre objects

Such mutilating processes lead to the production of *beta*-elements and bizarre objects. When alpha-function fails, sense data, which has not been assimilated, accumulates intolerably. These 'undigested' events are referred to by Bion as beta-elements. The psychotic mind develops in order *not* to think and *not* to perceive. 'What should be a thought, a product of the juxtaposition of preconception and negative realisation becomes a bad object, indistinguishable from the thing in itself, fit only for evacuation... The end result is that all thoughts are treated as if they were indistinguishable from bad internal objects; the appropriate machinery is felt to be, not an apparatus for thinking thoughts, but an apparatus for ridding the psyche of accumulations of bad internal objects'. (Bion, 1962b, p. 112) This model follows on from Freud's (1911b) paper 'Formulations on the two principles of mental functioning', in which Freud suggested that ordinarily thinking, connected to reality and to language, should take over from motor discharge connected with the pleasure principle.

The ejected fragments of the perceptual apparatus invade external objects, in a magically omnipotent way, to form highly persecutory objects, termed bizarre objects. There is the real external object, but it has become surrounded by a piece of the personality which has been ejected and engulfed it. The character of the bizarre object, Bion points out, 'will depend partly on the character of the real object, say a gramophone, and partly on the character of the particle of the personality that engulfs it. If the piece of the personality is concerned with sight, the gramophone when played is felt to be watching the patient. If with hearing, the gramophone when played will be felt to be listening to the patient' (Bion, 1956, pp. 39-40). The schizophrenic lives therefore in a bizarre egocentric world, persistently treated by bits of himself projected - mis-seen and mis-heard in everything.

The severe splitting and fragmentation in the schizophrenic makes it difficult to perceive reality. But Bion unlike Freud, suggests that the ego is never wholly withdrawn from reality. 'I would say that its contact with reality is masked by the dominance, in the patient's mind and behaviour, of an omnipotent phantasy that is intended to destroy either reality or awareness of it, and thus to achieve a state that is neither life nor death.' (1957a, p. 46)

In the schizophrenic, the ego's tenuous access to reality has to be constantly attacked. The patient wants nothing to do with his embryonic capacity for thought, which he dreads because it threatens to bring home to him his real *feeling* of pain, catastrophe and insanity. Regression to the paranoid-schizoid position is inevitable as it holds out the possibility of destroying the source of that pain by omnipotent evacuative attacks on reality, truth and thought, and the obliteration of the pain and suffering that would happen if things were allowed to come together, be linked-up and thought about. We will return to this psychotic dispersal of feelings.

As noted above, thinking is concerned with linking, on the prototype of the mouth-nipple link, or the penis-vagina link. Such intercourse or coupling is attacked and destroyed by the envy derived from the unassimilated death drive. This envy extends to the parental couple (in the primitive Oedipus), the analytic couple, ultimately to any creative process. Linking involves the capacity to use symbols. Bion (1957) suggests that, what he calls 'ideographs', exist from the outset. A thing becomes conscious by coming into contact, or linking with the verbal images that correspond to it. This is consistent with Freud from as early as his work 'On Aphasia' (1891) and 'The Project' (1950 [1895]). Bion points out, however, that:

> not only is primitive thought attacked because it links sense-impressions of reality with consciousness but, thanks to the psychotic's over-endowment with destructiveness, the splitting processes are extended to the links within the thought processes themselves... All these are now attacked till finally two objects cannot be brought together in a way which leaves each object with its intrinsic qualities intact, and yet able, by their conjunction, to produce a new mental object. Consequently the formation of symbols which depends for its therapeutic effect on the ability to bring together two objects so that their resemblance can be made manifest, yet their difference left unimpaired, now becomes difficult'. (1957,[1967] p. 50)[2]

As a result, articulation through language becomes difficult or impossible. Bion indicates that 'agglomerations' can occur, but the links are impregnated with cruelty. Repression becomes impossible since the psychotic core has destroyed the apparatus needed to carry out the repression.

According to Bion (1953)[1967], the process of symbolisation requires, (1) whole objects, (2) the abandonment of the paranoid-schizoid position with its persistent splitting processes, and (3) the *bringing together* of splits and the ushering in of the depressive position. Verbal thought requires integration, and is therefore linked with depression, and the awareness of destruction within, as Klein has emphasized. At this point of depressive realisation, the psychotic patient, as we have noted, is likely to regress into increasing fragmentation.

Furthermore, on language, Bion states: 'If verbal thought is that which synthesizes and articulates impressions, and is thus essential to awareness of internal and external reality, it is to be expected that it will be subjected, on and off throughout analysis, to destructive splitting and projective identification. I described the inception of verbal thought as appertaining to the depressive position; but the depression that is proper to this phase is itself something to which the psychotic personality objects and therefore the development of verbal thought comes under attack.' (1957a[1967] p. 60)

Hallucinations

Further illuminating the psychotic process, Bion describes hallucinatory phenomena. Here, he suggests, bodily movements and gestures themselves can represent the hallucinated expulsion and ejection of fragments of the self. Here, as noted above, Bion is following Freud's (1911b) description of motor activity, before the establishment of the reality principle, which unburdens the mental apparatus of noxious stimuli. In the example of the patient, in his paper, Bion notes that, 'The patient jerked convulsively and I saw him cautiously scanning what seemed to be the air around him. I accordingly said that he felt [hallucinated being] surrounded by bad smelly bits of himself including his eyes which he had expelled from his anus.' (1957a [1967] p. 56) He had lost various ego functions, such as his sight, his memory—he had anaesthetized these and any ego capacity that could make him realise pain. The analyst contains the patient's ego functions, and the patient needs to repair his ego, which has been damaged by excessive projective identification. Skilful agglomerations begin to occur, with approximations to ordinary verbal thought, more contact with reality and concern for the analyst as a human being. But the taking back of the expelled particles is felt to be very painful, an assault, a 'memory torture' as this patient described the increasing sense of depressive anxiety.

In another case Bion tries to understand the gestures and movements of an hallucinating patient. In relation to hallucination, Bion notes that perception is a *two* way process in the psychotic. Sense organs can *expel* as well as receive. 'If the patient says he sees an object it may mean that an external object has been perceived by him or it may mean that he is ejecting an object through his eyes: if he says he hears something it may mean that he is ejecting a sound - this is *not* the same as making a noise.' (1958 [1967] p. 67) Similarly, 'the unburdening of the psyche by hallucination, that is by the use of the sensory apparatus in reverse, is reinforced by muscular action which may be best understood as being an extremely complex analogue of a scowl; the musculature does not simply change the expression to one of murderous hate but gives effect to an actual murderous assault.' (ibid. p. 83)

Of the same hallucinating patient, Bion says, 'Each syllable that I uttered seemed to be felt by him as a stabbing thrust from me.' (ibid. p. 71) In what Bion calls a bad session, the patients says that he has placed (hallucinated) a gramophone on the seat, in place of Bion himself. And Bion comments that he began to realise that the patient was now hallucinating, 'he was so manipulating the analysis and myself that I felt I was no longer an independent object, but was being treated by him as an hallucination. My suspicion was that when he said he had placed his gramophone on the seat, he was denying me life and independent existence... treating my interpretations as auditory hallucinations.' (ibid. p. 75) Bion interprets this protective move, and the patient's response is to move his head from side to side, 'as if my words were visible objects which were passing over his head to become impacted on the opposite wall... On previous occasions I had interpreted his behaviour to mean that he saw my words as things and was following them with his eyes.' (ibid. p. 75) The patient agrees that the analyst's words were indeed being seen as 'evacuated objects like bits of faeces'. Bion continues that 'it had seemed to me that the hallucination had a reassuring quality in that my interpretations, felt as persecutory objects, were seen to be passing harmlessly overhead.' (ibid. p. 75) Indeed, Bion feels that his words are being taken in by the patient's ears, cruelly and destructively, and ejected by his eyes. The patient then reports that he feels very frightened and that he is fading away. The analyst interprets that he is afraid because he feels that he is destroying the analyst, as well as his words, and that he cannot not get enough good interpretations to cure him - save him from fading away. Bion had the experience with this patient, that whenever the analyst's interpretations were for some reason unwelcome, the patient appeared to strain forward and focus his attention on a far corner of the room.

Of such patients, Bion concludes: 'He wishes to love. Feeling incapable of [tolerating and thinking about] frustration he resorts to a murderous assault, or a token assault, as a method of disburdening his psyche of the unwanted emotions. The assault is but the outward expression of an explosive projective identification by virtue of which his murderous hatred, together with bits of his personality [including the perceptual apparatus itself, and with it the capacity for judgement], is scattered far and wide into the real objects, members of society included, by which he is surrounded. [Ironically] He now feels free to be loving, but is surrounded by bizarre objects each compounded of real people and things, destructive hatred, and murderous conscience ... the violence of the explosion leaves him denuded of his feeling of love.' (ibid. p. 84)

Finally and ominously in this paper, Bion warns analysts and therapists, that, with these sorts of patients, the analyst's attempt to rejoin these cruel fragments and bring the patient to the depressive realisation of his murderous intents, can lead to an incurable *secondary* splitting and minute fragmentation and the real danger of suicide.

Bion spent his professional life trying to hypothesize and theorize about the psychotic process which is driven by the unassimilated death drive, or as Freud noted, the essence of instinctuality itself, in its most extreme form, namely, the reduction of tension (feeling and thinking) to zero, the radical intolerance of delay, and the 'use' of the perceptual apparatus to destroy rather than perceive reality. Bion's insights have enabled us to think in a bizarre way about an essentially anti-life process, which in some individuals, designated as either borderline or psychotic, is the preferred solution when confronted by the pain or the insult, as Winnicott says, of reality. Furthermore, Bion has elaborated, what has been called the psychotic core within the *normal* and the neurotic personality, which can disrupt individuals and groups.

He has set the stage for seeing individual and group activity as a dramatic battleground between mind and anti-mind, between mindfulness and mindlessness, between communication through language, symbol and metaphor, and degrees of violent projective violation of all these. He has developed a terminology which is bizarre in its own way, to disrupt our normal rational ways of thinking, so that we can approach mental life perhaps afresh, 'without memory or desire', with unsaturated preconceptions to always be fleshed-out anew.

Like Melanie Klein, he has blurred the distinction between conscious and unconscious with his concept of linking which is undoubtedly unconscious, but not exclusively so. He has driven psychoanalysis back to its limit of conceptualisation in his attempt to formulate and understand primitive *affective* processes that arose from the 'primitive catastrophe' of infancy arising from the immanence of the death drive. Insofar as these 'events' were not structured (subject to alpha-function) they are always potentially present as beta-elements, as 'things-in-themselves', threatening and malevolent, *outside* the mind.

Probing 'O' and the catastrophe

Bion's reworking of Kleinian concepts has further radicalised the analyst's role. In order to analyse the patient's psychotic largely unstructured affective processes, the analyst also has to have the capacity to become temporarily but not actually psychotic, herself. In his book, *Attention and Interpretation* (1970), Bion elucidates his now famous injunction that analysts be 'without memory, desire or understanding'. Here paradoxically, the container of understanding can *also* be death bearing. '*Falsity*', writes Bion, 'is the characteristic of thought within an individual, or thought within a container.' (ibid. p. 117 my italics) 'The more successfully the word[3] and its use can be 'established', the more its precision becomes an *obstructive rigidity*' .(ibid. p. 80, my italics) For Bion the 'establishment' whatever form it takes represents 'rigid adherence to an existing framework.' (ibid. p. 111)

Clearly, the container must not always be marked with a positive sign. Bion refers to the conflict, 'between the container and the contained thing in which they both seem to be on very destructive terms, where either the container gets split apart, or the object that is put into the container gets destroyed. This seems to be a theme that occurs over and over again.' (In F. Bion, 1992, p. 356) Further on, speaking of ideas that are too big to be put into words, Bion comments, 'Either the speech, formulation, grammar [container] is destroyed, or the vocabulary and grammar get the upper hand - in which case the idea [contained] is destroyed.' (p. 356) Interestingly, in the case of the stammerer, 'The words that should have represented the meaning the [stammering] man wanted to express were fragmented by the emotional forces [derivatives of the death drive] to which he wished to give only verbal expression; the verbal formulation could not 'contain' his emotions, which broke through and dispersed it as enemy forces might break through the forces that strove to contain them.' (1970, p. 94)

Earlier in 1957, Bion (1957b) has indicated that the container of pride and self respect becomes 'arrogance', as the rigid container, where the death drive predominates. This leads to what Bion symbolises as a *minus* container-contained of the psychotic personality, or we could say, anti-growth, and the re-creation of *beta*-elements. Here, then, the excessive nature of envy can burst the container-breast. Or, the always limited breast container is constrictive when it comes to the *extreme* of desire.

In chapter twelve of *Attention and Interpretation,* Bion talks about the reciprocity of the container-contained. For instance, 'A word contains a meaning; conversely, a meaning contains a word - which may or may not be discovered.' (p. 106) Presumably in the latter, there is a feeling, or an intuitive stage *within* which we may or may not find a word. Or meaning is much larger than the words that might contain it. He goes on to give a number of commonplace examples of where the container squeezes the life out of the contained. For instance, the analysis that is continued so long that the patient cannot get any meaning out of it. Or, the analyst whose memory is 'saturated' kills off the possibility of making new observations.

Similarly, Bion advises that the analyst must be aware when he is the container and the patient the contained, and vice versa. This requires a certain capacity to play and to change vertices. And what type of link between the container-contained is there - commensual (harmless coexistence), symbiotic (growthful) or parasitic (mutually destructive)? For instance, Bion cites the greedy (parasitic) patient, who as container denudes the contained object (the correct interpretation), or conversely who, as contained object, takes the life out of the container (the analyst feels drained).

Of necessity, Bion says that 'psycho-analysis cannot "contain" the mental domain because it is *not* so much a container, but a "probe".' (1970, p. 73) Bion claims very paradoxically, and contra Lacan, as we shall see, that all that pertains to the psychoanalytic domain lies *outside* the mental container of all that is the sensuous, memorable, understandable, representable. These fundamentally are present only in 'O' - Ultimate Reality, which is ungraspable with the relative opacity of our senses and memorising. The analyst, à la Bion, is involved in a certain secular form of what Bion refers to as Faith (F). Freud, quoted by Bion, had spoken about artificially blinding himself 'to focus all the light on one dark spot.' (ibid. p. 57) Bion goes on to add, 'This provides a useful formulation for describing the area I wish to cover by F. By rendering oneself 'artificially blind' through the exclusion of memory and desire, one achieves F; the piercing shaft of darkness can be directed on the dark features of the analytic situation. Through F one can 'see', 'hear', and 'feel' the mental phenomena of whose reality no practising psycho-analyst has any doubt though he cannot with any accuracy represent them by existing formulations.' (ibid. pp. 57-58) Clearly, from this point of view the container (which remembers, which knows) veers towards omnipotence, which *constricts* meaning. So-called 'transformation in K [knowing] must be replaced by transformation in O, and K must be replaced by F.' (ibid. p. 46) This requires a mental '*un*saturation', or *un*possessiveness.

This is not to say that the analyst at this point *is* psychotic. Firstly, Bion emphasises, the analyst is only partly severed from reality; secondly, this is part of a *conscious* discipline which the analyst has a measure of control over; thirdly, the analyst wants to contact psychic reality, whereas the psychotic, conversely, wants to destroy contact. (ibid. pp. 68-69) Nevertheless, this discipline requires of the analyst what Bion calls 'patience', where the analyst is prepared, by her own analytic experience (i.e. the experience of being analysed), to enter the paranoid-schizoid position. Patience retains the notion of suffering and the toleration of frustration, but is not pathological. The corollary to patience is 'security', when pattern evolves in the session, analogous to Klein's depressive position. He goes on, 'I consider that no analyst is entitled to believe that he has done the work required to give an interpretation unless he has passed through both phases - "patience" and "security". The passage from one to the other may be very short, as in the terminal stages of an analysis, or it may be very long. Few, if any, psycho-analysts should believe that they are likely to escape the feelings of persecution or depression commonly associated with the pathological states known as the paranoid-schizoid and depressive positions.' (ibid. p. 124) Such an experience can contain these elements that Bion lists: '(1) feelings of persecution, (2) a mass of apparently unrelated facts, (3) an inability to find a selected fact, or perhaps to believe it would be any good if one could, (4) an inability to see any value in the facts, to regard them as dead particles, bits of faeces.' (In F. Bion, 1992, p. 221)[4] Such an approach, Bion notes, leads, perhaps painfully, to 'an increased awareness of the unique nature of every psycho-analytic experience and of psycho-analysis itself.' (in F. Bion, 1992, p. 296) By expressing this viewpoint, Bion stresses that he is not setting things in opposition to logic and reason, but he is saying that 'the analyst may have to cultivate a capacity for *dreaming while awake*, and that this capacity must somehow be reconcilable with what we ordinarily conceive of as an ability for logical thought.' (p. 215, my italics)

Logical thought, indeed psychoanalytic models, or whole psychoanalytic theories, can be constraining containers, parasitic containers of outworn and clichéed ideas with a deadening effect, whereby they become lifeless contents awaiting the larger container, the infinite container, of F. This resistance *of the analyst*, and the ever-present tendency to force one's ideas into the patient as container, will be part of a countertransference repetitive process of the analyst *with knowledge*, rather than the analyst who waits in O. Hence, Bion's invocation of the *capacity* to dream, which is not the same as *having* the memory of a dream, but instead, 'the experience of the dream which seems to cohere as if it were a whole, at one moment absent, at the next present.' (1970, p. 107)

For Bion, therefore, the depressive position (D) is not superior ethically (integration, reparation, growth, etc.) to the paranoid-schizoid position (Ps), as is the case in Klein. For Bion, the arrow between D and Ps, goes *both* ways, fragmenting can be just as creative as joining together. They are part of an overall rhythm of life which is prior to the relationship container-contained. The tendency to seek a container, as we have noted, forecloses the coming together/falling apart rhythm. The first elements of thinking, as we have noted, are affective *signals* (not symbols) of distress and horror, the baby's scream that signals the need for immediate attention. These are beta-elements which carry with them a sense of catastrophe. Indeed in so far as they are linked at all, they are linked by a sense of catastrophe. For Bion there is catastrophe at the very heart of our being. The self could not form without a sense of catastrophe and catastrophe would not exist without a sense of self.

The first prophylactic task of the psychic apparatus is to signal the catastrophe (*Hilflosigkeit*). As Michael Eigen says, 'A toehold is achieved in catastrophic oblivion and the oblivion of catastrophe by the growth of elemental signals for one's predicament.' (1985, p. 323). The first elements, as we have seen, are non-thoughts that grip the subject in terror (persecution). The subject *must* suffer (tolerate frustration) the tension of these elements if the thinking process is going to grow and become less toxic. However catastrophe for Bion is the bedrock of existence and suffering. Once there is some minimal differentiation or discontinuity of a proto-mind from the cosmos, the zero, there arises the first signs of catastrophe. The sense of catastrophe proves that there is a self, however rudimentary. The subject needs to maintain contact with this sense of suffering as what Eigen calls an essential feedback mechanism. In the case of the psychotic, the suffering can pervade the subject's whole life, or, in face of this horror, the psychotic becomes mindless and anaesthetises the pain.[5] As Eigen says, 'In time the subject adapts to it and the sense of catastrophe grows dull and blank... It may be possible for a whole culture to do this on a grand scale. We lose our sensitivity to our most pressing dangers, much as the toad boils to death without noticing as the heat in its water gradually increases.' (ibid. p. 329)

Bion's paradoxical position of F in O guards against this losing of ourselves and getting caught in the oblivion we are trying to deny. As the subject enters the circuit of life (Eros), he moves away from the sense of suffering towards the external world of containing objects and language, only to be caught in the repetition compulsion (due to the death drive) - the all pervasive reminders of the oblivion from which he has temporarily emerged. Commenting on F in O, Eigen says, 'faith presents itself as catastrophic to the various security systems[6] we have erected over the abyss.' (ibid. p. 330) The analyst in Bion's formulation keeps faith with the abyss.

Discussion

Through his notion of psychoanalysis as a probe, Bion is invoking not so much 'the talking cure', but the cure by faith in O, which is by definition *beyond* words. The criticism levelled at Klein, cited at the end of the last chapter, is also applicable here. The shift has been made from the Freudian emphasis on words, speech and representations to *process* - to generalised primordial affective processes (the catastrophe), from which spring such fundamental defensive strategies as introjection, projection, projective identification, splitting, fragmentation, integration, denial, etc., all at the behest ultimately of the death drive. Appeals are made to the 'healthy self', the 'tyrannical self' or the 'psychotic core', and there is a danger it seems that the analyst may fall into the trap that Bion was cautioning against - too much knowing, too much interpretation, too much containing. Clearly, the analysand in a Bionic analysis is brought through a deep *emotional* experience, where ultimately the words are not important, but merely vehicles, no more than passing containers, which enable the process to continue through to some sort of resolution of psychotic anxieties through toleration of suffering.

With this approach, less and less emphasis is placed on the subject's actual history it seems, and indeed his particular style of reporting that history. From a more orthodox Freudian point of view history does not begin until there is language as the subject emerges out of the Oedipus complex. The Kleinian analysis is preoccupied with the substratum of pre-Oedipal, preverbal, pre-subjective and intensely affective 'experience', and in particular where this experience has become traumatic because of (1) extreme intolerance to frustration, due to external circumstances (neglect, etc.), or, (2) internal causes: variation in stimulation due to the [death] drives, and/or, (3) variations in tolerance to this stimulation, all of which ultimately must be genetically based, or, (4) less reductively, the suffering that arises from the primitive catastrophe of being alive not dead.

According to Hinshelwood, 'Kleinians have a taste for very remote forms of experiencing' (1994, p. 236) revealed firstly through work with children and then to psychotics over the past sixty years. It is not so much the neurotic levels of the personality that interest Kleinians, but, since Bion, precisely how the higher levels of the mind and the capacity for understanding and judgement can be damaged by remnants of psychotic processes. These psychotic anxieties are re-experienced in the *present*, and are interpreted in 'the here and now' of the transference and countertransference.

The early adversarial style of the Kleinian analysts and the so-called deep interpretations of envy and greed, psychotic attacks upon the self, and so on, which alarmed non-Kleinian colleagues, has given way to more balanced formulations, which are less reductive in terms of part-object (breast, penis, anus), less combative, emphasising love as well as hate. Partly as a result of Bion's influence, the analyst is now seen more as an understanding containing object, who can articulate for the patient the terror of fragmentation due to the death drive.

Close attention is given to the *response* of the analysand to the analyst's interpretation. I think it would be true to say that there is an *immediacy*, a rapid to and fro, in the Kleinian approach, quite different from say the Lacanian (silent) emphasis on *mediation* through language. The Kleinian is emphatically dyadic (container/contained), and there appears to be little emphasis on the *third* pole corresponding to the Oedipal triangle, the so-called big Other of Lacanian psychoanalysis. However, less enigmatically, the third pole for the Kleinians is *truth*, which Bion emphasises is nourishment for the psyche. He says: 'The Idea that is nourished by love develops from matrix to function in Language of Achievement; from which it can be transformed into [actual] achievement.' (1970, p. 127) Against this process belonging to Eros, Bion makes one of his strongest statements about envy and pathological splitting. The idea splits and splits again repeatedly sponsoring a superficial interest. But the multiplication is not development but a *cancerous* growth. Each split grows independently of the others. As Bion says: 'ostensibly these 'bits' appear as 'different' ideas. In fact they are all a cover: ideas - impulses - One impulse [...] "proliferation of fragmented envy"' (ibid. p. 128)

Although, according to Bleandonu (1994), for a substantial part of his life Bion lived alone, it is his preparedness to encounter the radical unknown suffering of *emotional* life that marks his special contribution. In Bion's later work we come across the notion of psychic birth. The infant, as has been emphasized, is entirely dependent on the early environment to overcome its primary helplessness. It soon develops fantasies of omnipotence which provide the *illusion* of emotional control over the real world. Subsequently, mental growth takes place in sudden and potentially catastrophic changes when the psyche is threatened with the terror of disintegration and collapse, at adolescence, marriage, the onset of old age and death. Anxiety also accompanies every act of creativity (see chapter six).

The primordial break is the 'caesura' of birth. Bion speculates that something of the mental life must exist in the intrauterine state, which subsequently becomes lost to consciousness. The caesura of birth may be so intense that it prevents us from thinking about the 'proto-mind'. But Bion wants to emphasise the continuity of different and indeed opposite states of mind. Nothing really ever disappears, it is only split off into unconsciousness.

Bion's preoccupation with the emotional life is what is central to our argument here, whether the emotionality arises as a result of (1) the activity of the drives - the death drive in particular - or, (2) the absolute helplessness of the infant[7]. Bion was impressed by the fact that radio astronomy was discovered by slightly de-tuning the radio and listening and making sense of the background noise - the invisible radio signals from distant galaxies. The task of psychoanalysis is to make sense of what is beyond the senses, the affective 'noise', in, around and behind the analysand's discourse.

This approach could not be more different from Lacanian psychoanalysis to which we will now turn.

4. LACAN: SPEAKING AROUND DEATH

This chapter enters upon a separate world. While each psychoanalytic system develops its own language, its own terminology, that developed by Jacques Lacan represents more of a departure, indeed a radical critique or subversion of both classical psychoanalysis and object relations theory. Lacan's relentless criticism of The International Psychoanalytic Association, earned him expulsion from that organization in 1953. Lacan opposed orthodoxy, standardized trainings, organizational discipline in the transmission of psychoanalysis, anything that he felt was deadening its vitality as an autonomous discipline; this included the standard length of the analytic session itself. It was his so-called 'short sessions' that was the focus of the most controversy and his fitness to train analysts. (Turkle 1992, p.107) Lacan is credited with or accused of, depending on your point of view, of 're-inventing' psychoanalysis. Within a short time he himself was being accused of being *le Maître* with his own elite, his own dogma.

Briefly, his doctrine emphasized the subject as against the ego, language structure rather than affect, listening as against empathy, punctuation not interpretation, lack rather than integration, desire over and against need and demand. He was against current aims of growth, cure, adaptation, adjustment, maturity, resolution, fulfilment. It therefore makes no sense to try to integrate Lacanian psychoanalysis into any of the other languages of psychoanalysis, as all these base themselves on progressive notions of psychological health. Lacanian psychoanalysis is a very different form, in fact Lacanians have frequently claimed it as the only form of psychoanalysis[1].

Lacan regarded Freud's notion of the death drive as central to psychoanalysis Unlike Klein, who took the death instinct as a biological given, and other analysts who regarded it as irrelevant as a concept, Lacan came to see it as an essential condition of subjectivity and as an inevitable effect of our insertion into language.

For the later Freud, Klein and Bion, the death instinct comes from the inside, from the id, and via an external detour into parental figures who are introjected as violent internal objects. For Freud the sadistic internal object is the Superego formed at the dissolution of the Oedipus Complex. But it is people and objects into whom the death instinct is deflected, and although their image will be magically and fantastically distorted by this deflection, it will be in these internal imagos that the death instinct will be found, and for the Kleinians in particular, interpreted frequently during the analytic sessions.

Not so for Lacan, as he comes to relegate all this kind of psychoanalytic object-relational theorising to the register of the *Imaginary*. For Lacan, the structuralist, it is *language* that poisons, or the symbolic system into which we are born and have to be situated. He therefore re-situates psychoanalysis within a continental philosophical framework and tradition. By emphasizing human subjectivity, not the human ego as such, Lacan claims to be returning psychoanalysis to its Freudian roots, and away from what he regarded as revisionist medical notions of an adaptive ego which, he claimed, is the basis of British and American psychoanalysis, based on object relations and ego-psychology, respectively. This is Lacan's well known return to *early* Freud, the Freud of the first topography, *The Interpretation of Dreams, Jokes and their Relation to the Unconscious*, and *Studies on Hysteria*.

Original organic incoherence

According to Lacan, something that seems like death is 'experienced' by the very young infant, by the specific prematurity of its birth. He says in his article, *La Famille*, 'We must not hesitate to recognize a positive biological deficiency in those early years, nor to consider man as an animal who is born prematurely'. (Lacan, 1938, p. 9) Lacan will later come to refer to this deficiency as a 'lack' *(béance)* which is fundamentally bound up with having to speak, with being a child of language, and therefore separated or cut off from the totality of Being. But this lack has a biological substratum, connected with the organic incoherence of the child before its entry into language. He also notes an appetite for death which represents the immense power of the maternal imago, which, he says, 'must be sublimated so that new relationships can be introduced with the social group and new complexes integrated into the psyche. To the extent that it resists these new exigencies, which are those of the progress of the personality, the imago, which is salutary in its origins, becomes death bearing'. (ibid. p. 11) Lacan notes clinically in the anorexic or the addict, for instance, the subject is abandoning himself to death and attempting to rediscover the imago of his mother. In these so-called 'non-violent suicides', the desire to return to the maternal womb is made manifest. This aim is also present in our nostalgia for wholeness and in our inclination towards universal harmony, social utopias, and totalitarian dependency. All these are 'derived from the longings for a paradise lost before birth and from the most obscure aspirations for death'. (ibid. p. 13)

At this point in Lacan's work, we are not far from Freud or Klein. Lacan was clearly influenced by Klein's new ideas and her descriptions of the fragmentary nature of early development. For Lacan, also, aggression is primary. But for him, the primary nature of aggressivity is rooted not so much in biology, but more in a *mental* identification with the other as rival. It is here that Lacan's reconcepualization of psychoanalysis is clear. Jealousy for Lacan, is the archetypal social sentiment. He cites St. Augustine's observation in *Confessions* of the little boy observing his foster brother at the breast, who became pale and envious. Here, Lacan points out, the little boy, who could not speak, is confronted by his counterpart, as if in front of a mirror, which evoked in him his primordial frustration. 'The image of the unweaned sibling only attracts a special aggression because it repeats in the subject the imago of the maternal situation and with it the desire for death ... Thus the non-violence of the primordial form of suicide engenders the violence of the imaginary murder of the sibling'. (1938, p. 18) At first it was *him* who had to undergo the pain and loss of being weaned from his mother. Now he sees the *other* and identifies with him. He imagines the other's satisfaction, the other's desire for death, which evokes in him the intense pleasure and pain, deficit and satiation, of that time; and he imagines achieving mastery over that painful experience of the prematurity of his birth, by *eliminating* the other.

The mental image

This real or imagined violence is *not* biologically based. It is not connected to the struggle for life, or rooted in a Darwinian competitiveness. Referring to the 'fort-da' of Freud's grandson, 'the object that aggressivity chooses for its primitive death games is in fact some toy or scrap which is biologically indifferent. The subject does away with it gratuitously, as if for the sheer pleasure of it, and thus brings to completion the loss of the maternal object'. (1938, p. 18) We should note here that Lacan sees this game with presence and absence as the beginning of symbolisation and it marks the child's entry into language. The urge to destroy triumphantly what reminds him of his weaning complex is greatly assisted by his narcissistic capture by his own image, as represented to him by the mirror. The mirror for Lacan, is a powerful metaphor, by which we recognize ourselves in our image given to us by our mother, our family, our social position, and so on. However, firstly let us understand the basis for this narcissistic need.

The psychological tensions built up during the months of prematurity, the subject's incapacities, his lack of motor co-ordination, his fragmented state, all of which have been discovered by the analysis of the unconscious, in phantasies of dismemberment of dislocation of castration, place a special emphasis on an urgent search for affective *unity*, a desire to restore a lost unity. This progress is determined by the predominance of the *visual* function, a means by which he can represent to himself, or *see* a unified identity. It is this mirror image that evokes his longed for unity. 'However, before the ego affirms its own identity, it confuses itself with this (mirror) image which forms it, but also subjects it to a primordial alienation'. (ibid. p. 22)

With Lacan's paper in 1949 on the mirror stage *(stade du miroir)*, his confident radicalisation of psychoanalysis, and indeed of all psychologising based on the Cartesian tradition in European philosophy, was well under way.

For Freud, the transition from initial autoerotism to narcissism required 'a new psychical action' (1914, p. 77) to take place as development proceeds towards relations with objects in the outer world. This problem of the initial cohering of the ego in its first formations is addressed by Lacan's mirror stage. The infant between six and eighteen months old, sees its image (Gestalt) in the mirror and is captivated by it, delighted with it, for it gives him a sense of unity and completeness that he has been in need of. The mirror becomes a metaphor for recognition and narcissistic completion.

> The *mirror stage* is a drama whose internal thrust is precipitated from insufficiency to anticipation - and which manufactures for the subject, caught up in the lure of spatial identification, the succession of phantasies that extends from a fragmented body-image to a form of its totality that I shall call orthopaedic - and, lastly, to the assumption of the armour of an alienating identity, which will mark with its rigid structure the subject's entire mental development. (Lacan, 1949 [1977], p. 4).

Thus, in Lacan's view, all subsequent relations with reality will be fundamentally marked by this imaginary *capture* in an external image, an idealized unity, which covers, masks and substitutes for the initial deficits to do with the prematurity of birth and the fragmented body. This identification of the subject's own body with this external image, with what is, after all, himself as 'other', structures the subject *as rival with himself.* This essential discordance affects all subsequent social relations. He is captured from very early in his life by the regard of the other, by the mother in the first instance. He will always be preoccupied with how he appears to the other, and how others see him. He will become dependent on the desire of the other. On the one hand, there is the *subject's* fragmented way of being, always aggressively deficient, and on the other, there is the *ego's illusion* of autonomy and integration in the assumption of the human form.

The doomed ego

Lacan's controversial point of departure from the rest of psychoanalysis rests to a considerable extent on his denigration of the ego. For him, the ego is a fiction, a spectacle, a fabrication, devised to patch things together or to paper over the cracks. The ego may be necessary, but it is marked all the time by a fundamental *méconnaissance*, a misperception of the world based on the illusion of a narcissistic fullness of closed image. The image may be all good or all bad. This (mis)perception corresponds closely to the Kleinian paranoid-schizoid position discussed in chapter three.

However, in complete contrast, developmental psychologists and many psychoanalysts have rejoiced in the infant's initial, indeed foundational (positive) mirroring experiences as being the core of mental health, as we have noted, for instance, in the good object of Melanie Klein. And Winnicott tells us of 'the mother's role of giving back to the baby the baby's own self'. (1967 [1971a] p. 118) He asks: 'What does the baby see when he or she looks at the mother's face? I am suggesting that, ordinarily, what the baby sees is himself or herself.' (ibid. p. 112) Ideally, Winnicott says, there begins 'a two-way process in which self-enrichment alternates with the discovery of meaning in the world of seen things.' (ibid. p. 113) Thence begins the wider and wider ranges of enriching identifications with significant others in the environment of home and school and later the wider society. These mirroring identifications are seen by non-Lacanians as optimal for growth and maturation of the ego in its classical encounter with the id, the superego and the external world.

Lacanians reverse this positive optimistic *perspective* on developmental progress. Instead, every developmental phase of growth, involving the whole dialectic of (narcissistic) identifications with external images, and the attempt at circumscribing the self in terms of the look, the admiration and recognition of the other, reveals, for Lacanians at least, the constitutional narcissism in which the subject takes on board the *frustration* of being in a sublimation of himself. The child's adaptive developmental process is, at the same time, an *ontological* constriction. While being obliged to fashion himself with reference to and in rivalry with an other, or to wait for recognition/judgement from the other, all kinds of aggression will arise, including envy, jealousy, mortal negation of self and other. Here we are very much in the Kleinian paranoid-schizoid domain. It is in this alienation[2] and normalisation of his aggressive and sexual drives that the origin of human aggression is to be sought. By taking on, believing in, being enchanted by, and valuing above all his image, he is marked paradoxically by a sacrifice of Being close to suicide. Lacan says of the subject, 'that at every moment he constitutes his world by his suicide ...' (1948[1977], p. 28) He alienates himself in his double (the mirror image), just as Narcissus drowned trying to rejoin his own image. As the ego proliferates in form and structure, it becomes less and less in Being. Rather than solving and reconciling life's problems, as we formerly believed of the ego, Lacan tells us, 'This ego, whose strength our theorists now define by its capacity to bear frustration, is frustration in its essence ... Frustration by an object in which his desire is alienated and which the more it is elaborated, the more profound the alienation from his *jouissance*[3] becomes for the subject.' (Lacan 1953, [1977] p. 42) The ego, Lacan tells us, is based on a *passifying* image, and therefore, 'The aggressivity experienced by the subject... [is]... the aggressivity of the slave whose response to the frustration of his labour is a desire for death.' (ibid. p. 42) Man assiduously devotes himself to his own death and consummates it in his social and cultural assertions. This is, in broad outline, the Lacanian critique of social adaptation, and the pursuit of, and seduction by image, which we will make more of in later chapters.

But Bowie points up the Lacanian extremism, 'caught between delusional wholeness and infernal disintegration, the ego leads a doomed life. Whatever it is that gives the ego its normal buoyancy, and allows the individual to do such straightforward things as formulate and execute a plan, has been moved to the margins of the theoretical picture.' (1991, p. 28) Lacan is referring to only the most immature and paranoid *origins* of the ego, as if it was composed of only two dimensions. There is no credence given here to the ego's mature power to think, to contemplate, to delay - in short to do all the things we expect a mind, in Bion's sense, to do. Instead, the ego is narcissistic, caught between omnipotence and impotence, a constricting container, in a Lacanian version of the paranoid-schizoid blindness, without hope, it seems, of ever attaining the depressive position. Thus conceived, the ego is engaged in resisting the chaotic flow of life, as if we might be able to hold onto an (ideal) picture of ourselves, an identity or self esteem. The whole register of the imaginary is an attempt to illusionize the world, to render it safe in terms of past memories and pleasures. Here, sameness and repetition is privileged over difference. The series of irretrievable losses, emphasized as we have noted by Klein in particular, to which the subject is heir (the breast/mother, the faeces, the phallus, etc.), makes for a compensatory desire for completeness, for hankering after old pleasures and satisfaction, even clinging to symptoms rather than facing loss and uncertainty. *Jouissance* is the (intense) pleasure that collects around these points of loss thus creating the deathly resistance to change and truth.

Cut by language

Not only is the subject alienated in some version of an ideal image to which it always pitifully tries to aspire, but entry into language, into an entire Lévi-Straussian symbolic system,[4] involves a further alienation. Language structures what is meaningful in life. But it can never be all inclusive. Other meanings fall *outside* of language. While language, in this structuralist over-arching symbolic sense, places, positions and vivifies the subject, it also confines, limits and constricts. Language is the *only* way in which the subject can be represented to the world. According to Lacan, language has deathliness within it. It becomes an ordering principle of Otherness that dominates and alienates, and takes no heed of us. It was there before we were born and it will be there after we die. It is therefore totally unmindful of us. Lacan connects this symbolic register with the death drive. The symbolic order, says Lacan 'tends beyond the pleasure principle, beyond the limits of life, and that is why Freud identifies it with the death instinct.' (1988 [1954-5] p. 326)

In his seminar on *The Formations of the Unconscious*, Lacan speaks about the *abolition* of the subject in masochism, in the beating phantasies outlined by Freud in his paper '"A Child is being Beaten": A Contribution to the Study of the Origin of Sexual Perversions' (1919). The difficulty is for the child subject to situate himself in the Symbolic register. Elaborating on masochism, Lacan comments: 'I would say that the very form which comes into play in the phantasy, namely the whip, the cane, has something which...is expressed by a stroke, ... something which bars[5] the subject... strikes him out... [it is here] that something of the signifier intervenes'. (12.2.58, p. 10) It is this symbolic character of being barred that is eroticism. In the beating phantasies that Freud elaborates, the whip remains a constant, and in the final form of the phantasy - the others are beaten - Lacan derives the notion generally, that 'human beings are as such all under the rod..[all] to suffer from this something which exists beyond,... the law.' (ibid. p. 12)

Following Oedipus at Colonus, and Oedipus' utterance, 'better not to have been born', Lacan goes on to consider how unwanted children, children who were not conceived in erotic desire, have no Imaginary register to protect and shield them from a deadly definition and fixing in the Symbolic, and that they are prone to suicide. These children above all demonstrate the difficulty of accession to the Symbolic. They demonstrate the 'irresistible slide towards suicide, in this quite specific character of the negative therapeutic reaction... it is in the very measure that there is better articulated for them [in analysis] that which would make them approach their own history as subjects, they more and more refuse to play the game... They do not want anything to do with this signifying chain into which they were only reluctantly admitted by their mother'. (ibid. p. 14)

Paradoxically, Lacan goes on to note, the position of being an unwanted remainder specifies in an absolute and final way our desire for recognition: 'the more a subject affirms himself with the help of the signifier as wanting to get out of it [the Symbolic], the more he enters and integrates himself into this signifying chain. If he abolishes himself, he is more of a sign than ever, for the simple reason that it is precisely from the moment when the subject is dead that he becomes an eternal sign for others.' (ibid. p. 14) Lacan refers to the 'horrific beauty' or the 'contagious beauty' of suicides and their absolute condemnation by moral authorities.

Lacan demonstrates the subject's enmeshment in this signifying system and the impossibility of his escape from it. 'from time to time he refuses it, he says no, I will not be an element of the chain... [but] what does he do every time he refuses in some way to pay a debt that he has not contracted? He does nothing other than to perpetuate it, namely [precisely] *by* his successive refusals to make emerge again the chain of what is always more [or less] linked to the *signifying* chain.'

(ibid. p. 15, my emphasis)   Even the refusal is stated in terms of the chain. This is the essence of the repetition compulsion. Consequently for the masochist, in contact with the whip or the rod, his subjectivity is refused. He is an object, abolished, desecrated, but also, even here, is recognition, as Lacan says, 'in so far as it becomes from that moment the relationship with the Other, with the Other that one must be loved by.' (ibid. p. 16)

Once the signifying chain has marked the subject, it is barred from its own existence, but not from his actual existence. 'Like the 'messenger-slave' of ancient usage, the subject carries under his hair the codicil (supplement to a will) that condemns him to death [and] knows neither the meaning, nor the text, nor in what language it was written, nor even that it had been tattooed on his shaven scalp as he slept.' (Lacan, 1960, [1977] p. 302)

By conceiving language in this way, Lacan is addressing what he sees as a fundamental misconception both within the empiricist psychoanalytic tradition and outside, namely, the commonplace notion (narcissistically imbued) that language comes along as an afterthought to help to explain the world. When speaking or using language, we believe that we are in charge and can say roughly what we want to say, if we can find the right words - a matter of education. Language emanates from us. This view persists in spite of Freud's Copernican discoveries - namely, the unconscious, with its Other language. Lacan reverses all this: it is language, the wholly symbolic system of any culture - the law - that dominates *us*, that determines *us*. We are more spoken, than speaking. *It* speaks. The Id speaks. *Ça parle*. In order to understand this subjugating effect of the word, one might think of the language of economics, or of the legal system itself, and how in a sense, the individual is ignored, unrecognised and subordinated. Instead of words simply being life-promoting containers of meaning, meaning only arises problematically *between* the elements of language. Meaning arises elsewhere. As noted at the end of the last chapter, words as containers constrict meaning; containers like the symbolic can become deadening.

This is not to say that we are just pawns, subject to the whim of language, without ever being able to be part of life. For Lacan believes that on entry into the symbolic system, which is also the 'treasure house of signifiers', once we are prepared to assume the *position* of subject, we can begin to change from using 'empty speech', which is banal repetitive speech, to using 'full speech', which is performative and carries an evocative power. So, Lacan suggests, although 'our culture pursues its course in the shadowy regions beyond [any] creative subjectivity', nevertheless 'creative subjectivity has not ceased in its struggle to renew the never-exhausted power of symbols in the human exchange that brings them to the light of day.' (1953, [1977], p. 71) However, the Other is not one. That is, language is incomplete and full of holes. Lacan's symbol for the Other - that is, the big Other of language - has a bar through it (Ø). This indicates that the Other *lacks*, and it is this lack that institutes *our* desire to try always to articulate what we mean. Yet, what we say has many meanings, and often not the one we intended.

The divided subject and death

Thus, the Lacanian subject is all but lost, being variously described by Lacan as decentred, split, fading. As we have noted, 'The subject is no one. It is decomposed, in pieces. And it is jammed, sucked in by the image, the deceiving and realised image, of the other, or equally by its own specular image.' (1988 [1954-55], p. 54) The fundamental law of the signifier is that 'a signifier is that which represents a subject for another signifier...it functions as a signifier only to reduce the subject in question to being no more than signifier, to petrify the subject in the same movement in which it calls the subject to function, to speak, as a subject.' (1964 [1977], p. 207) A signifier is that inert material element of language which represents a subject, in the circuit of exchange, for another signifier. This little bit of language is commonly the personal pronoun 'I', or the forename, or the denomination 'son of'. So the only way the subject can be represented, is by a stand-in, which gives him a place on the one hand, but excludes him on the other. The subject is reduced to a signifier, to a name. Lacan makes clear that 'the fact of being born with the signifier, the subject is born divided. The subject is this emergence which, just before, as subject, was nothing, but which, having scarcely appeared, solidifies into a signifier'. (ibid. p. 199)

Lacan's dramatisation of the fading subject, who appears and disappears, who exists only by proxy, who is nothing substantial, flies in the face of all positivist (psychoanalytic, psychological) notions of self, identity, stability, security, self esteem, and so on. It could not be made more clear. Bion's notion of maternal reverie, or Klein's good object are no match for the incessant change and exchange demanded by the symbolic. However, when Bion notes the pulsation between Ps and D, part of the catastrophic real which is uncontainable, he evokes the same chill for the subject, who only feels himself to exist by virtue of an illusion.

Lacan speaks of *two* lacks in the subject. The first at the level of the signifier, 'by the fact that the subject depends on the signifier and that the signifier is first of all in the field of the Other'. Then he goes on to elaborate, that 'this lack takes up the other lack, which is the real, earlier lack, to be situated at the advent of the living being... [who], by being subject to sex, has fallen under the blow of individual death.' (1964, [1977] p. 205) Perhaps this is connected with the fact, noted earlier, that as *sexual* as opposed to asexual beings, we are subject to death, and to being born in a fragmented state. The effect of Lacanian teaching is to emphasise the inescapable incompleteness of human subjectivity. There are two deaths. The first is the death of the biological body. The second death is the summation of the losses, specified by psychoanalytic theory generally, and highlighted by the Lacanian register of the Symbolic. Language imposes a Law, a prohibition on pleasure reaching its climax during the Oedipus complex, when castration comes to represent the division with in the subject, inscribing him in a loss and separation from those objects of complete satisfaction, to which he will secretly aspire to return repetitively.

At this point, we can envisage the death drive as the energy which allows the counter-cathexis to bring about the *primal* repression that founds the unconscious. According to Laplanche and Pontalis (1973), this is the repression of very intense archaic experiences, of excessive excitation, as we noted in chapter one. So the death drive is implicated in, both, the intense experience *(jouissance)* itself, *and* its primary delimitation in language, as per Lacan's Symbolic register outlined above. Furthermore, this echoes Bion's assertion of the death drive being present in the container as well as the contained.

Lacan makes it clear that 'Freud says quite categorically that it is the pressure of what, in sexuality, has to be repressed [archaic excitations] in order to maintain the pleasure principle - namely the libido - that has made possible the progress of the mental apparatus itself, as such and, for example, the establishment in the mental apparatus of that possibility of investment that we call *Aufmerksamkeit*, the possibility of attention.' (1964, [1977] p. 184) Without this primal repression, there is no possibility of the modificatory containment of the drives, ordinary progress, attention and civilisation.

Lemaire, drawing extensively on Leclaire's work, summarises the Lacanian position on the death drive. The death drive is an active or 'ecstatic void met with by the subject in pleasure or in pain, and from which the subject is preserved only by the letter (not merely a linguistic term but a mnemic trace whose form may vary), which appears in order to support his organic and psychical coherence. The death instinct is the *attractive "zero"* around which the subject gravitates, the *antimony of the "one"*, which is also the subject when he has been able to maintain himself in consciousness with the help of some letter.' (1970, p. 167)

Lemaire quotes Leclaire: 'The death instinct is that radical force which surfaces in the catastrophic or ecstatic instant, screaming out its appeal for a word to veil and sustain it [to *contain* it in Bion's formulation]. It constitutes the basis of castration and allows the development of language, together with the possibility of desire.' (ibid. p. 167) Primordial signifiers *conceal* the void, establish normative desire and coherence. Thus there are two ways in which the death drive intervenes in the constitution of the subject. (1) It is that which inscribes the letter (the signifier) in the unconscious and *fills in* the primitive void. And, (2) that which leads the subject to language in the true sense by way of metaphoric function whereby the letter is replaced by (alienating) symbols - the so-called signifying chain.

So it is the death drive that kills desire in the *total* sense, yet supports it to make it human, tolerable, alienated because it is *structured* in language? It is death which creates the gulf, the lack, the castration of the subject so that he speaks and wants endlessly, without ever getting what he wants, or knowing what he wants. And it is also death that is the point that we have to go towards when we want to go right over the top in terms of desire *(jouissance)*. It is the *beyond* of language which can never be represented and which holds out for the subject the possibility of rejoining his lost desire. As Lacan says: 'when we wish to attain in the subject what was before the serial articulations of speech, and what is primordial to the birth of symbols, we find it in death.' (1953, [1977] p. 105)

One thinks of violent pleasures, of the moment of desire going to completion, in extreme states of supremely omnipotent behaviour, or states of manic denial. Consider the anorexic patient's supreme disregard for her ailing body. Think of living on that knife-edge, as in war, addictive states and so on. How contemptible seem ordinary pleasures obeying the law of homeostasis in comparison to the possibilities of an extreme pleasure, of the intense moment when the alienation of ordinary life is overcome. Once these moments have been experienced, there persists the desire to return. The addict always wants to return to the drug, the war veteran longs for the field of battle where he was living most intensely, on the margin of death, or in the presence of death. Here, the subject is toying with the idea of the completion of desire, of overcoming the intolerable alienation, distance and deadness of ordinary existence under the law of the signifier.

In summary, the death drive is required to create the lack so that desire can be circumscribed, limited, and forever self-perpetuating in demand expressed through language, and, it also seems to be what desire strives after - namely its absolute fulfilment, which, as we have seen Freud postulated, is the aim of all instinct, namely death.

Bowie comments that 'the Symbolic relentlessly pre-ordains and organizes human experience... It creates meaning, yet also withdraws it, it vivifies yet also mortifies.'(1991, p. 87) It is a deathliness written into the symbolic. Lacan indicates this: 'The symbol manifests itself first of all as the murder of the thing, and this death constitutes in the subject the externalisation of his desire.' (1953, [1977]) Bowie continues, 'Death is the eventual triumph of the Real (finally), but is already homeopathically present in speech. [Lacanian analysis which lays stress on the Symbolic], allows the individual's mortality to speak and be spoken; it allows him to be unillusioned in his desire...' (1991, p. 100)

Lacan returns us to the brink of the béance, the assumption of castration, of primordial loss, that creates the lack upon which desire is instituted, and without which there is no desire, when the desiring Other intervenes to say 'no'. To assume this castration is at once an acquiescence in this Other's law (the law of the father, the Symbolic), and an envious appropriation of his desire. The drives, the relatively fixed forms of desire, circulate around the lack, and therefore are marked by impossibility, seeking satiation, desire half pursues its own extinction. The death drive's action is immanent in the signifying chain. Being barred by the signifier, is to be poisoned with a sense of death. Bowie again, 'The drive, as it circles round the excavated centre of being, is pulled outwards towards the objects that promise gratification, but inwards too, towards the completest form of loss that it already knows.' (1991, p. 163)

In 'The Function and Field of Speech and Language in Psychoanalysis', (1953[1977]) Lacan, speaking about death in language. refers to the model of the torus; a torus is a cylinder joined at both ends into a ring. Bowie clarifies this image, 'Death is 'inside' speech in that speech encircles it, but 'outside' it too, for as soon as speech is figured as a ring, a tubular continuum, it can no longer be centred on a point falling inside its own volume.' (1991 p. 192) 'Death is both intrinsic and extrinsic to the words that speak us.' (ibid. p. 203) 'death is the ubiquitous condition of human speech, and the only opportunity we have for saying *no* to mortality lies, fragilely, in speech itself and in the actions it may provoke.' (ibid. p. 202)

Death haunts us. Lacan underlines the *ultimate* power of the death drive:

> What Freud's primary masochism teaches us is that, when life has been dispossessed of its speech, its final word can only be the final malediction expressed at the end of *Oedipus at Colonus*. Life doesn't want to be healed. The negative therapeutic reaction is fundamental to it. Anyway, what is healing? The realisation of a subject through speech, which comes from elsewhere, traversing it.
> This life we are captive of, this essentially alienated life, ex-sisting, this life in the other, is as such joined to death, it always returns to death, and is only drawn into increasingly large and more roundabout circuits by what Freud calls the elements of the external world.
> All that life is concerned with is seeking repose as much as possible, while awaiting death. That is what devours the time of the suckling baby at the beginning of its existence, with hourly segments, which allow him just to take a peep from time to time. You have to try bloody hard to draw him out of this for him to find the rhythm by which we get attuned to the world... the nameless desire can appear at the level of the desire to sleep - dozing off is the most natural of all vital states. (1954-55, [1988] pp. 232-233)

The Real

We shall turn our attention more specifically to Lacan's *third* register, the Real, which is always beyond the *humanly constituted* reality (of the Imaginary and the Symbolic). What human desire desires, according to the Hegelian scholar Alexander Kojève, is desire as such - desire of desire, or as Lacan will say, enigmatically: desire is the desire of the

Other. Desire is the attempt to solicit the desire of the other (their recognition), or it can be at the same time, to desire the other - the desire *for* the other. Mythically, two consciousnesses fighting to the death for mutual recognition, for each to recognize the other, for each to desire the other. That is a struggle for pure prestige. Therefore, fighting for nothing! This is the nature of human reality, which transcends, surpasses, negates, nihilates, the Real (given reality) - the natural substantial Real which Lacan tells us is seamless and complete in itself. The human reality (the Symbolic register) is torn from this Real, negating and paralleling it at the same time through discourse.

The humanly constituted reality, that of the image and that of language, are constituted by the death of some-*thing*. This 'thingliness' is left behind, but ever-present, *in the Real*. It is this very real reality that constitutes the trauma. Lacan tells us:

> Is it not remarkable that, at the origin of the analytic experience, the real should have presented itself in the form of that which is *unassimilable* in it - in the form of the trauma, determining all that follows, and imposing on it an apparently accidental origin ... at the very heart of the primary processes, we see preserved the insistence of the trauma in making us aware of its existence. The trauma reappears, in effect, frequently unveiled. (1964 [1977] p. 55)

Let us consider again, for a moment, the nature of this trauma. *Before* there is any 'real' trauma of sexual abuse for instance, there is what Laplanche (1987) calls 'primal seduction', where the adult (sexual) unconscious impinges on the infant in a way that the infant cannot integrate or symbolise. The psychoanalytical consensus is clearly, as we have seen in chapter one, that trauma is generated by the intensity of the drives against which the little primary vesicle has no *interior* defences. This is the real of the drives, which Freud emphasized, have to be inaugurally *projected* into the outside world.

In section IV of 'Beyond the Pleasure Principle', Freud says of the primary vesicle: 'Towards the outside, it is shielded against stimuli, and the amounts of excitation impinging on it have only a reduced effect. Towards the inside there can be no such shield; the excitations in the deeper layers extend into the system directly and in undiminished amount.' (1920, p. 29) Although Freud speculates at this point that these internal stimuli may be more or less compatible with the system's method of working, more so than its difficulties in dealing with energies from the external world, he goes on to suggest that 'any internal excitations which produce too great an increase of unpleasure [create]... a tendency to treat them as though they were acting, not from the inside, but from the outside, so that it may be possible to bring the shield against stimuli into operation as a means of defence against them. This is the origin of *projection* which is destined to play such a large part in the causation of pathological processes'. (ibid. p. 29) This is Freud's position that we have repeated from chapter one.

Contra Freud, Laplanche, following Ferenczi, privileges *introjection* over projection - the introjection of the mother's (sexual) unconscious which is of its very nature excessive and therefore traumatogenic. He asks: 'Can analytic theory afford to go [on] ignoring the extent to which women unconsciously and sexually cathect the breast... It is inconceivable that the infant does not notice this [excess] sexual cathexis.' (Laplanche, 1987, p. 126) Similarly, the observation of parental coitus is always highly frightening, seductive and enigmatic. 'For the child the so-called 'primal scene' is a seduction, a primal seduction. The sight of its parents having intercourse allows, or forces, the child to see images and fragments of traumatic scenarios which it cannot assimilate because they are to a certain extent opaque to the actors themselves'. (ibid. p. 127) He likens this idea to the Kleinian notion of the 'combined parent figure'. This opaqueness, seductiveness and enigmatic quality leads to the implantation of what he calls 'enigmatic signifiers', which in Lacanian terms are at the border of the of the Real, the so-called S1 signifier. They stimulate symbolisation - those sexual enigmas from the adult world - but they set the child an impossible task of translation.

Therefore, Laplanche envisages a series of traumas that are seductive and enigmatic. The first is the primal seduction, which is *unavoidable* and is the child's first contact with the Real. Here the child is confronted with its *hilflosigkeit*, a primary *passive* helplessness, which like the adult trauma has the sense about it of an accident, for which it was totally unprepared, psychically. Laplanche makes it clear that primal seduction has nothing to do with *actual* sexual assault, although he notes that precocious seduction (by the mother) and later paedophile seduction may be more likely to follow as a consequence. He makes clear that, 'Primal seduction does not take away the importance of the other two levels; on the contrary it provides them with their *foundations*'. (ibid. p. 128, my italics) This primally exciting lure of the Real inaugurates a seductive proclivity that will haunt us in an *unheimlich* fashion during the rest of our lives. This is the pull of the first moment of the repressed, the pull of what has to be turned away from, the primarily repressed. However, forever after, we will be endlessly capable of being seduced, drawn towards this enigmatic void[6].

We might also note here Laplanche's notion of the superego that can be a 'psychotic enclave' which is passed on across generations because it is untranslatable and constitutes an impossible traumatic encounter for each generation. This amounts to a Kleinian bad internal object. Thinking of the Superego as being like Kantian categorical imperatives, Laplanche says that 'they are certainly enigmatic in the same way that other adult messages are enigmatic... they are... in other words non-metabolizable. This means that they cannot be diluted, and cannot be replaced by anything else. They exist, and they are immutable and cannot be symbolised.' (ibid. p. 139) This is very close to the earlier discussion on the saturated nature of beta-elements, which remain very problematically in the margin of mental life and are unable to engage in linkages with other elements. These are 'thoughts without a thinker'. Similarly Laplanche asks: 'are the moral rules handed down by parents repressed, or are they *impossible to repress* or do they remain in the limbo of pre-repression...? And if categorical imperatives are, so to speak, trapped between the two stages of primal repression, should we not see them as psychotic enclaves inside the human personality as such?'. (ibid. p. 139, my italics) These messages are destined to repeat and repeat as they are not repressed, not dialecticised. They are death drive derivatives that wreak constant havoc by their ever-presentness and their *real seductive power*. The subject is therefore drawn to these and horrified by them simultaneously in his efforts to translate and decipher them.

Lacan summarizes: 'The place of the real... stretches from the trauma to the phantasy - in so far as the phantasy is never anything more than the screen that conceals something quite primary, something determinant in the function of repetition'. (1964 [1977] p. 60) The real is this, that we are obliged to stumble over it again and again in a seemingly hopeless attempt as assimilation. What am I supposed to do to stop this...? If it is the phantasy screen, it is also the dream, the dream in its fundamental function as a defence. 'The real has to be sought beyond the dream - in what the dream has enveloped, hidden from us, behind the lack of representation of which there is only one representative. This is the real that governs our activities more than any other and it is psychoanalysis that designates it for us.' (ibid. p. 60) Lacan says: 'Where do we meet this real? For what we have in the discovery of psycho-analysis, is an encounter, an essential encounter - an appointment to which we are always called with a real that eludes us'. (ibid. p. 53) This is 'what is nodal in the encounter, *qua* encounter forever missed'. (ibid. p. 60)

We encounter this real in a lack, a hole, in an empty place:

> A lack is encountered by the subject in the Other, in the very intimation that the Other makes to him by his discourse. In the *intervals* [my emphasis] of the discourse of the Other, there emerges in the experience of the child something that is radically mappable, namely, *He is saying this to me, but what does he want?*
>
> In this interval intersecting the signifiers... desire crawls, slips, escapes, like a ferret. The desire of the Other is apprehended by the subject in that which does not work, in the lacks of the discourse of the Other. (1964 [1977] p. 214)

There is something impossible in this (overwhelming) desire of the Other. What do you want from me? This desire is beyond words, beyond any symbolisation.

This can go to an extreme, as Lacan notes in his Seminar on Anxiety 'The anxiety of the nightmare is experienced properly speaking as that of the *jouissance* of the Other... It is this being who weighs with his whole opaque weight an alien *jouissance* on your chest, who crushes you under his *jouissance*..' (1962-3, 12.12.62, p. 7) This puts us in mind of the Kleinian envious internal object, against which the subject feels powerless. This desire of the Other is too intense, is too much. This is the crushing effect of the Symbolic to which we referred above - ultimately its deathly aspect. The question is whether or not the subject can interpose something imaginary, something illusory, at this point. Lacan goes on to say that the ego is warned (by signal anxiety) about this excess of desire of the Other. 'But it is not for the ego that the signal is given. It is quite obvious that if this lights up at the level of the ego, it is in order that the subject - one cannot call it anything else - should be warned about something... something which is a desire, *namely a demand that does not concern any need* (my emphasis), which does not concern anything other than my very being... let us say that it cancels it out.' (ibid. 27.2.63, p. 7). This constitutes the Real of desire, beyond the pleasure-reality principle, and it is death-bearing. Ultimately, it requires us to become a *lost* object, that, as Lacan puts it, may topple off the stage. Lacan goes on to add: 'All that is left to me is to use violence.' (ibid. p. 7) And violence is where we enter the whole Kleinian dialectic.

The lost object

Clearly, people can become the lost object when they fall out of the social, when there is no place for them in the existing cultural system. They cease to be a subject and become a discardable object. More generally, the register of the symbolic creates a remainder, a residue, or trace that cannot be symbolised or represented that falls through the 'holes' in the symbolic universe, and is therefore lost in the Real. This remainder or hint becomes the *cause* of desire - the kernel in the Real that the drives encircle. This kernel is the so-called objet *a*. Thus Lacan schematizes the central theme in psychoanalytic theory - namely, the theme of separation and loss. In *Inhibitions, Symptoms and Anxiety*, Freud lists the separations: the separation at birth; separation from the breast; from the faeces during the anal phase; from the treasured object of the penis by castration; and the fear of loss of love of the superego. These successive disappointments involve the subject in an intense longing for the irredeemably lost object.

Lacan even pinpoints the precise and most poignant moment of our severance. Listing the well known 'subtractions' that the subject undergoes, in addition to the breast, Lacan cites the placenta, that 'represents that part of himself that the individual loses at birth, which may serve to symbolise the most profound lost object.' (1964 [1977] p. 198) Here we are cut from *our own tissues* - the placental, the umbilicus, the amniotic membranes - which are left behind in the womb, and constitute the 'afterbirth'.

We will briefly look at how Lacanians have thought about this object that has been cut out and from which the subject must always be separated, and yet, crucially, it remains the support (in the Real), or the cause, or the motor of desire. The subject is cut off from this object, yet joined to it unconsciously in phantasy. For Lacan, the object is never completely lost. It necessarily fills up the real, and prevents the subject from experiencing an unbearable void[7].

Charles Melman expands on this notion of the objet *a* (in an unpublished lecture in 1988). He says that it is the object which disgusts us because it shouldn't be there. We feel we should be separated from it, and to the extent that it is present, it causes anxiety, as in phobia for example. There are a number of possible objet a's. These are the ones that determine the different drives. The object of the scopic drive (the gaze), the oral drive (the breast), the anal drive (excrement), the object that invokes or evokes (the voice).

Melman explains the relationship between pleasure and the objet a. Pleasure always stops before something that evokes pain, a psychological constraint which is associated with feelings of dissatisfaction or unpleasure. *Jouissance* goes beyond the pleasure principle towards complete satisfaction, transgressing the Law. When pleasure goes beyond the limit it meets this objet a. Lacan calls it the 'plus-*de-jouir*', the 'more than pleasure'.

The objet a is that which is *cut out* when we enter the register of the symbolic. This is the phenomenon of castration, and what he calls, 'some sort of demon in the world, a pure effect of the symbolic chain'. He gives some examples to illustrate the association of the objet a, its emergence, and the simultaneous occurrence of extreme anxiety.

For instance, the arrival of a baby can be an intense pleasure for the mother, a pleasure that takes priority over any other, and one that it becomes impossible for her to renounce. In this particular *jouissance*, the child must always remain a baby, to be the sole support of the mother's desire. Melman says, 'The baby becomes like a cork; the world becomes closed with that baby; nothing else exists, nothing else has any value'.

Here is an instance in which one sees the object of desire emerge, and every thought becomes tied up with this. The emerging *presence* of the object can cause a psychosis, as this object tends to undo or indeed abolish the subject. Perhaps, he suggests, 'this phenomenon is responsible for post-puerperal psychosis, or the extreme guilt of a mother who has to get her child minded, or the murderous feelings towards children, whom one loves. For these mothers, this object is *too much*, it is an excess'. Sometimes in the case of still-births, Melman notes, the mother can have an excess of erotic attraction for the midwife or the obstetrician.

Melman also points out how our knowledge of the objet a is essential for understanding drug addiction. He says: 'The addict wants to go to the limit with his make-believe pleasure, he wants to die of it. He looks for death because this would be the peak in pleasure, and that is why there is a great danger when the drug becomes the objet *a* for the addict'.

In terms of the obsessional, Melman notes, 'The child thinks that the faeces cause the pleasure of the mother, as she acts as if they were a real gift. So this becomes an object that he would like to enjoy himself, and so he can get into a cycle that becomes mad, with the eroticisation of the intestinal and anal life - a condition of what is called cleanliness in our culture. The obsessional doesn't renounce this object, and he always gives the impression of being dirty. He has the problem of separation and this separation is not completed. In spite of everything he still contaminates'.

Czermak (1989), in an unpublished lecture, further underlines the point, that the subject can only remain in existence, if the objet *a* remains veiled or hidden. If the object emerges for the subject, then he will disappear in extreme (automatic) anxiety. In Lacan's formula for phantasy, every desire is destined to be unsatisfied. The object of desire should always be *metonymical*, moving from one object to another, from a', to a'', to a''', etc. The barred subject is always turning around an object that is never the right one.

Czermak gives examples. Objects like the voice and the gaze, in normality, leave us in peace: we do not hear the interior monologue, the voice in your head, the echo, the commentary. Also, we cease to realise that we are looked at *more* than we look. However, in the case of the paranoiac, the gaze, or the voice is unveiled, in their terrifying reality. Czermak considers a more limited delusion like a revenge or an erotomania. For instance: 'A woman is certain that a man loves her. It doesn't matter about the actual circumstances of the man, the woman subject has found her object. Schreber became the object of a divine erotomania. He loved the rays from God: the subject has found his object, and cannot let it go. The hypochondriac has not lost the object (his symptom), it has not fallen away, he is full of anxiety about it'.

We might summarise the Lacanian position on extreme anxiety, by linking it to the forbidden emergence of the objet *a* from the Real, which gives rise to an excess, a *jouissance*, a horror, an impossible desire - the death drive. The subject becomes 'unstrung' and is on the point of disappearing, as repression fails altogether, and a psychotic breakdown occurs.

Terminal freedom

Lacan recognises our final freedom in the death drive. 'Empedocles, by throwing himself into Mount Etna, leaves forever present in the memory of men this symbolic act of his being-for-death.' (1953[1977] p. 104) This negation is a final triumph, 'depriving of his victory the master whom he abandons to his inhuman solitude.' (ibid. p. 104) Lacan says:

> ... [It] is not in fact a perversion of instinct, but rather that desperate affirmation of life that is the purest form in which we recognize the death instinct. The subject says "No!" to this intersubjective game of hunt-the-slipper in which desire makes itself recognised for a moment, only to become lost in a will that is the will of the other. Patiently, the subject withdraws his precarious life from the sheeplike conglomerations of Eros of the symbol in order to affirm it at last in the unspoken curse. (ibid. pp. 104-5)

In his seminar on Ethics[8] (1959-60) Lacan speaks about Antigone and her 'unbearable splendour' that endlessly captivates and fascinates us. Antigone evokes the *'unwritten unalterable law'* (Sophocles, [1947] p. 138) in her implacable opposition to Creon's refusal to allow her traitor brother Polynices a proper burial. In deadly defiance of Creon, she will bury him herself. She lives in the house of Creon, her uncle, and has witnessed the death of both her brothers. She is subject to Creon's law, and this she cannot bear. She is concerned with *chthonic* laws, the laws of the earth and blood relations - 'my brother is my brother'. Her fate is to commit a crime against Creon's tyrannical order. In contrast, Lacan comments on how de Sade, 'goes as far as forging the strangely extravagant notion that through crime man is given the power to liberate nature from its own laws. For its own laws are chains.' (1959-60[1992] p. 260) Hence Lacan's concept of the 'second death', which is: 'death insofar as it is regarded as the point at which the very cycles of the transformations of nature are annihilated.' (ibid. p. 248) This is the destruction of life itself, the end of the natural cycle of life and death. This 'crime' is our ultimate freedom, 'the fantasm involved is that of eternal suffering.' (ibid. p. 261) Lacan quotes Sade: 'The reign of the law is, therefore, evil; it is inferior to anarchy.' (ibid. p. 221) Antigone, as a tragic hero, is *beyond* the limit (of the signifier), beyond the law. That she shows neither fear nor pity is apparent at every point. 'Something beyond the limits of *Atè* [atrocious] has become Antigone's good, namely, a good that is different from everyone else's.' (ibid. p. 270) In an almost Kleinian moment Lacan suggests that, 'Analysis shows clearly that the subject separates out a double of himself who is made inaccessible to destruction.' (ibid. p. 261) In what Lacan believes is a clear illustration of the death drive, Antigone says of herself that she is *already* dead in life, and desires death, 'She is there in spite of herself as victim and holocaust.' (ibid. p. 282)

Antigone alone *assumes* the crime that founds her family. Antigone's *absolute* power is shown in the play when she says in bitter irony to Ismene: 'You chose: life was your choice, when mine was death... No, no. You live. My heart was long since dead.' ([1947] p. 141) The only complete desire is the death drive. Ismene's life drive, by comparison, seems to lack conviction, to be weak and vacillating. The desire of the mother (Jocasta) is the founding and fatal desire ('the curse departs not but falls upon all of the blood' [ibid.p. 142]), the criminal incestuous desire (Jocasta and Oedipus) that brought into the world Eteocles, Polynices, Ismene and Antigone. The criminal desire is perpetuated when Eteocles clings to power and is avenged by Polynices. Her two brothers are dead, one honoured, the other an unburied corpse, there is no resolution to this problem. As Lacan says: 'Antigone is someone who has already set her sights on death.' (1992 [1959-60] p. 286) Antigone alone, isolated, tragic, in her *sovereign* desire, 'chooses', as Lacan says, 'to be purely and simply the guardian of the being of the criminal as such.' (ibid. p. 283) The chorus says of Antigone: 'For what presumption of man can match thy power.' ([1947] p. 142) By comparison, man, even Creon, is a weak creature, *human*, clinging hesitantly to the life drive. And as Lacan says, ironically, 'Only martyrs know neither pity nor fear. Believe me, the day when martyrs are victorious will be the day of universal conflagration. The play is calculated to demonstrate that fact.' (1992 [1959-60] p. 267)

The simplicity of the death drive *de-* fused (the pure culture of the death instinct), sublime, serene to the zero point, is beautifully illustrated by the chorus at the beginning of Anouilh's *Antigone*:

> The machine is in perfect order; it has been oiled ever since time began, and it runs without friction. Death, treason and sorrow are on the march; and they move in the wake of storm, of tears, of stillness...Tragedy is clean, it is restful, it is flawless... In tragedy nothing is in doubt and everyone's destiny is known...

That makes for tranquillity... and the reason is that hope [Eros], that foul, deceitful thing, has no part in it. (Quoted in Cuddon 1977, p. 985)

In the introductory remarks to the play, Pol Gaillard is summarised as seeing Antigone's gesture as entirely devoid of *human* value: 'Antigone thus dies for nothing; Creon survives, believing in nothing, and the whole play expresses the failure of human effort in general.' (Landers, 1954, p. 26)

Foreclosure

Before we end this overview of the Lacanian contribution, we must examine one more theme within Lacanian thought which is relevant to our focus on the death drive.

What in Lacanian terms serves to designate what Kleinians refer to as 'pathological splitting'? Here we will consider, in some detail, the Lacanian term, 'foreclosure' *(foreclusion)*, which is theorized by Lacan as the determinant of psychosis. Is foreclosure analogous to pathological splitting? Both, after all, are implicated in psychosis and the death of the subject.

Freud spoke of 'repudiation' *(Verwerfung)* as being a defensive process, *different* from repression. In 'The Neuro-Psychoses of Defence', Freud states apropos psychosis, 'There is, however, a much more energetic and successful kind of defence. Here the ego rejects the incompatible idea together with its affect and behaves as if the idea had never occurred to the ego at all.' (1894 p. 58) And, 'the ego breaks away from the incompatible idea; but the latter is inseparably connected with a piece of reality, so that, in so far as the ego achieves this result, it too, has detached itself wholly or in part from reality'. (ibid. p. 59) In the 'Wolf Man' (1918), Freud asserts that the young Serge repudiates castration.

Freud, however, had difficulty in assigning a defence specific to psychosis. He sometimes refers to disavowal *(Verleugnen)*. He also used *ablehnen*, to fend off, and *aufheben*, to abolish. In Schreber, clearly Freud is not talking about simple repression, when he says, 'What was abolished internally returns from without.' (1911a, p. 71) In the same work he talks about the psychotic withdrawal of cathexis from the external world, and the loss of reality.

These are clearly psychotic mechanisms because they involve some loss of contact with reality, some withdrawal of libido from reality. Freud speaks of a delusion being 'applied like a patch over the place where originally a rent had appeared in the ego's relation to the external world such that neurosis is the result of a conflict between the ego and its id, whereas psychosis is the analogous outcome of a similar disturbance in the relations between the ego and the external world.' (1924b p. 149).

But Lacan uses Freud's paper on 'Negation' to help clarify the nature of foreclosure. In this paper, Freud postulated a mechanism of defence that involved, 'the content of a repressed image or idea [making] its way into consciousness, on condition that it is *negated.*' (1925 p. 235) Thus: 'You'll think I mean to say something insulting, but really I've no such intention'. (ibid. p. 235) Or, that image in the dream? Well, it's definitely not my mother, anyway!

Lacan took up this idea of the *two* operations. Firstly an affirmation, or *Bejahung*, an introduction into the subject or a symbolisation; then, an expulsion from the subject, a 'symbolic abolition' - that is, a *not* symbolising what ought to have been symbolised. The expulsion that is spoken of is not into the unconscious but into the Real. And so Lacan formulates the phenomenon of hallucination in similar terms to Freud in Schreber, quoted above, 'what has been foreclosed from the Symbolic reappears in the Real.'

So to be clear, some perception has been taken on board (e.g. castration), but the idea, instead of being repressed (symbolically preserved, albeit unconsciously) is *abolished* into the external world, from whence it returns in the form of a hallucination. 'For, in order that its irruption into the real should be beyond question, it has only to present itself, as it usually does, in the form of a broken chain'. (Lacan, 1955-6 [1977] p. 183) There was, for instance, the Wolf-man's hallucination of his severed finger as the castration, which had been abolished, returning in the Real. And it is significant that this hallucination of the cut finger produces a state of 'unspeakable terror', indicating clearly the original problem of symbolising something which is terrifying.

The failure to symbolise leaves a 'hole' in the Symbolic. Lacan emphasized the 'rent' that appears in the psychotic's relation to the world - 'the rent in the order of the world' as Schreber puts it - and the nature of the 'patch' that is applied over this rent. Leclaire quoted in Lemaire gives a vivid image to clarify the distinction between repression in the neurotic and foreclosure in the psychotic:

If we imagine experience to be a piece of material made up of criss-crossing threads, we could say that repression would figure in it as a rent or a tear which can still be repaired, whereas foreclosure would figure in it as a *béance* due to the weaving itself, in short a primal hole which will never again be able to find its substance, since it has never been anything other than the substance of a hole and can only be filled, and even then imperfectly, by a patch. (1970 p. 231)

Therefore a lived element, that has been foreclosed, can never be re-evoked. The experience may have been lived, but no judgement which would symbolise and register it, i.e. link it alphabetically in the mnemic systems of the unconscious, has been made on it. Foreclosure takes place before there is any possibility of repression, in fact foreclosure is a failure of primal repression. (ibid. pp. 230 and 235) Primal repression, as we have seen, grounds and establishes the symbolisation that makes discourse possible. In so far as the psychotic does not make this primal repression, he is therefore excluded from the Symbolic. In primal repression, the subject distances himself from both the Real, and from the substitute which he gives it. Unless he can make this separation he is caught in an imaginary dyadic trap. He must be able to name the things, which will therefore situate them as exterior to himself.

According to Lacanian theory, the subject is helped in this process by a *third* term, the so-called 'Name-of-the-Father', or the paternal metaphor[9], that during the Oedipus complex comes in between mother and child and insists on the substitution of the symbol for the lived experience of desire for the mother. This enforces a renunciation of the possession of the mother, and established the third dimension - the Symbolic, as well as the other two, the Imaginary and the Real.

Lacan writes:

Following Freud, I teach that the Other is the locus of that memory that he discovered and called the unconscious, a memory that he regards as the object of a question, that has remained open in that it conditions the indestructibility of certain desires...

It is in an accident of this register and in what takes place in it, namely the foreclosure of the Name-of-the Father in the place of the Other, and in the failure of the paternal metaphor, that I designate the defect that gives psychosis its essential condition, and the structure that separates it from neurosis. (1955-6[1977] p. 215)

Further on, Lacan states that, 'It is the lack of the Name-of-the-Father in that place which, by the hole it opens up in the signified, sets off the cascade of reshapings of the signifier from which the increasing disaster of the imaginary proceeds, to the point at which the level is reached at which signifier and signified are stabilised in the delusional metaphor.' (ibid. p. 217)

It is the requirement by the the Name-of-the-Father, that desire be represented or symbolised, which saves the subject from being lost in a confusion of the Imaginary and the Real. The paternal principle *mediates* or makes possible the throwing together (Greek: *syn*, together, *ballein*, to throw) of a thing in the concrete real, with an abstraction, a signifier, for a subject. Without this abstract representation - language in the largest sense - the subject is lost in a concrete universe, with no third point of reference., This is the position of the psychotic subject.

Lacan asks this question: 'how can the Name-of-the-Father be called by the subject to the only place in which it could have reached him and in which it has never been?' He answers his question, enigmatically. 'Simply by a real father, not necessarily by the subject's own father, but by A-father'. He goes on, 'It is enough that this A-father should be situated in a third position ...' (ibid. p. 217) Further, he gives some examples of this third position. For instance, it may be the husband's face for the woman who has just given birth, or the figure of the priest for the person confessing their sins, or her boyfriend's father for the girl in love.

Czermak, writing about the onset of psychosis, states that, for the psychotic subject, speech appears in the Real, from the outside. The father's voice is not heard by a subject; it is not a transaction between an 'I' and a 'Thou', but arrives as a disembodied terrifying command.

> An encounter with a pure voice is much more frequent than clinicians think. Our insufficient tests and examinations often miss it. We can find it, however, in the terrible sound of the shofar, horn of the primordial ram, symbol of the ancestor who demands a sacrifice...
> Since the subject is absent before the question, the voice of the ram will be the one that kills *(tue)* because it cannot say "thou" *(tu)*.

> The automatism... is to be found in the act through which the body, commanded by the voice and the look, disarticulates itself and tries to rearticulate a sentence that was never articulated. The attempt to articulate the relation of "Son" to a "father" who has never occupied his rightful place, forces the object-a, voice and look, to emerge in the hallucination. The object emerges so well in the hallucination that the subject now circulates between the voice and the look. (1977 p. 173-4)

He goes on to say that 'the psychotic subject questions himself about the hole in the real in order to deny this incredible possibility. In so doing he misapprehends his own symbolic catastrophe by evoking a disaster that will eventually take place in the real.' (ibid. p. 175)

Failure of Alpha-function and the Paternal metaphor

Following this Lacanian formulation of foreclosure, we might therefore tentatively link Lacan's notion of the paternal metaphor with Bion's alpha-function. As we have pointed out in chapter three, it is alpha-function that renders raw experience (concrete unmediated reality) meaningful and workable with, consciously or unconsciously. Foreclosure prevents this process from happening. Foreclosure pre-empts symbolisation.

But how does foreclosure come about and how does alpha-function fail? Clearly, foreclosure comes about by the exclusion of the paternal metaphor. The mother refuses to acknowledge the Name-of-the-Father, the Law, and prevents the symbolic castration of her child, thus preventing him from repressing the immediacy of his desire. He is kept fixed in an imaginary phantastic world without relation to the Other. He is unable as we have seen to be properly the object of desire, or a desiring subject. The child fails to develop an unconscious. This can be formulated conversely. The child refuses, perhaps with the collusion of the mother, to be symbolically castrated, preferring to remain in the *totality* of his desire - the special objet *a* for the mother, as pointed out by Melman above. In either case, his access to the Symbolic, to the law that differentiates, divides and that makes reality sensible, is severely disturbed. The balance between all three registers is upset. Too much is expected of the Imaginary as a fragile and intensely narcissistic support for an identity. It is indeed applied like a patch, in desperation against the disrupted Symbolic's invasion from the Real. At this point we are close to the starting point of our discussion on Lacan, where the child may be drawn regressively towards sleep and death.

For Bion, the alpha-function mediated access to language is brought about by the mother's capacity for reverie - that is for toning down and detoxifying the infant's projected drives. (Bion, 1962) Through her capacity for emotional thinking, she is able to render safe the anxiety due to the infant's massive erotic and destructive impulses. This alphabetising process breaks down, when the mother herself has not had sufficient access to the symbolising process - the paternal metaphor/alpha function is inadequately established in her own life. The converse holds too. The infantile drives may be too urgent to be contained, and the alpha-function/paternal metaphor is continuously destroyed by the excess.

To come back to our earlier question about the relationship between foreclosure and splitting, foreclosure preempts repression and access to the Symbolic. I think that Kleinians would agree that the more severe forms of splitting, brought about destructive impulses (either innate, or as a result of environmental failure, or both) would have the same effect, namely, attacking the links *between* signifiers, preempting symbolisation and making repression more or less impossible. The result is the same, although arrived at by different theoretical routes. The Kleinian route is an *economic* one to do with the failure of taming excessive energies (the death drive), while the Lacanian one is essentially *structural* - the failure to stabilise a structure, a structure that is *already there* but which has been foreclosed. Either way, access to language-mediated human reality is severely impaired. The fabric of experience is irremediably torn, and the subject remains tortured by the split-off or foreclosed elements which hit him, as it were, in horror, from the outside. He is no longer a subject, because the unlinked signifiers or beta elements control him from the Real.

Here is a brief summary of the Lacanian contribution:

(1) The prematurity of birth, and the 'experience' of fragmentation is the biological substratum of the death drive.

(2) The passive desire to sleep, to die, is one pole of the experience with the mother - the desire to return to non-being.

(3) The assumption and capture of the subject by his mirror image constitutes the bedrock of his ego, which introduces a fiction, a death-like falseness, a closure on truth. The subject is caught in a dualism

which is really a sameness, an eternal aggressive rivalry with himself and the other.

(4) The insertion of the subject into the Symbolic, into language, gives him a representation on the stage, but at the cost of his unity. He is torn and divided with respect to himself. The symbolic is overpowering and negating. It grinds on without us. The psychoanalytic shorthand for this is castration.

(5) The symbolic, itself, is an expression of the death drive (arising as it does from the dead father of prehistory), it constricts and limits. It (we) can never say what it wants to say. The Other is not one.

(6) The drives always tend towards death, in that they want to go beyond language, to resist entrapment and homeostasis, and to go towards completion *(jouissance)*. Thus as Lacan says all drives are death drives.

(7) The drives circle repetitively around the lost objects in the real. However, refinding the object involves the death of the subject.

(8) The death drive is the great refusal to give up on desire, the refusal of all oppression, the absolute 'No'.

(9) The foreclosure of the Name-of-the-Father during the Oedipus complex brings about the psychotic experience of *un*mediated reality.

5. ENTROPY, HELPLESSNESS AND APOPTOSIS.

In our search for the significance of death and more especially the death drive, we will now divert our attention from psychoanalysis to biological discourse, regarded increasingly as a metadiscourse which subsumes all others. Psychoanalysis has borrowed from biology, and here we will do so again.

Anti-entropy

Biologically speaking life is anti-entropic. Life opposes entropy. In the natural course of events in the universe, entropy increases, there is an increase in randomness. This is Lacan's seamlessness, or lack of differentiation within the Real. Life processes are involved in reversing, going uphill against this ubiquitous trend. Briefly, energy is captured from sunlight and fixed by plants during photosynthesis. During this process small molecules like carbon dioxide and water are joined together, using the sun's energy, into larger molecules called carbohydrates. Carbohydrates can then be transformed into other large molecules like proteins, fats and nucleic acids, by enzyme systems within the plant cells. Animals take these ready-made large molecules and transform them by first breaking them down in their own digestive systems into smaller soluble units which are absorbed and rebuilt into macromolecules characteristic for that particular species.

The cells of living things, therefore, are composed of large complex molecules, the most intricate and sophisticated of which are proteins and nucleic acids. And indeed these molecules are also grouped into further functional units, such as ribosomes and chromosomes and other cell organelles. Complexity and diversity increases, and therefore in any particular organism entropy is being reversed, for a time at least. This increasing complexification is clearly what Freud had in mind when he talked about Eros or the life drives.

The whole process is controlled and orchestrated by the genetic material in the nucleus of each cell, the deoxyribonucleic acid (DNA). Since Watson and Crick elucidated the structure of DNA in 1953, there has been a revolution in our understanding of biological systems. One of the outcomes of our new understanding has been that we now understand life as a *unity*. Basic life processes, in whatever organism, are structured fundamentally in the same way. Organisms that contain certain pigments, normally chlorophyll, can fix sunlight and make carbohydrates (plants); other organisms without this ability (animals) take those macromolecules and restructure them into animal tissues. All these processes are regulated by their genes.

Further back, more fundamentally, biological theories about the origin of life on earth envisage the abiotic formation of these macromolecules such as DNA and proteins from inorganic sub-units in the 'primeval soup' of some 3 or 4 billion years ago. Various external sources of energy will have sponsored these processes, in the context of a hostile environment of ionizing radiation which would have degraded the molecules as fast as they were formed. This abiotic process perhaps took 1 to 2 billion years before the first primitive proto-cells were formed and were subsequently found in the fossil record. Once life gained a foothold against the destructive forces, it was able gradually to modify its earthly habitat (The gaia hypothesis). The earliest plant-type organisms through their photosynthesizing activities split water molecules to release oxygen which eventually became available in sufficient quantities in the atmosphere by about 600 million years ago, to enable the well known explosion of life forms that occurred at the beginning of the Cambrian period and the beginning of evolution as we have come to understand it through Darwin.

With this essential updated 'de Chardin' vision of evolution, we can see in all these processes the gradual emergence of life in the midst of an entropic environment which threatens destruction, the return to the inorganic state. Life has emerged against all the odds, we might say, against all those forces that would tend toward randomness. In all probability, life emerged and was destroyed many times in the first two billion years of the planet's history, in what is now understood as a dynamic equilibrium between primitive life forms and their destruction before the Cambrian period. For a very long time evolution was on a knife-edge.

Death required

There is a paradox, in that life needs death to sustain itself. The entropic forces, which result in decomposition, the reversal of life processes, the reduction of macromolecules to their inorganic components, are required so that new life forms can grow and develop. Life requires death. For the new trees of the forest to grow, the old ones must be decomposed by saprophytes and their inorganic components recycled via the soil to the roots of the young saplings. Life literally feeds on death. In fact the process of feeding *itself* is a very destructive process, a point not missed by psychoanalysts. Feeding, digestion and assimilation involve the wholesale destruction of living tissue for its use in building new living cells.

There are also destructive cells in our own bodies that act in the service of life. The cells of the immune system, particularly the neutrophils, are capturing and destroying 'foreign' cells at all times. These white cells carry powerful packages of destructive enzymes, which when released on another foreign cell, will in fact destroy both cells. Sometimes the immune system for unknown reasons can become overactive and start to attack the ordinary healthy cells of the person's body, giving rise to the so-called auto-immune diseases, such as rheumatoid arthritis.

Modern biology would confirm that life and death are mutually interdependent, and I think that biologists would have no difficulty with the notion of a life drive; after all we understand that all organisms must inherit a built-in programme to survive - any that did not would have been selected out long ago. But the notion of a death instinct *per se*, seems nonsensical. Why should organisms have a desire to die? That death is essential and inevitable is beyond question, but to have a innate desire for death cannot be conceived of by biologists. One cannot think of an organism that should desire its own end. Of course, destructiveness and predation are observable facts, but these deathly activities are in the service of life. This is other-destructive, not self-destructive. It is therefore within the realm of biological reason. Any organism that desires to destroy itself would, by definition, have not survived.

Fight or flight

To come back to our central point, we are still left with the clinical findings in psychoanalysis that (some) people are self destructive and lust for death and cruelty in the extreme. For some psychoanalytical thinkers at least, they do seem to desire their own death, beyond any reasonableness or beyond any logic of their early environment.

We have considered (chapter two) the fate of the 'fight or flight' response in the human organism, inherited from our vertebrate ancestors. The biological base of the response to a predator would be the same as any other animal. The subject would be precipitated into a state of terror, fear, dread and a potential fight to the death, or flight from death. These experiences have much in common with the Kleinian description of the paranoid/schizoid position, with its dominant *persecutory* anxieties. The infant comes into the world with the capacity for this kind of response to his environment. It is part of psychobiological inheritance. And if Klein is right, this response remains central - only rarely, it seems, is the depressive position attained.

What happens to the human infant under favourable circumstances is that his *innate* tendency to respond to the environment in this paranoid, fight/flight and terror-stricken way, even more so in view of the fact that the *human* infant is the most helpless of all creatures, is modified by the benign presence of the mother as a container for his fear that he might die, his annihilation anxiety. He is gradually able to come to terms with his destructiveness, to feel guilt and concern about it, in the depressive position, to realise - that is in reality over against phantasy - that his mother loves him more than she hates him, and finally be able to use his capacity for aggression for constructive assertiveness in the service of the life instinct.

When this benign environment of the early infant does not exist, or is faulty, or simply cannot contain the infantile onslaught due to constitutional factors, then the infant is left to a greater or lesser extent exposed to his raw unmodified paranoid anxieties and dreads (Bion's nameless dread, chapter three). There is little or no protection from the terror and fear of imminent death and destruction.

I have argued that culturally this situation is becoming more and more common in the West. (Weatherill, 1991, 1994, 1995) Increasingly, it appears, human destructiveness is on the rampage, unbound, defused, unmodified by the environment, or its internal representative, the ego. As we have seen, it can be lodged in others who become terrifying persecutors, or it can be turned against the self in the clinical manifestations described by those who work with borderline and psychotic individuals. Here, argue the developmental psychoanalysts, the human infant has been left exposed and uncontained in a relatively primitive condition. In this sense the death drive, or the fight or flight response, is archaic and primary. It is a fundamental *biological* given. It only becomes integrated into normal and healthy assertive aggression in the service of the life instinct in good-enough early development.

The desire for death and destructiveness in its most malign form occurs by default, by an accident of early and radical environmental failure. The intensely vulnerable human infant is left in an extreme state of persecutory anxiety, at the mercy of the innate predator/prey reaction which precludes emotional development, precludes an attachment to life, leaving him, as Winnicott puts it, all the time on the brink of unthinkable anxiety. To be involved in violence and a death dealing struggle of one kind or another, is all that is left to him. To be able to enter Lacan's 'Symbolic register' the sphere of human culture and human reality, the sphere of language and sociality, required initially a container for thinking unbearable thoughts, or the introjection of the good breast, the experience of a good enough mother, or the undamaged background object. Instead, without these, he is left with the continuous need to evacuate unbearable feelings, beta elements, bizarre objects that attack and fragment. He has not been enabled to integrate his animal inheritance and enter the world of human object relations with a capacity to hate and to love. He is left in a delusional world which echoes his prehistory. Here is a 'pure culture' of the death instinct, devoid of influence by the life instinct, in complete defusion. It is the predator/prey, fight or flight response in its most extreme form, activated in an extreme necessity by the most radically helpless creature, the isolated human neonate.[1]

As is well known, such violent madness is never encountered in nature, because there is never a vertebrate animal that is ever as helpless. The 'cruelty' one finds in nature is always more or less appropriate to a real situation programmed into the species by natural selection. It is necessary for survival and in keeping with the struggle for existence. This is why, as has often been pointed out, animals rarely kill members of their own species. They spar and fight, but not to the death.

Two developmental crises

It is the *excessive* vulnerability and prematurity of the human infant that leaves it acutely and uniquely aware of and sensitized to the quality of its environmental provision. *All* analysts agree on the essential prematurity of the human neonate at birth. Blomfield (1987) in his essay on human destructiveness has pointed to two developmental crises that the human infant has to negotiate. The first is familiar, Rank's birth trauma. Here the foetus makes, or is obliged to make, the profound transition from 'placental parasite' (Blomfield following Giard) and the instinctual programming appropriate to uterine existence, to a radically different existence and instinctual requirement *out-*

side the womb. The second crisis relates to the new-born's immature brain. At birth, the brain is under-developed. The nervous system has a basic integrative function, and yet the human infant is born with incomplete myelination of the central nervous system. This, Blomfield suggests, represents the extra-uterine phase of human gestation. The possibility of many complex integrated actions and experiences dependent on brain maturity are delayed until *after* the first year of life. Blomfield quotes Wallon when he describes the infant's experience of this time as being one of fragmentation, which will only slowly be replaced by one of integration following on neurophysiological maturation. For a long time the infant is unable to co-ordinate his experience, and this period of brain deficiency corresponds well with Melanie Klein's paranoid/schizoid stage which precedes the more integrated experience of the depressive position. It also corresponds well with the 'mirror stage' of Lacan (1949), which is not surprising, as Wallon was also an inspiration for Lacan. The findings of neurophysiology correlate well with those of psychoanalysis.

Pressure for closure

The implications of these two developmental crises are profound. Entry into the world in a perceptually and experientially chaotic state, and with a residual parasitic intentionality, poses unique problems and opportunities in human maturation. They provide an urgency and a dynamic towards the creation of unities, syntheses, symbolisation, the acquisition of language, the development of secondary process, and logical linear type thinking. They imply a demand to repress ambiguity in favour of an instrumental view of the world. Survival demands certainty, and the tendency towards premature warding off of unconscious meanings. And yet the life drive demands access to the unconscious. The repressive barrier must be permeable in both directions otherwise the sources of our creativity dry up. There is a requirement for some flexibility and toleration of anxiety. If the experience of being in a state of traumatic fragmentation can be symbolised, dreamed about, written about, mythologised about, thought about, and so on, then human culture and the imaginative life is greatly enhanced. However, this involves a toleration of a kind of madness. The new science of *chaos* (Gleick 1987), for instance, the computer simulations of chaotic systems, is just one recent illustration of an awareness of a reality beyond the reality of order, rationality and linearity.

If, on the other hand, there is an excess of destructiveness, due to radical environmental failure, or later trauma, or genetic endowment, or the nature of drive itself, the predator/prey response in its archaic unmodified form becomes manifest as a last ditch defence again annihilation. Destructiveness which has not become transformed into constructive aggression (the death drive fused with Eros), attacks the ego from within, destroying the repression barrier, or alpha-function, and bringing about the return of the foreclosed in the shape of psychotic fragmentation and breakdown. Or, in the reverse: the threatened re-emergence of archaic fragmented states into consciousness, brings about the reactivation of the primitive predator/prey response and a desire energetically to destroy these terrifying perceptions. There is an active evacuation or repudiation of proto-mental contents which only serves to reinforce the disintegrative processes.

At this stage, there is no possibility of the primary processes being used creatively. Consciousness has been hijacked by destructive forces, there is no longer any distinction between conscious and unconscious and nothing creative or constructive can possibly occur.

Such a disintegrative and morbid process belongs to the domain of severe mental illness. But it would be a grave error to confine it to a psychiatric category. For clearly, Kleinian psychoanalysis has demonstrated that normal and neurotic people contain a psychotic core which may never be made manifest, but remains a potential to be activated under the appropriate traumatic conditions. There is a hint of this when one, for a brief time, 'goes to pieces' or 'freaks-out' or 'becomes beside oneself with rage', and so on. The dreams of normal and neurotic people contain terrifying sequences, sometimes of perverse brutality. Similarly in intoxicated states, psychotic regressions can occur.

The fear of uncertainty (the Real), the tendency towards premature closure, leads the ego to react to the split off and catastrophic threats to its integrity by omnipotent denial and idealisation of its capacities. As an extreme measure to reinforce its own unacknowledged alienation, it resorts to massive imaginary demonstrations of its invulnerability. Globally, omnipotence has put its faith in science, technology and totalitarian systems, in which the subject does not exist. This is the triumph of negative narcissism (Rosenfeld 1987), in which the death drive is incorporated into a perverse structure whose aim is to block-off any awareness of weakness, dependency and human vulnerability (subjectivity). This is an *in*human and a precarious structure, given to violent reactions against any *re*-presentation of its own incompleteness.

We have made mention of perversion, briefly in chapter four, when Lacan spoke of the child being under the bar (or the whip) of the symbolic. It is the terrifying autonomy of this register in which the subject is almost emptied that makes perversion so widespread. Perversion is connected to a sense of humiliation and helplessness. Behind these eroticized repetitions is *hilflosigkeit* - the never to be re-encountered primary helplessness. Classically, perversion is the reverse of neurosis, and is evidence for a universal 'polymorphously perverse disposition' in human (infantile) sexuality, prior to, and hidden behind, the dominance of genital organisation. But perversion is nothing *natural*. Perversion is a sophisticated *structure*, that, as it were, *knows* about castration and the Law, but repudiates both. In a brilliant essay, Janine Chasseguet-Smirgel speaks of the pervert's belief that its pregenital desire is preferable and superior to the father genital desire. The disavowal of Oedipus leads to the 'Erosion of the double difference between the sexes and the generations.' (1985, p. 2) Perversion is the elimination of difference and the Law that founds difference, and the consequent 'destruction of all values.' (ibid. p. 10) Chasseguet-Smirgel envisages the pervert's creation of an anal-sadistic universe that eliminates all difference and is a parody of the genital paternal universe. For Freud (1917), the anal-sadistic stage was a 'trial gallop' on the way to the genital organisation of the libido. The pervert literally 'turns-around', this reality (ultimately the Judeo-Christian tradition), replacing it with sacrilege. That is, 'All that is taboo, forbidden or sacred is devoured by the digestive tract, an enormous [anal-sadistic] grinding machine disintegrating the molecules of the mass thus obtained in order to reduce it to excrement.' (ibid. p . 4) This represents the jouissance of destruction, as a veil for the terror at the heart of things, designated by the term castration in psychoanalysis. Consequently, Fromm speaks of sadism as exerting absolute control over another, creating the illusion of omnipotence, but having no *practical* aim, instead it is '"devotional ... it is the religion of psychical cripples.' (1974, p. 386)

On the personal level, the fragility of the self is manifest in the massive growth in recent years of multi-layered security systems, insurance policies, personal alarms, to achieve closure into a perfect private world against the dereliction perceived without. On the macro-level, there have been (and still are) weapons of mass destruction, the secret police, and death camps, and more recently, renewed racial conflict, retrenchment and fragmentation. Here the death drive is manifest not so much as chaotic violent disintegration, but, against this imminent

Emptiness, Hopelessness & Apoptosis 111

possibility, frozen into rigid control systems of oppression and tribalism, which are always prone to implode into acts of barbarity and internal disintegration.[2] Deadly solutions are envisaged for life's problems. Extremism increases. Pornography increases world-wide. As real life gets harder, the *image* of perfection proliferates everywhere. We will return to these themes in chapter seven.

To summarise: life, at least as defined biologically, is anti-entropic in that it opposes the inevitable increase in randomness and chaos which *is* the universe. The anti-entropic process par excellence is photosynthesis, on which all plants and animals ultimately depend. But we have noted here that death is essential to life. Decomposition leads to regeneration. The tail of the tadpole is autolyzed and the digestion products become the frogs legs. The cells of the caterpillar are metamorphosed into the adult butterfly. Eating requires the death of one organism so that another may live. All is constant flux and change. Only the imaginary perceives stasis.

In so-called normal infant development the threat of death, derived from the drives themselves, is detoxified by maternal reverie and language and transformed into constructive aggression, fused with and put to the service of the life instinct under the governance of the pleasure/reality principle. The infant grows up with the very necessary illusion of protection by a background object, *our* family, *our* tradition, *our* people. There is both on the level of the individual and the species a developmental pressure to integrate perception, *to make familiar* what is fundamentally alien, to domesticate life, to develop language and to abandon, or leave behind the real (ecstasy) of death, for the sake of the deadly peace of normality. But in certain circumstances (which may be increasing), this background object becomes damaged or injured, it loses its protective shield and the subject is in danger of coming face to face with the event horizon of catastrophic anxiety. Thus, the subject is re-presented with the foreclosed or abolished image of the fragmented body, the totally alien Thing-in-itself *(das Ding)*. Biologically speaking, the subject, or more likely the organism, reacts to this terror by invoking a predator/prey response which in the extreme attacks perception and consciousness itself, so as not to see and not to know, or the perverse 'solution' which seeks erotic pleasure in playing with the fragmented body of the other, thereby invoking the entropic forces it was attempting to combat.

Apoptosis

However, modern biology gives an unexpectedly close parallel with that of the human predicament. What follows is a useful intersection between psychoanalytic theorising on the death drive on the one hand, and the recent findings of cell biology on the other.

It has been noted since the 1940s that some cancers, instead of proliferating out of control, spontaneously regress and even disappear for no apparent reason. Up until recently, the focus in cancer research has been on discovering the genes which switch on cell division allowing cancers to grow out of control. But during embryological development, it has been known that some cells are *programmed* to die. As organisms develop, some cells or groups of cells abort according to a programme laid down genetically. We have already made reference to the frog and the tadpole. These examples have been known for years.

In the 1970s, John Kerr and his colleagues, pathologists working at the University of Aberdeen discovered that normal cell death was strikingly different from cell death caused by injury or accident. Injured cells tend to swell and burst inflaming neighbouring cells (a process termed necrosis), whereas, when normal cells die, they shrink and condense and are devoured by white cells long before they have a chance to cause inflammation or tissue damage.

Programmed (normal) cell death is termed *apoptosis*, which means falling, as in withered leaves. Apoptosis had been noted in these earlier years, it had attracted some attention, but rather at the level of an epiphenomenon. It happens in some tissues, it is difficult to detect because the dead cells leave no traces behind them. Many biologists were reluctant to conclude that cell death was widespread. It was not regarded as an important mechanism. Research into this area lay dormant for many years.

Instead, what had always seemed to be more interesting was why some cells resisted internal controls and started to divide uncontrollably leading to cancers. However, an interesting question was raised during the 1970s: do the genes which switch on cell growth *also* cause cells to die? This question was sponsored by a frequent yet rather bizarre observation: cells that are rapidly dividing out of control in cancers, also appear to be dying in very large numbers in these same aberrant tissues. Modern biology understands that cells do not die by a slow wind-down process, an ageing process, but by an *active* programme of death. Death is programmed genetically into the organism, and, what is new, and very relevant for our discussion here, is that this programming appears to be *universal*.

Martin Raff (1996), of London University, studying brain cells called oligodendrocytes showed that when grown singly, in artificial isolation on the petri dish, these specialised nerve cells died. These cells isolated from their neighbours, yet provided with all environmental requirements, unaccountably die within a very short period. Cells *in vivo* are not normally isolated and therefore *receive continuous signals* from other cells that maintain them in life. They are *not* allowed to die by virtue of their neighbours' continuous signalling. Even cells of the same tissue (Raff chose retinal cells and cartilage cells), where there is just *one* type of cell, are maintained by signals from neighbouring identical cells. If these cells are artificially separated then they too will die, for want of signals from other cells which - ordinarily - prevent single cells from automatically taking the suicidal path. Raff concluded that what holds for retinal and cartilage cells, will hold for all *cells in every tissue*.[3]

The revolutionary idea, that has taken at least twenty years to become widely accepted, is that all cells are *continually trying to die* unless they receive a signal to the contrary. But what selective advantage could there be for this mechanism? Firstly, any cell that ends up in the wrong tissue during development will be eliminated because it will not get the right signals to keep it in life. Secondly, this mechanism enables the right balance to be struck between cell death and cell division. If the level of signals in a tissue were set at a particular value, if too many cells were produced by cell division, some would not receive enough stimulation and would abort. Such a mechanism would ensure that cells survive only when and where they are needed. Recent work on a range of widely different animals indicate that the mechanisms of cell death and its prevention are the same or very similar across the board, indicating just one more mechanism out of a long list of fundamental biological processes[4] that have been present since early on in evolutionary history, and subsequently inherited by modern life forms.

The body's health is ultimately controlled by death. Paradoxically, growth genes added to cell cultures increase cell proliferation, but also increase cell death. These genes can act as accelerators for growth *or* death. The path taken will depend on the signals from neighbouring cells. With signals, growth will proliferate; without signals, cells will die in vast numbers. Why would cells be so structured genetically that whenever they start dividing there is also a programme built in to kill them? It is now argued that a major way of controlling cancer in the body is by this cell division/cell abort mechanism. It therefore becomes very difficult for a cell to become a proliferating cancer cell because the whole process that is driving it to proliferate, is also driving it to die. As I indicated earlier, the only reason that cells do not die is because they get signals from other cells not to go down the death route. Proliferation and death, therefore, are intimately linked - the same gene(s) essentially programming the cells in life and death.

In reality, in the living organism, there are the so-called protective genes (for example, the p53 gene)[5] that monitor DNA damage in cells from environmental influences, and decide if the damage can be repaired, or, if the cell should go down the death pathway and commit suicide. Cells deemed to be too damaged will be allowed to follow the death pathway for want of life-giving signalling. Animals specially genetically engineered without these protective genes develop excessive cancers early in life because there is no mechanism for abortion of damaged cells. Cancers cells that manage to continue proliferating have therefore lost the ability to die by apoptosis (either by making more cell death suppressing proteins, or, by deactivating the p53 gene, or because p53 has mutated - a factor in half of all human cancers). Without their protective genes, cells that should die because they are damaged, are not able to do so. In terms of the major modern diseases, there is on the one hand, cancer, which involves a failure of cell death, while on the other hand, there are the neuro-degenerative diseases and AIDS where cell death happens when it shouldn't.

From this new vantage point, we understand cytotoxic drugs, used to treat cancer, as being an extremely crude method of hitting cells and turning them towards the death pathway. Cancers that develop on the inside of the body, in the lymphoid tissues and the blood system for instance, are easier to treat because the cytotoxic drugs seem to be able to reverse the process of cell proliferation relatively easily because of the tissues' lowish threshold to damage tolerance. These tissues, protected on the inside of the body, are not used to being damaged by environmental stimuli. Therefore any cells that appear to be minimally damaged and different are allowed to enter the suicide pathway. The most difficult tumours to treat are in the epithelial tissues that cover the inner and outer surfaces of the body, the lungs and the colon in particular. These tissues are exposed to continuous damage from environmental influences and they have to survive, so their threshold before engaging in cell suicide is high, whereas in the bone marrow, for instance, the threshold is much lower. Therefore, oncologists have been effective in treating those tumour cells that would die readily, as they already had a programme that would enable them to die easily. The tumours not so easily affected are those tumours where the cell death programme is not readily engaged because their threshold is set at a relatively high level. In these latter intractable cancers, employing treatments with cytotoxic drugs, damages the normal tissues that die readily, and the tumour cells coming from these tougher tissues tend to survive because their threshold is that much higher.

The relevance of this modern biological research to our present discussion will be immediately apparent. There is a *similarity* between the human subject and its relation to its own death, and the individual cell and its own death[6]. Both, on their own, are in a radically helpless state, and are in imminent danger of death. Both, as it were, need to be led away from the inevitable route towards death by entering the circuits of exchange of their respective communal worlds. Both need to be signalled to, in order that they remain alive. Isolated and alone, both will die. As Lacan has shown, the failure to enter the Symbolic via the paternal metaphor leaves the human subject in a perilous state ultimately akin to death. Similarly, the failure of the cell to engage in the biochemical 'language' of its surroundings leads to death.

Psychoanalysis has shown how necessary are these human signals (the maternal reverie and containment, in the first instance, of a long line of identifications with the other) in order to bring about the substantial constitution of human subjectivity. This cannot be taken for granted as an automatic process of growth and maturation. The self is not pre-given in any sense. The self only comes into being on the basis of object *relations*, that is, in the context of the *fabric* of social relationships. What the new discoveries in biology 'confirm' analogously is that omnipotence cannot work. Without this great effort of bringing the infant, the child and the adolescent into the social, impoverishment and death are real possibilities. Object relations theorists have been in the forefront of this research, paid lip service to by parents, teachers and state agencies generally, but in practice children may be being increasingly left to fend for themselves, as yet another category of autonomous consumers in a global market. And if *within* psychoanalysis there is no consensus, for example, the object relational emphasis is relegated by Lacanians to the Imaginary, and by extension the self is merely an illusion, so in some quarters there may already be sufficient justification for *more* child autonomy. The consequences for the integration of the drives and the death drive in particular are already apparent.[7]

There is another important analogy here, also, namely, that the apparent aliveness of cells - their growth and proliferation beyond the normal in the tumour - is also a death. The meaningless directionless *excess* of growth is in fact the drift towards death. As we discussed at the end of chapter one, Freud's interest in the immortality of the protista, their perpetuation of sameness, is also death. The protista divide asexually and therefore they never die and no new genetic information is added. This mechanism of asexual reproduction ensures perpetual survival but no diversity and no evolution (except that occasioned by mutation). This is like the stasis of the Lacanian Imaginary.

Just as in human communities there has to be repression, containment, a partial death, so also, in cell communities there is this limit or break on excessive growth, or a submission to an overall law and structure laid down in the genetic code. Therefore in the metazoa (multicellular organisms), controls are placed on cell division and differentiation as the organism develops. This coincides evolutionarily with the phenomenon of sexuality and the arrival of genetic difference. A certain limited death is placed on all cells and maintained by intercellular signalling for the sake of a controlled life and living within the confines of homeostasis, and soon enough the death of the individual, for the sake of the genetic rejuvenation of the species offered by the sexual process. The human *biological* organism is subject to the *language and structuring* imposed by the genetic code in an analogous way to the human subject's structuring by the symbolic order envisaged by Lacan. Both are necessary deaths so that life can proceed, diversify and evolve, or, are inescapable alienations from an excess of life. Both cover, control and conceal a deeper tendency - a death drive towards abundance, cancerous growth and suicide. This excessive growth is not simple, it is wild, unstable and volatile, as it carries within it the seeds of its own destruction, in the shape of the cell abort mechanism.

But I think that what comes out of this new research and what has been resisted by biologists for so long is the propensity for *all* cells to die, and the propensity for damaged cells, to a greater or lesser extent depending as we have seen on their positioning within the organism itself, to die, not by accident, but according to an ever present *inner* programme. We have noted a similar resistance among psychoanalysts, oriented towards life, growth and Eros, to seeing the drive towards death in human subjectivity, unless some saving influence is

Emptiness, Hopelessness & Apoptosis 117

brought to bear that will divert the subject for a time into life and adaptation.

Such analogies are tempting, but are only analogies, and we must leave them in the background as exciting and interesting. We will resist the temptation to biologize human desire any further.

We will summarise some crucial points.

(1) Life resists the Real of entropy. Living processes, operating as a unity, reverse the universal tendency of everything to randomise. Life emerges against all the odds.

(2) Yet life needs death and decomposition to sustain itself. However living beings do not appear to desire their own death.

(3) We have inherited from our vertebrate ancestors the fight/flight mechanism as a terror response to predation. This reappears and coincides with the Kleinian paranoid/schizoid position of earliest infancy.

(4) This biological given can only be problematically integrated by maternal containment. Without this primary illusion, the death drive emerges by default.

(5) Legendary human cruelty arises out of our primary helplessness and our premature birth.

(6) The return of the residual parasitic intentionality (intra-uterine 'experience'), and the earliest post-uterine phases, may lead to psychotic disintegration.

(7) The evolutionary pressure, ontogenetically and phylogenetically, is to develop secondary processes and the repression barrier, but with *enrichment* by primary process, that is access to abandoned signifiers in the unconscious. This is the basis of creativity, homeostasis.

(8) There is the recurrent danger of contamination by destructiveness. Here, the primary process is seen as dangerous and contaminating, *not* enriching. Rigid containers.

(9) The endopsychic perception of dangers inherent in survival, demands *certainty*. Ambiguity, therefore, must be destroyed by closure, especially now. Here is the logic: survival=certainty=control=omnipotence and the illusion of transcending the terror of the limitations of human existence: hence, orality, envy, greed and perversion.

(10) The persistent and chronic inability to analyse and understand foundational anxiety, leads to chronic repetitive forms of destructive acting and thinking.

(11) Modern biological findings show that cells, on their own and isolated, die for want of signals from their neighbours to keep them alive. All cells are programmed to die. This is termed apoptosis. The

parallel with human subjectivity is interesting.

(12) Protista and cancers cells are immortal - they have lost the ability to die, but their very 'aliveness' is death bearing.

(13) Paradoxically, the arrival of sexuality early in evolution imposes 'repressive' controls and mortality on the cells of multicellular organisms for the sake of genetic diversity. Omnipotence does not work. There has to be the encounter with sex and death.

6. *ENJOY* DEATH: INITIATORY PROCESSES?

> There is a woman who dreamed that *she stood before a forest and saw that it was completely dead. She was afraid to enter because she was sure something terrible would happen to her if she did. However, she decided to enter, and in doing so came upon a beautiful pasture where she found a white shepherd.* The dream says: as things are now everything is dead and sterile, but if you have the courage to enter, it may open up. (Whitmont, 1969, pp. 92-93)

Consumers of psychotherapy think of the process as being about something more, about growth, about potential and celebration. True, but theorists of the process would say that the increments come about via a paradoxical and dark encounter with one's own mortality. The space provided by a psychotherapeutic situation, the silence, the attention, inevitably evoke one's own finitude and the potential proximity of death - *your* death. The implicit question is: what does death, our own death, do to every moment in our lives? This chapter concerns itself in general terms with death in a symbolic sense as part of a transformative and regenerative process - deaths that enhance life - a theme that is widespread today in transpersonal psychologies.

Rebirth, renewal

From here, one might go on to think of the universality of the themes of death and resurrection or creation in religion and mythology. Here death is taken on symbolically or almost literally in order for a rebirth to take place. Death is regarded as the supreme initiation into the new life, by all the great religions. Death is seen as a source of renewal. Encounter death; enjoy death!

Dissociations of the sense of identity occur in many states of mind: mystical bliss, psychotic states, near death states, in accidents and severe illness, as well as drug-induced states. 'In the deepest and most lasting forms of ego dissociation and re-formation the willing and judging egos become separated from the sense of personal identity and are so changed as to produce a sense of being "reborn". This transformation can occur within the religious frame of reference and in the individuation process of depth psychology.' (ibid. p. 233) Any change of psychic structuring is reacted to by the ego as a death-like experience (Bion's catastrophic change). The ego resists its dissolution.

Around mid-life however, the Self, which in Jungian theory created the ego and then withdrew, now returns as a compensatory function with images of the *transcendental*. The subject is on the downward trajectory to its aboriginal source.

Jung says:

Many young people have at bottom a panic fear of life (though at the same time they intensely desire it), and an even greater number of the ageing have the same fear of death... We are so convinced that death is simply the end of a process that it does not ordinarily occur to us to conceive of death as a goal and a fulfilment...
From the middle age of life onward, only he who remains vitally alive is ready to *die with life*. For in the secret hour of life's midday the parabola is reversed, death is born. The second half of life does not signify assent, unfolding, increase, exuberance, but death, since the end is its goal. The negation of life's fulfilment is synonymous with the refusal to accept its ending. Both mean not wanting to live, and not wanting to live is identical with not wanting to die. Waxing and waning make one curve. (1960, paras. 797-800)

This death is not the death drive of Freud. For Gordon (1978), for instance, the death drive provides the self with a frame for life, a frame for its unfolding and transformation. There is an intimate connection between death and creativity. The general Jungian view seems to be that: 'The death instinct is experienced subjectively via imagery and emotional states - oneness, floating and oceanic, dreamy, a creative reverie, nostalgia. Crucial to this reading of the death instinct is that regression, whether benign or malign, is as much a part of life as growth and progress. Death as a psychic fact, therefore occupies an individual all of his days and not just towards the end of his life'. (Samuels, Shorter and Plant, 1986, p. 40)

Jung himself, on the day that his mother died, had a frightening dream of a wolf-hound commanded by the Wild Huntsman to carry away a human soul. On travelling home he experienced great grief alternating with music, dance and laughter. 'The paradox can be explained', says Jung, 'if we suppose at one moment death was being represented from the point of view of the ego, and at the next from that of the psyche.' (1963, p. 345) Jung acknowledges, 'death is indeed a fearful piece of brutality... This is a cruel reality which we have no right to sidestep... From another point of view, however, death appears as a joyful event. In the light of eternity, it is a wedding, a *mysterium coniunctionis*. The soul attains, as it were, its missing half, it achieves wholeness.' (ibid. p. 346)

Initiations

For example, initiation rituals in traditional societies mark the transition between boyhood and manhood. Typically the young boy was taken into the forest to confront terror, suffering and torture. Here he was to enter the unknown, the darkness, the unconscious. The boy may have been taken there by an animal ancestor or indeed swallowed by one (like Jonah or Tom Thumb) symbolising a regression to a foetal state, but it is also a return to the beginning of the world before creation. In some practices, the initiates are laid out in newly dug graves and are made-up to look dead. They are also tortured by the mythic ancestors, by being made to drink blood, to suffer bodily mutilation such as circumcision, subincision, extractions of teeth, cutting off of fingers, tattooings and so on. One can see in these practices the theme of castration and initiation into the Symbolic order. Further, one can note the forced regression to confront annihilation anxiety and the image of the body in pieces. The boy is 'reborn', he may acquire a new name, may be taught a new language, a privileged or secret language, and fed like a child. In some instances an animal will be sacrificed and the boy enclosed within the dead animal's skin from which he will be 'born' and cry like a new-born infant.

For girls, the initiation begins at the first menstruation. She is immediately isolated and separated from the rest of the community. She must enter a hut in the bush and remain out of the light of the sun. She must enter her 'shadow', her unconscious. During her seclusion she will be educated in certain traditions of her tribe and the secrets of sexuality. Spinning and weaving symbolise the omnipotent magical powers of fate and destiny. The moon spins time, it is she who weaves the lives of humanity. At this time some of the old women will teach the initiates, ritual, erotic dances and songs, which will reveal the sacredness of the feminine and the sources of life and fecundity. She will be encouraged to fully identify with and celebrate her child-bearing capacities, the mysteries of creation and giving birth. Some feminine secret rituals at this time involve running wild, dancing and shouting, eating and drinking. Eliade (1960) points to some African traditions that involve aquatic symbolism. Here the young girls have their clothes taken away by their 'mothers', and are made to plunge their heads into water, to the verge of suffocation, sometimes their bodies are beaten, and later the 'daughter's' head is held over a fire, and she is made to dance, an erotic dance, and then pass between the woman's legs in a symbolic act of rebirth. In one tradition, the girl is symbolically killed by a leopard, then the leopard is killed and the girl is liberated from its body. This means that she is reborn to a new spiritual existence.

From our perspective, these initiations were brutal. For modern adolescents, there are no culturally ordained rituals, bar the transition from primary to secondary school - *secretly* and unpublicly painful as that can be. Menstruation is marked only by its absence - the whiteness and the invisibility of the tampons the young woman is expected to effortlessly use. However, adolescents create their own initiations[1]. They enjoy the proximity of death in their own way. Increasingly, to judge by the dramatic rise in suicides, this enjoyment *without limit* can go too far - tipping over the edge. Death is the only barrier now that adolescents have, as every other barrier has been thrown off. Death is the only challenger now. Formerly, structures of authority *represented* death to rebellious youth. Now there is little left of this old repressive morality. Adolescents are left to themselves a great deal to find their own boundaries. This could not be more different from traditional practices.

However, to return to the argument here, one archetypal theme repeats itself: the need for regression, the death of a former self, the return to origins, to chaos, the re-entry into Primordial time, for the sake of new life and creativity in Historical time. We live in two worlds, and that in health we must be able to move freely between them. One world is broadly speaking the world of the ego of secondary process, conscious or preconscious thought, asymmetrical consciousness and historical or profane time and existence. The other world is unconscious[2] to us, it is timeless and infinite, symmetrical, outside of history. It is the Beginning, the Origin, the chaos at the beginning of Creation, when the world was without form. To move from the first world to the second is to be involved in death or some symbolic equivalent, which psychologists refer to as regression.

It will be important to comment at this point on the largely negative connotations connected with the term regression. For instance, Rycroft defines regression as a 'defensive process [involving] the return to an earlier stage of libidinal and ego development... [marked by] fixation points such as the oral or anal stages of infantile development.' (1968, pp. 138-9) Such a return to immature functioning is often regarded as pathological. There is also a psychoanalytic literature on creative regression to which I refer later. Regression here is being viewed as *progression* of the unconscious into consciousness, or a temporary surrendering of conscious controls to the unconscious. This is a process that is potentially dangerous, but, under certain conditions, life enhancing. The arguments developed here are mainly concerned with the life enhancing aspects of regression.

Psychoanalysis is a *modern* form of initiation. There are rituals: strict times; the couch; lying down; regular payments; the analyst's words; impossible theories and mysteries; the mask of incognito; and so on. The analysand is encouraged to free-associate, by suspending his normal historically determined consciousness, by being directed to pay attention to his dreams and phantasies and other unconscious processes. He will come to encounter suffering, anxiety and dread, the deathly power of primary envy and hostile internal objects, and through this process he will come to learn a *new* language, perhaps his own 'full speech' in the Lacanian sense. He will enter the chaos and timelessness of the unconscious, and learn the traumatic connection between, sexuality, his coming to be, and death. Jung claims that: 'The only 'initiation process' that is still alive and practiced today in the West is the analysis of the unconscious as used by doctors for therapeutic purposes.' (CW 11, para. 842)

On this initiatory journey as envisaged by some psychoanalysts, the analyst will be his guide and guarantor. Through the analyst's toleration of anxiety, chaos and not-knowing, his capacity to suffer with the analysand via the latter's evacuatory and communicatory projections, he will bring to consciousness the insatiability of desire and its lack. By maintaining a disposition of the Freudian 'evenly suspended attention', 'without memory or desire' (Bion, 1970), he may bring to birth via 'selected fact' new integrations and knowledge (K) about Truth (O), which will again be disassembled into chaos, in an unending dialectic of deaths and new beginnings. He will activate within the analysand his own nascent internal analyst/shaman, who wants to know truth, and who reveals to the ego its ultimately shallow, provisional and fictitious nature.[3]

The ego resists truth. But the analyst is asking the ego to give up its controls, or at least suspend them in the session, to re-enter chaos, a death, in order to gain insight. The emotional impact of true insight is a feeling of new life. Bion always spoke of truth as food for the mind. What the analyst is doing, optimally, is enabling the analysand to tolerate deathliness homeopathically or prophylactically. In contemplation of death and all its symbolic equivalents, we come to apprehend non-being and the source of our basic anxiety. Being becomes the stronger the more non-being it can absorb. The death drive can then be reclaimed for Eros, thought about, dreamed about, phantasied about, reintegrated and re-fused with it. The more this fusion can occur, the less unintegrated destructiveness there will be to oppose life and creativity. This residual destructiveness exists *outside* the ego until it is symbolised in the depressive position, whence it can be employed creatively. While it is outside, it can act independently (in the Real) in a mindless catastrophic way (literally without a thinking mind to contain it). Instead of thinking and speaking about being destructive, the subject is impelled to act-out the destructiveness in his behaviour. The implicit hope in all 'talking cures' is that the drives and ultimately the death drive itself can brought within the orbit of speech and more broadly the whole range of representational processes (art, music, drama, etc.).

Often, however, this destructive acting-out is quite silent. Freud cautioned us about the silent and dumb nature of the death drive, making its destructive activity often difficult to appreciate. In analyses we are aware of it as a hidden, but chronic ego-syntonic resistance, subtly opposing the progress of the analysis, hollowing it out from within. Here are just a few instances of the many that could be described of our apprehension of the death drive: the unaccountable depression of the analyst; the patient who never showed a flicker of recognition of the analyst; the excessive morality, or excessive adherence to a doctrine, in either patient or analyst; the analyst's growing realisation that the sessions are very hard work and probably pointless; the leaden atmosphere in the room...

Always alienated

However, there is a dilemma here. Is it ever quite so simple? Clearly the death drive, the radical end of desire, could never be *fully integrated* into Eros. According to the very nature of the structure of the ego, this little bit of life that has of necessity had to separate itself from the universe, is therefore forever alienated and defensive, unsure of its position, *essentially* paranoid as Lacan and Klein have shown us. This intense narcissistic vulnerability requires the subject to fight off truth and achieve certainty. However much we tend to come to terms with this dilemma, through analysis or other life experiences, fundamentally we are left with a perception of our own limitedness. In fact, the more we face it and think about it, the more it becomes apparent to us. While we require an egoic view of the world, at the same time, we are involved in defending it. If one accepts the ego as a necessary instrument of functioning *in* the world, one accepts a corresponding aggressive defensiveness of its territory. Can all this can be described under the heading of healthy aggressiveness? From a certain point of view (that expressed by the ego-psychologists) this is true. The ego, if it is worth anything, must maintain its integrity. In the case of psychoanalytic treatment one would say, blandly, that a certain amount of resistance is normal or healthy. But we cannot escape the fact, as we have emphasized in the previous chapter, and as the Jungians emphasize, that ultimately the ego is founded upon an illusion of unity, a *premature* closure in an omnipotent and omniscient mode. When pushed it will fight and fight to defend its position. This is part of healthy assertiveness, as understood by the ego-psychologists of adaptation. The Jungians ultimately understand this also in a positive sense: the process of individuation, this circumambulation of the self as *the* centre, involving an ultimate unity, synthesis and wholeness. The emphasis is on oneness and *in*-dividuality, or a separate indivisible unity or whole. This is 'nothing less than to divest the self of the false wrappings of the persona.' (CW. 7, para. 269).

The psychoanalytic position, that we have emphasized here, is different. The normal and neurotic personality includes a residual psychotic core which hates reality and will destroy the perceptual apparatus involved in the judgement about that reality. This is more extreme than the Jungian position. Moreover this holds whatever the circumstances of the birth and early environment happen to be. Normatively, good enough mothering holds and contains infant psychotic distress by the development of alpha-function and the repression barrier which divides consciousness from unconsciousness, sanity from insanity. Of course, if maternal reverie fails the psychotic core remains a terrifying *daily* reality. Clearly, the maternal (environmental) response is of crucial importance for psychic health, harmony and integration. With it, life is worth living and fighting for. Without it, life is not worth living, but death is well worth striving for. Nevertheless, so-called ego autonomy (however deep it reaches) rests on an almost permanently occluded primary madness.

With this proviso of the *relativity* of ego-autonomy, let us proceed positively. Later, we will explore the weakness or perhaps the naivity

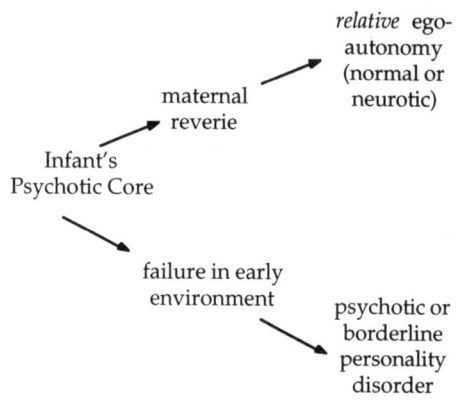

```
                                    relative ego-
                                    autonomy
                                    (normal or
                   maternal          neurotic)
                   reverie    ↗
                         ↗
Infant's    →
Psychotic Core
                         ↘
                   failure in early
                   environment     psychotic or
                               ↘   borderline
                                   personality
                                   disorder
```

of this position. But for the present state of our argument, it will be clear that normal and neurotic individuals can temporally regress 'in the service of the ego' to a transient chaotic state without any danger, because of the relative intactness of their ego autonomous functions. In fact the whole burden of this chapter points to the necessity and spiritual value of this periodic return to chaos and Primordial time. The necessity is occasioned by the ultimately fictitious and superficial nature of the ego itself. The ego has to be frequently 'dissolved' by symbolic deaths, otherwise it becomes a dried up mechanical fragment stuck in the imaginary, increasingly out of touch with vitality, thereby increasingly beleaguered and prone to breakdown. Psychoanalysis and psychotherapy can be seen as a method that sponsors creative regression. However the periodic return becomes increasingly problematic for the psychotic or borderline personality for whom chaos and primordial time are too terrifyingly present without relief.

It is implied here that failure to repeatedly regress in this way which we are calling creative, leads ultimately to pathological and destructive regressions by default. Hence the need of all people at all times, in all historical periods, to periodically re-enter chaos and death, to remain in touch with death. Dare we say enjoy death symbolically? Failure to do so leads to a fatally destructive acting-out. Let us go on to examine the myriad ways in which this creative regression can take place, even in modernity where we have universally replaced ritual with reason.

The ordinary sacred

The ancients felt the existential necessity of grounding themselves in the sacred mysterious realities of sexuality and death, creativity and chaos, historical or profane time, and Primordial time as it was at the Beginning before the 'fall' into historical time. The periodic ritualistic re-entry into cosmogony, into the process of creation, was a sacred imperative.

Much of this has been lost, as all aspects of life have become secularized in the modern period. But some traces still remain. The celebrations that accompany birthdays, marriage, death, Christmas, the New Year, and to a lesser extent, holidays, weekends, and so on, mark an abrupt transition from ordinary humdrum existence into an awareness, however limited, that transcends egoic consciousness. We move from ordinary time, into a concentrated intensified time with laughter, music and dance. There is an element of the return to the 'new beginning', a pleasure in returning to an unintegrated state of freedom and spontaneity, licence and permissiveness.

There is the same intensity at concerts or football matches, where the roar of the crowd brings a feeling of togetherness, a benign sense of the boundary-less state in which one is transported by the energy of the moment. The feelings of well-being which accompany one's involvement in such events testify to their profound psychological importance.

Something of the same happens when we get 'lost' in a book, a conversation, a poem, a painting or any aesthetic form. For a time we are removed from secondary processes and we enter the world of myth, narrative, of beauty of form, which points us towards our origin. If we get deeply involved and then have to return to ordinary existence and attend to tasks in hand, we can feel strangely dislocated and bereft. A lot of time may have passed, or very little. At any rate we have lost perception of ordinary time, because we have been immersed to a slight degree in the Great Time. Again the effect can be if one reflects on it, a sense of the affirmation of life and one's existence, and a minimal *forgetting* of oneself. Something worthwhile has happened and at these moments, in however small a way, we feel slightly more alive. Liberated for a time from the narrow confines of modern separated existences in space time, we participate to some small degree in the timelessness of a cosmic reunion which has a deeply re-creative effect.

Playful illusions

Only a person who has been sufficiently contained, developed alpha-function and the repression barrier can safely proceed to enter the regressed state for the purposes, however unconscious, of recreation. Such a person can make full use of the dialectic between the ego and participating in the trans-cosmic 'self', of being a form embedded in formlessness, of being conscious and unconscious, of using language and being immersed in the musicality or the rhythm of language, of need and ineluctable desire. Here there can be a certain drift and carelessness.

From the point of view of psychotherapy, which, as has been pointed out, is fundamentally concerned with this dialectic, Winnicott famously spoke of the capacity to play:

> Psychotherapy takes place in the overlap of two areas of playing, that of the patient and that of the therapist. Psychotherapy has to do with two people playing together. The corollary of this is that where playing is not possible then the work done by the therapist is directed towards bringing the patient from a state of not being able to play into a state of being able to play. (1971a p. 38)

Such an ability originates in the safety of that transitional area between the mother and her child in which the child can become lost in his own reverie. Optimally, he can also get enraged and anxious without it becoming a disaster, because of the abiding presence of the good internal object. Insofar as this has not been established, the child will feel anxious and inhibited, threatened by the space and unable to regress creatively.

At this point it will be worth noting that there is a vast literature much of it emanating from the British Independent tradition (Rayner, 1991) on the therapeutic value of regression and the whole question of creativity. The theme that is crucial amongst these theorists is that of self/object de-differentiation. A return to Milner's (1952) 'illusion of unity', or Little's (1960) 'basic unity', or the 'primary love' of Balint (1952), or the merging, fusion and transitionality of Winnicott (1951).

However when we come to consider the borderline or psychotic, he has such a tenuous hold on his integrative and perceptual capacities, that the invitation to enter into the creative regression of the celebration becomes an invitation not so much representing symbolic death, but the terrifying threat of real death and annihilation, a vivid experience of 'going to pieces'. Regression in this sense becomes pathological.

One analysand who took some cannabis at a party, on going to bed forced himself to stay awake with the light on, because he was in the grip of an overwhelming fear that something terrible was going to happen. He felt he would be overtaken by evil within himself, or that he might injure himself badly by cutting his wrists with the scissors in the bathroom cupboard, or that he might be forced to break his back over the headboard of the bed in which he was lying. He would then be paralysed, reduced to a state of utter helplessness.

In such situations psychic space becomes potentially traumatic. It is as if the space re-invokes the absence of the mother's containment function, which in the case mentioned was not sufficiently secure and stabilised to be relied upon. As it fades, beta-elements threaten to invade the empty space, and will take over if they can, hijack the dream, and the ego will be overwhelmed and out of control. As beta-elements proliferate, they corrode stable realities and induce a consciousness of dread without limits.

In a nightmare, a woman patient felt she was being pursued by an elderly woman with a knife, who was trying to stab her. The dream scene shifted many times, from rooms, to corridors, to streets, but always this murderous woman would suddenly reappear from behind doorways, alleyways, lamp posts and so on. Each time she dreamt this dream, the murderous double seemed closer and closer.

The precariousness and insecurity involved in this pathology means that the subject can only live a highly circumscribed life. The requirement always is to keep a measure of control, and to restrict vitality, or sometimes to break out in impulsive excess and chaos. Free association, never easy, seems surrounded by barriers or cliff edges that corral the material into stereotypical paths. The therapeutic task is to make that space, now the analytic space, less persecutory, by the reliving of the archaic fears in the transference. Playing then becomes a tentative possibility and the dialectical interplay between the ego and the cosmos, between historical time and the Great Time, can be resumed.

Regression in dreams

Such an interplay is most properly illustrated as Freud emphasized, by dreams. Sleep is par excellence a benign regression. Freud suggested that we dream in order that we may continue sleeping. The modern view (Jones, 1970) is that we sleep in order to dream. Lewin pointed out that sleep is unconsciously equated with refusion with the mother. In 1950 he hypothesizes states where the mother's breast is the dream screen. Nightly we return to our origins for regeneration. This is apparent in the so-called hypnagogic state, where thoughts without containers and containers without thoughts roam, effortlessly slipping and sliding over each other in turbulent profusion. Try to focus on meaning at this point and it is disturbingly absent.

But in the dream proper, desire, forever frustrated by the censorship, requires earthly forms, the day residues, in order to surface. But they can only surface via a *regressive* pathway towards visualization. Conscious experience is disassembled, purloined by the unconscious for its own purposes, to gain expression on the dream screen. Such a complex processing of external and internal reality is essential for psychic health, irrespective of whether or not the dreams are remembered. Thus, wakefulness is enabled by day and sleep by night. When this complex and mostly unconscious synthetic process of great complexity is damaged, the capacity to dream is compromised, and the subject feels tired all day and stays awake all night.

The child who has introjected the maternal containing function, the alpha-function, now contains within himself a capacity to process the chaos of daily life which is not safe until it has been dreamed. With this function intact, one has confidence that the stresses of everyday existence can be re-worked, processed and stored for future use. This is the conservative function of the dream, which involves healing and homeostasis. But the dream also puts us in touch with what we lost when we descended into historical time/space. Grotstein following Bion, states that the dream as experienced is only a tiny holographic image of O, universal truth. It 'is a vent in the shield that separates our two worlds, the outer world of the conscious, asymmetrical experience and the inner world of infinite symmetry and inner cosmic vastness'. He goes on to clarify a point that is highly relevant for the argument being developed here: 'The term 'unconscious', the proper name for this system of inner cosmic vastness which contains a wealth of 'myriad consciousnesses', is therefore an unfortunate term because it belies the awarenesses implicit and inherent in this system. The truth of the matter is that what we call unconscious is really unconscious *to* us but itself never unconscious of us.' (1979 p. 402)

The unconscious is always trying to make itself known. Regression as exemplified in the dream is the return of the unconscious to the surface in a highly enigmatic and compromised form demanded by the censorship which guards consciousness from traumatic overload by the reservoir of the repressed. Thus, concentration on external reality is made possible, confident in the knowledge that the slights and hurts that are suffered by day will be contained and transformed continuously by alpha-function by day and by night. The world of consciousness and the timeless vastness of the unconscious world are kept separate, although they exist in a dynamic equilibrium.

Such a homeostatic view may satisfy the need for *total* adaptation to the demands of external reality. It is exemplified by those who say they never remember their dreams and that they don't mean anything anyway. This shows the psychical apparatus working as it should, creating a dissociation of consciousness from the unconscious - a state of normal enough alienation. All this is fine because dreams are indeed nonsense in that they successfully and continuously conceal their meanings and their significance, as we go for days without remembering any of them.

The dreamer who attempts to understand his dreams is seeking individuation. However, this so-called understanding must have the lightest touch, otherwise it becomes pretentious. There is no attempt at mastery of the meaning of the dream. Jung stressed the *experiencing* of the dream. The value of this attempt cannot be underestimated. In some measure the subject gives up omnipotence in asking the question of meaning. Here is an opening to the progress of the infinity of unconscious meanings. A highly successful professional person who dreamt very vividly of meeting a small neglected dirty little street kid was sufficiently struck by the experience to ask himself what it might mean. He was able to make the link with his own humble origins, and a childhood fantasy of freedom he had long forgotten, all of which he had forsaken through educational pressure and later financial success. Herein lies the potential at least to start *experiencing* experience. Dreams can be arresting. Here too is the possibility of increasing alpha-function, experiencing and conserving life.

Dreaming is creative regression. Experiencing the dream and what it evokes by free association encourages, however slightly, the regressive progression towards universal truth, 'O'. Whatever method one uses to approach the latent content, whether it be Freudian, Jungian ('amplification', 'active imagination') or Gestalt therapy (identification with each dream object) or any other method where the process is potentially regenerative. The dream seeks an audience, some reciprocation by an alienated ego, which must die a little in the intercourse between the two worlds.

Psychotics, as noted earlier in the chapter are scarcely able to dream. The dream screen has been damaged or attacked, giving the action a bizarre or fragmented nature. Psychotic dreams tend to be immediate, intense, momentary, as if bearing witness to the notion that the death drive tends to reduce time and space to zero. Omnipotent characters take over the dream, become a law unto themselves, and the dreamer feels himself to be a part of someone else's dream. He is so un-alienated from unconscious and primitive forces, that he cannot live sanely in the external world. Dream-life and waking life become too interfused. The veil that should separate the one from the other is torn. There is no possibility of creative regression to origins for the purposes of regeneration, but only a fear of destructive overwhelming and catastrophe.

In this rather simplistic division that we have, the normal or neurotic subject can relax and contemplate the opening up of levels of consciousness, envisaged by Grotstein, approaching the mystical 'O', and experience some degree of regeneration, apparently without danger. Whereas, on the other side of the divide, the psychotic is condemned to free floating catastrophe, the truth of the Universal Real, as the real of *suffering*. Winnicott (1945) makes the distinction between unintegrated and disintegrated states. In neither case is there a strong sense of self or of being together, but in the former the drifting like reverie is benign, while in the latter the drift is towards the abyss.

A question

An important and difficult question occurs at this point, a question which disrupts this notion of an unceasing rhythmic harmony of dispersal and integration, of a benign Ps <—> D. The question is: *where is the 'Other scene', as Freud referred to the unconscious, located?* Is it the dynamically repressed unconscious, the repressed personal domain of abandoned childhood wishes, the world of Otherness, the register of the Symbolic? No, clearly not as we have intimated already, as this

Other, as we have seen, is the *barred* Other, the Other that is *not one*, not a unity or a divine support. Or is it the greatly expanded world, the cosmic world of the *un*-repressed unconscious, which perhaps coincides with a benign Lacanian Real - a world of *no* signifiers, of mystery, of silence and nothingness. Or is it *not* the Real but the Imaginary, or more precisely *our compensatory imaginarization of the Real* - the Real as we would dearly love to see it - our beautiful *vision* of the cosmos, as sustained by all the major religions, and more recently, following Jung in particular, their psychotherapeutic successors.

The Lacanian theorist, William Richardson, asks the interesting question: 'what if we conceived of a God that is not merely symbolic, but that would 'reside', so to speak, in the real, emerging from it through whatever imaginary or symbolic representations that might manifest him, a God of contradiction (in Claudel's phrase) - would not such a God at least be possible for psychoanalytic speculation and compatible with the rigour of its theory? ... psychoanalysis ought not in principle exclude the possibility of such a God.' (1994, pp. 133-134)

Humour

Laughter and humour illustrate well the symbolic cycle of death and rebirth. Golan, Rosenheim and Jaffé (1988) in assessing the role of humour in psychotherapy note many clinicians who have shown that humour can bring about catharsis, alleviate anxiety, enhance interpersonal intimacy, increase flexibility and reduce perceptual rigidity and stereotyping.

Festivals and celebrations are accompanied by much laughter and humour. In Freud's book on jokes he showed how 'the joke-work receives its most powerful stimulus when strong purposes reaching down into the unconscious are present, ...which may explain to us how it is that the subjective determinants of jokes are so often fulfilled in neurotic people.' (1905 p. 178) Humour and jokes allow 'free play to modes of thought that are usual in the unconscious.' (ibid. p. 203) The pleasure obtained in jokes, the comic and humour are all derived from economies of expenditure of psychical energy, i.e. a relative suspension of secondary process mentation in favour of reaching 'the mood of a period of life in which we were accustomed to deal with our psychical work in general with a small expenditure of energy - the mood of our childhood ...' (ibid. p. 236) The release in laughter is an escape from the effort of ego activity involving restraint, thought, inhibition and control. In order to laugh we have to have the capacity to transcend our ordinary concerns, and re-enter if only for a moment the other world. Freud pointed to the nature of this return when he connected the pleasure in laughter, to the smile of the infant satiated at the breast and about to fall asleep. (1905, p. 146 footnote)

Lacan connects laughter *directly* with desire:

> It is enough to observe a child to perceive that before the word, the communication... namely communication with the beyond of what you are before him as symbolised presence, is laughter. Before any word, the child laughs. He laughs when the laugh is of course linked to smiling and to relaxation, and the whole physiological mechanism of laughter is always linked to a certain satisfaction... but the child... laughs... precisely in a certain relationship of course with his satisfaction of desire... it is to this beyond of this presence... that it contains in itself something that accords with [the infant's] desire... *before* speech, these first laughs in the presence of certain presences which look after him, which nourish him, which respond to him.
> Laughter corresponds... to all these maternal games which are the first exercises in which modulation, articulation, as such are put before him. Laughter... is beyond the immediate, beyond any demand. (1957-8. 16.4.58, p. 13)

Umberto Eco refers to Aristotle's lost second book of the *Poetics*. 'Comedy is born from the komai - that is, from the peasant villages - as a joyous celebration after a meal or a feast. Comedy does not tell of famous and powerful men, but of base and ridiculous creatures, though not wicked... It achieves the effect of the ridiculous by showing the defects and vices of ordinary men... through witty riddles and unexpected metaphors, though it tells us things differently from the way they are, as if it were lying, it actually obliges us to examine them more closely.' (1980 p. 472). The second book of Aristotle, 'perhaps really did teach how to distort the face of every truth, so that we could not become slaves of our ghosts. Perhaps the mission of those who love mankind is to make people laugh at the truth, *to make truth laugh,* because the only truth lies in learning to free ourselves from insane passion for truth.' (ibid. p. 491)

Nietzsche's Zarathustra: 'I myself pronounced my laughter holy. I could find no one else today strong enough for that... Zarathustra the light one, who beckons with his wings, posed for flight... Zarathustra the soothsayer, the southlaughter...' (SZ, Part IV)

Humour has been regarded as a high level defence (Vaillant, 1970), pressed into the service of a denial of painful reality (truth). However, what is emphasised here is that the capacity for humour is *central* to life. It is no mere epiphenomenon. The most disturbed patients cannot laugh, they cannot stand outside themselves, because they feel forced to take themselves too seriously. One cannot laugh when in the grip of anxiety, hatred or fear. One could say the same for analysts caught in the grip of orthodoxies and trainings. Should the analyst laugh in the session? Or does this automatically mean that they are not taking the patient's suffering seriously? Frankl comments that 'humour deserves to be mentioned as one of the basic human capacities.' (1946 p. 140) Humour is always implicitly involved in his behavioural technique of 'paradoxical intention' in logotherapy, in which a person is encouraged to do in an exaggerated way the very thing that they most fear.

Humour involves flexibility, humility, a surrendering of grandiosity and omnipotence, and an acceptance of the incongruities, stupidities and complexities of existence. The fact that humour has become commodified and packaged by the media and has become a means of escape and entertainment should not distract us from seeing it in a deeper light.

Writing

Let me now take the example of writing, to illustrate the continual and necessary oscillation between death and new creative forms. W. H. Auden remarked in a private conversation to Rollo May that 'The poet marries the language, and out of this marriage the poem is born.' (1975 p. 85) The ego of the poet has to become immersed in language, the unconscious, for the sake of the new creation. The same creative struggle is implied by Seamus Heaney when he writes of the poem, that 'in the process of its own genesis, [it] exemplifies a congruence between impulse and right action, so in its repose the poem gives us a premonition of harmonies desired and not inexpensively achieved.' (1988 pp. 93-4) Here the 'impulse' of the unconscious and the 'right action' of the ego are fused in a new harmony, but not without considerable cost.

Therefore, in order to write something worthwhile there will be of necessity considerable inner turmoil. The process starts in a fragmented way, with bits and pieces of thoughts and ideas which, in time, begin to coalesce into something closer to what the writer wants to say. There are perhaps inner conflicts and contradictions which upon further thinking can be reconciled to a greater extent. Something is beginning to take shape. In Bion's (1963) terms there is a movement from Ps to D. A container is being formed in which thoughts can be held and communicated. It started with chaos, a paranoid/schizoid state of being in pieces, which is benignly persecutory. There is great anxiety and excitement at this stage, a wanting to get going, to get something formed, to get something down on paper. However, it is important not to rush and be omnipotent, in exactly the same way as it is important not to give an interpretation too early in an analytic session. The waiting in chaos, although sometimes very difficult to hold and bear with, leads to a better resolution or interpretation. The time span can obviously vary from a few minutes to a number of years. A book may emerge only after many years of incubation in this inchoate state. On the other hand, as many writers have advised, it is important to *start* writing. Letting it write itself, letting the effect be the cause, like free association, a benign 'Ps' position with minimum coalescence.

Something is eventually written on a page. The chaos of the unconscious primary process has been transformed via selected fact into secondary process formulation with primary process enrichment. There is a feeling of satisfaction, of resolution and peace. Later in the day, further thoughts or ideas will come into the mind, as if they have been thought about unconsciously, while attending to other things quite unconnected with writing. A notebook is useful to jot down further points that will appear to consciousness often unbidden. Again and again ideas and thoughts will come to the mind ready-formed as a result of unconscious thinking, connected to alpha-function, which enables the subject to dream while awake. Here, the unconscious ego demonstrates its formidable powers of synthesis. For a time, there can be elation about what has been produced, Milner refers to this as idealisation, and Winnicott has spoken of the ego-orgasm.

Then out of the blue comes anxiety. Now this anxiety might be quite realistic and related to the depressive position. The manuscript is incomplete on a further reading. There are many faults with it, much that is left-out, or poorly formed. Others have written better on the subject. Others have written about the same subject. Therefore, what has been newly written is of only limited value. It may represent only a small contribution or none at all. There is no getting away from this, for any piece of writing is finally a commitment to paper of a point of view, a story or an interpretation, and as such one choice has been made which necessarily eliminates an infinite number of other possibilities.

The worry about the work's validity and usefulness, may require a complete revision, or even abandonment. Here the work will return to the unformed state (Ps) looking for a new container, a new formulation, which again will be somewhat incomplete and limited (D). The continuous revision may involve catastrophic changes with painful transitions between structure and chaos. Such movements require immense tolerance of anxiety and a willingness to live among the pieces. Without this preparedness to tolerate the birth-death-rebirth cycle, the Independents talk similarly of differentiation and fusion, without an overall containing function, the loosest of containers, nothing creative or worthwhile will be produced. The analogy with the analytic session is useful. The preparedness, that we noted in chapter three, to go into persecutory anxiety is the essential prerequisite for analytic interpretation. One is prepared for this, but when it happens it is always experienced as a shock, a collapse of confidence, or a feeling of panic and incompetence. Some element of courage in face of this symbolic death is required. Ultimately, there is no guarantee that one will emerge from it.

A patient of a narcissistic disposition frequently reported that he wanted to write. He was an avid reader, reading all the reviews in the book sections of all the quality newspapers. He wanted to read these latest books as soon as they appeared in book shops. He wanted to write, yet he never put himself to the test. And he got no satisfaction out of his avaricious reading. Too strong a drive element in it always left him empty and unsatisfied. He was trying to know everything, in keeping with a hidden illusion born of his mother's desire that he was perfect. And to write something would entail a catastrophic limitation of his narcissism: saying the *one* thing and not the infinite number of alternatives, and being forced to acknowledge his incompleteness. By never writing he could hold to the unconscious imaginary notion of perfection.

The creative writer has to be able to tolerate the anxiety involved in the oscillation Ps $\longleftrightarrow$ D, the deaths and rebirths, vital to the creative process. To believe that one can be creative without this necessary suffering leads to work that is sterile or to nothing at all. We come back to the original premise which has been illustrated in various ways: there can be no life without the death of something; the more deathliness is contained, the greater the capacity for vitality.

The triumphant assertion of this vitality is clearly stated by Conrad, in the preface to *The Nigger of the Narcissus*, when he describes his technique in respect of the art of the novel: 'To snatch... a passing phase of life is only the beginning of the task. The task approached in tenderness and faith is to hold up unquestioningly, without choice and without fear, the rescued fragment before all eyes in the light of a sincere mood. It is to show its vibration, its colour, its form; and through its movement, its form, and its colour, reveal the substance of its truth - disclosing its inspiring secret' (Conrad, quoted by Paul O'Prey, 1983, pp. 16-17).

Finally, T.S.Eliot movingly describes the struggle for form.

And so each venture
Is a new beginning, a raid on the inarticulate

...

There is only the fight to recover what has been lost
And found and lost again and again: and now under conditions
That seem unpropitious. But perhaps neither gain or loss.
For us there is only the trying.

...

We must be still and still moving
Into another intensity
For a further union, a deeper communion
Through the dark cold and the empty desolation,
The wave cry, the wind cry, the vast waters
Of the petrel and the porpoise. In the end is my beginning.

(*The Four Quartets*, section 5 of East Coker pp. 203-4)

Prayer

Let us take one more theme to illustrate the thesis being expounded here. We will consider prayer and meditation. Harry Williams considers three types of prayer: 1) prayer as petition; 2) prayer as intercession; 3) prayer as contemplation. Williams, who was analysed himself, suggests that prayer rightly understood is a process that can, and must of necessity, take on board, depression, anxiety and hate - the death within: 'Prayer is an acceptance of the reality of evil and suffering and death.' (1975 p. 84) 'Christ sometimes invites us, especially when we pray, (though not only when we pray) to share His conflict with Him. Our feelings of anger, worry, depression or whatever, are signs that for the time being Christ is calling us to stand with Him in the thick of the battle, to face within us the forces of destruction.' (ibid. pp. 46-7)

Similarly, this prayer invites the acceptance into consciousness of split-off sides of the self.

> Prayer is an act of opening,
> An act of opening one's spirit.
> Amidst the turbulence of hostile feelings,
> Prayer is the opening of one's spirit to the forgiving,
> Healing, recreative power of love.
> Prayer is the opening of one's self to the larger Self
> Who seeks to make us whole, ...
> An act of dedication, an act of transformation,
> An act of reconciliation joining what is sundered in the soul'.

(Author unknown. *The Fellowship of the Tryst* No. 18, 1971).

Happold points to the essential polarity between the ego and the unconscious, and the necessity of going beyond the purely rational, 'Contemplation is a method of apprehending the nature of things which is not antagonistic to rational, analytic thought, but complementary to it.' (1971 p. 86) 'Man's real and enduring self, his Greater Self, is not the phenomenal self. His real self is bound up with the Divine Essence, a spark of divinity within him.' (ibid. p. 91). Prayer affirms the existence of the Greater Self, and recognises the continual need to come at one with it for the sake of psychic integration, reconciliation, the attainment of the depressive position.

Prayer brings us in contact with Grotstein's notion of the 'Background object of Primary Identification', which, he informs us, is ultimately God. Following the later Bion and his notion of the caesura, he says, 'I perceive the human infant to experience himself as incompletely separated from a mythical object behind him, his rearing or background object, his object of tradition which rears him and sends him forth ... [a] backwardly departing soul or spirit of comforting protection, and ultimately, to a religious, spiritual, or divine essence on one hand and a sense of tradition and background certainty on the other.' (1979 p. 369)

The background object, then, guarantees our sense of containment through all transformations. It is the unifying function that we take for granted in non-psychotic illness. Grotstein believes that there is sense to be made of the apparently random free associations, that there is some organising principle at work despite resistances. Grotstein comments: 'It is my belief that the organiser of associations is the messiah within.' (ibid. p. 361). There is some hidden orchestration in the unconscious which throws up dreams, jokes, bungled actions, symptoms, and so on, in the continual hope that we might come a little closer to embracing 'O', Universal Truth. Perhaps psychoanalysis - indeed psychotherapy generally - and prayer have this faith in common: there is a Container, however obscure, that ultimately can, 'Beareth all things, believeth all things, endureth all things'. (1 Corinthians: 13, v 7)

What stands between the subject and such faith is narcissistic omnipotence - the subject's compulsive belief, born as a defence against the pain and humiliation of separation/individuation, that he can go it alone, relying on the *self*-creativity of his own ego. forced continually to deny the existence and the need for the Other.[4] This is the final source of resistance in psychoanalysis. It is also the source of resistance to religion and prayer.

True, we have little difficulty in merging with the good object, the breast, the background object of primary identification. Here we experience to a greater or lesser degree, the 'oceanic feeling', induced in the religious setting by prayers, hymn singing, ritual incantation and so on. Here, at a paranoid extreme against ambivalence, is the euphoria of the charismatic Christian and all those who have 'found Jesus'. The difficulty comes when one is forced also to consider religious hatred, bigotry and schism.

The subject is faced with the power of the bad object, the damaged, absent, greedy or envious breast, who is malevolent, filling us with dread, hatred and defensive omnipotence. Religious people believe that, through prayer, God can receive these derivatives of the death instinct and transform them. It requires of us, 'an act of opening one's spirit, amidst the turbulence of hostile feelings, ... the opening of one's spirit to the forgiving, healing, recreative power of love'. In the pain of the depressive position, we acknowledge the 'reality of evil, suffering and death'. [anon.]

In the same way, albeit on a human scale, the analyst suffers with the analysand, continuously trying to contain and transform the latter's projections to increase the range and scope of alpha-functioning. For the analysand, the analytic space becomes the re-encounter with archaic trauma and the attempt at resolution. For the religious, what we might call the prayer space can be similarly transformative. Just as the process of psychoanalysis gradually leads to the development of the analyst/analysand-couple (analogous to the thinking-couple) within the analysand, so the practice of prayer leads to the internalisation of the one who hears the prayer, and therefore the development of the prayer-couple within the one who prays.

Critique:

The foregoing puts in very broad terms the secular and transcendental position in relation to death. One end of the psychoanalytical tradition links here with this humanistic approach.[5] It rests ultimately on a broad faith in the synthetic power of the ego-Self axis in the individuation process. It seems, if we can spread the therapeutic net wide enough, that we can capture all the demons, which will be transformed, albeit with difficulty, in the act of creative capture. Our *salvation* will reside in the unconscious - in myths, dreams, symbols, imagery of all kinds both personal and universal. According to Whitmont, 'The centre of gravity of the Jungian approach thus could be said to rest upon the purposes and guidance of the unconscious.' (1969, p. 294) We must be able to avail ourselves of the 'counsel of the unconscious'. This means that therapy would allow us to understand and have our own *personal* religion. Whitmont continues: 'Jung credits the psyche with a potentiality towards self-healing. The idea that the unconscious contains also the *healing potential* and not only the disturbing elements was one of Jung's unique and revolutionary discoveries.' (p. 295, my italics).

However, Rieff attacks Jung's theorising as a 'private religion' and an 'anti-science'. He says: 'Jung developed a fresh rhetoric of spirituality, without the bother of churches or the imposition of consequential ethics.' (1966 p. 98) Rieff suggests that Jung created a 'charming cosmos, full of interesting people.' (ibid p. 98) His enduring appeal is to a post-religious propertied class. 'Jungian theory proposes to every disaffected humanist his 'personal myth', as a sanctuary against the modern world... [It] proposes an aristocracy of feeling.' (ibid. p. 102) Similarly, 'Just there, in the unconscious, are those superior illusions that would compensate mankind for the barren interdicts of Christianity and the almost equally barren interdicts of psychoanalysis.' (ibid. p. 104) Rieff understands that 'Jung legitimates the demonic and destructive as having rights of their own on the strength of their therapeutic potential.' (ibid. p. 95)

Why did Freud not embrace Romain Rolland's position on the religious sensibility in man? Rolland was a brilliant exponent of the transcendental and its capacity to heal the world. They corresponded closely for sixteen years. (Fisher 1991) Why was Freud not persuaded by transcendental spirituality? Rolland agreed with Freud's (1927) critique of orthodox religion, but beyond this, Rolland felt himself to be in touch with the eternal. He says: 'It is a *contact*. And since I have recognised it to be identical (with multiple nuances) amongst numerous living souls, it has allowed me to understand that there was the true subterranean source of *religious energy* - which next is tapped, canalized, and *desiccated by the Churches:* to the point that one could say that it is inside the Churches (wherever they are) that one finds the least of true 'religious' feeling.' (in Fisher, 1991 pp. 42-43)

In opposition to Freud, Rolland offered a powerful argument that man was capable of achieving wholeness - the perfect realisation of the 'highest joy'. Freud acknowledged that he had never experienced these religious sensations: 'From my own experience I could never convince myself of the primary nature of such a feeling.' (Freud in Fisher, 1991 p. 47) Instead Freud concluded that such feelings were derived from the earliest phases of the ego to do with 'the intimate bond' between the child and its surroundings, the desire to fend off 'feelings of unpleasure', and the continual desire for the father's protection. Freud says, in the first section of *Civilization and its Discontents:* 'The origin of the religious attitude can be traced back in clear outlines as far as the feeling of infantile helplessness. There may be something further behind that, but for the present it is wrapped in obscurity.' (1930, p. 72) The oceanic feeling is interpreted by Freud as religious consolation, 'as though it were another way of disclaiming the danger which the ego recognises as threatening it from the external world.' (ibid. p. 72) Rolland's response is: 'It would be strange if mental joy were a sign of error. The mistrust shown by some masters of psychoanalysis for the free natural play of the mind, rejoicing in its own possession -

the stigma they imprint upon it of 'narcissism' and 'autoerotism' - betrays in them unknowingly a reverse kind of religious asceticism and renunciation.' (in Fisher, 1991 p. 52)

Freud's espousal of the death drive theory, his non-experience of the religious sensation, his apparent lack of interest in music, his rationalist outlook, his pessimism, and above all his interpretation of religion as infantile, has separated him and barred him ultimately from inclusion in the whole gamut of the pan-religious post-Freudian psychotherapies that have flourished in his wake, counselling and consoling us with the, 'river of the soul, flowing from the dark unplumbed reservoirs of our Being, the conscious, realized and mastered Being... From the source to the sea, from the sea to the source, everything consists of the same Energy, of Being without beginning and without End.' (Rolland quoted in Fisher, 1991 p. 51)

> I am the one who says: Whether the world is eternal or not, there is birth, and death, and suffering, and woe, and lamentation, and despair. And what I do teach is the means that lead to the destruction of these things. *Majjhima Nikaya* 1.63 (*The Upanishads*, p. 22)

Brahman is the universe of God. Omnipotence? Or Faith? This is the psychology of reconciliation, of redemption. Why is the modern religion of humanistic psychotherapy, *not* the answer? Because, indeed, there is *no* answer? Only a multiplicity of signs and representations *and then a remainder.* We must consider the remainder. Freud, as we now understand him, centred his theory around the traumatic ultimately unsignifiable beyond - the Real beyond the real. Here, there is no symmetry between life and death, no gradual and creative absorption of death by life, no enjoyment of death. The background object, or the good object, or the container, or language, the 'Vorstellungen', *fail in the end.*

The psychotherapies which emphasize growth are being unethical. The profession has been hugely oversold in a world-wide evangelism of human potential, which has taken flight from any notion of the brute real. What can be done to alleviate suffering is small. This much should be done. To pretend more is to completely misunderstand the nature of suffering, that the subject is born in suffering and remains stubbornly attached to suffering, via the symptom and the repetition compulsion. As Lacan says: 'Is not the dream essentially, one might say, an act of homage to the missed reality - the reality that can no longer produce itself except by repeating itself endlessly, in some never attained awakening?'. (1973[1979], p. 58) What we do not want to know and therefore keep repeating in total disbelief, as it were, is that *loss drives life* into an endless substitutive search for the lost cause.

To emphasize growth and integration whether by psychodynamic interpretation, body work, group work, behavioural strategies, reality therapy, hypnotic suggestion, psychodrama, divine wisdom, or whatever, is to try to lure the drives into acquiescence or capitulation, which may be laudable from an educational, medical and social management point of view, but which may also spawn the *death* drive as blind refusal. No matter how soft and seductive these strategies become, no matter how precisely matched to the client's needs for empowerment and autonomy, will they not, or indeed *should* they not, from an ethical point of view, become impaled on the gratuitous cruelty of the real? The proliferation of these strategies (400, 600 types of therapy and counselling?) bears not so much on their success, but the appalling real against which they are silently committed. It seems to me in this context that we have to read and reread Lacan's 'passion for the negative'. (Roustang, 1986, p. 84) The real is there. According to Roustang, Lacan's real is 'no longer connected to anything at all. Its only remaining option is to drift towards death. Does this mean the kind of death the sages and mystics have in mind when discussing the human world? Definitely not, for the Real we are now dealing with is not an unthinkable that could conceivably flow back into the Symbolic and the Imaginary in order to start afresh in rethinking them; it is the end of the line with no turning back.' (Roustang, 1986, p. 101) This chapter will end with diverse examples, which evoke, either the (death) drive towards the void or the horror itself.

Robert Frost in his poem 'Home Burial':

... The nearest friends can go
With anyone to death, comes so far short
They might as well not try to go at all.
No, from the time when one is sick to death,
One is alone, and he dies more alone.
Friends make pretence of following to the grave,
But before one is in it, their minds are turned
And making the best of their way back to life

And living people, and things they understand
But the world's evil.

(Summerfield 1968, pp. 100-101)

For Schopenhauer, speaking of the subject in time:

> His real existence is only in the present, whose unimpeded flight into the past is a constant transition into death, a constant dying. For his past life... is entirely finished and done with, dead, and no longer anything... just as we know our walking to be only a constantly prevented falling, so is the life of our body only a constantly prevented dying, an ever-deferred death. Finally, the alertness and activity of our mind are also a continuously postponed boredom... Ultimately death must triumph... and it plays with its prey only for a while before swallowing it up. (*The World as Will and Representation*, Vol. 1, p. 311)

As if echoing the psychoanalytic discovery being emphasised here, Schopenhauer, quotes Ecclesiastes, i, 18. 'He that increaseth knowledge increases sorrow', going on to say, 'It [suffering] first appears in a high degree with the complete nervous system of the vertebrate animals, and in an ever higher degree, the more intelligence is developed. Therefore, in proportion as knowledge attains to distinctness, consciousness is enhanced, pain also increases, and consequently reaches its highest degree in man...The pain possible in the dull animal consciousness is related to the violent grief that becomes possible only through distinctness of knowledge.' (ibid, p. 310)

Further on, he says:

> Just as the boatman sits in his small boat, trusting his frail craft in a stormy sea that is boundless in every direction, rising and falling with the howling, mountainous waves, so in the midst of a world full of suffering and misery the individual man calmly sits, supported by and trusting the *principium individuationis*. (ibid, p. 352)

The astronomer, Paul Merdin, the discoverer of black holes, said in a radio interview (September 1994):
I feel directly connected through the giant telescope to these

distant objects, this star or galaxy that is sending this signal towards me. I leave the telescope monitor, and go outside and look up into the sky towards the region that I have been studying, and think of all those light particles that are travelling across space and coming down into the telescope. And I dream about the photons that are travelling almost parallel to the ones I am collecting, and which have gone past the earth to some civilisation behind me, to be collected some thousands or millions of years later. And I think of the poor photons that are neither the one thing nor the other, but just miss being collected by the telescope. Their entire destiny, after travelling through a thousand million light years of space is to heat up the earth just a fraction. They have no destiny at all really.

Like Bion's beta-elements, thought particles, 'things-in-themselves', dispersed in an 'uncertainty-cloud' in the void, travelling at prodigious speeds, desperately seeking a container with alpha-function within which they can at last realise themselves. All they can manage is to heat up the earth a fraction.

John Moriarty, the modern Irish mystic, speaks of the terror, the absolute dislocation, he felt when as an adolescent, growing up rooted in the bounded traditional culture of the West of Ireland, he discovered Darwin's *The Origin of Species*. He describes running out of the farmhouse, seeing by chance a piece of paper blown across the yard, chasing it across the road, over a ditch, a hedge, into the fields beyond, chasing it on and on, in desperation, to see if he could find written on it, the face of God. This chasing, he says, has been his whole life's work.

I will end this chapter with three extended quotations from modern writers, without comment, which turn around this catastrophic void at the heart of things.

Ian McEwan:

> He was struck by the recently concluded war not as a historical, geopolitical fact but as a multiplicity, a near-infinity of private sorrows, as a boundless grief minutely subdivided without diminishment among individuals who covered the continent like dust, like spores whose separate identities would remain unknown, and whose totality showed more sadness than anyone

could ever begin to comprehend; a weight borne in silence by hundreds of thousands, millions, like the woman in black for a husband and two brothers, each grief a particular, intricate, keening love story that might have been otherwise... For the first time he sensed the scale of the catastrophe in terms of feeling; all those unique and solitary deaths, all that consequent sorrow, unique and solitary too, which had no place in conferences, headlines, history, and which had quietly retired to houses, kitchens, unshared beds, and anguished memories... what possible good could come of a Europe covered in this dust, these spores, when forgetting would be inhuman and dangerous, and remembering a constant torture? (1992, pp. 164-5).

The end of Chekhov's, *Uncle Vanya:*

Sonia: Well, what can we do? We must go on living! [a pause.] We shall go on living, Uncle Vanya. We shall live through a long, long succession of days and tedious evenings. We shall patiently suffer the trials which Fate imposes on us; we shall work for others, now and in our old age, and we shall have no rest. When our time comes we shall die submissively, and over there, beyond the grave, we shall say that we've suffered, that we've wept, that we've had a bitter life, and God will take pity on us. And then, Uncle dear, we shall both begin to know a life that is bright and beautiful, and lovely. We shall rejoice and look back at these troubles of ours with tender feelings, with a smile - and we shall have rest. I believe it, Uncle, I believe it fervently, passionately...[kneels before him and lays her head on his hands, in a tired voice.] We shall have rest!

We shall rest! We shall hear the angels, we shall see all the heavens covered with stars like diamonds, we shall see all earthly evil, all our sufferings swept away by the grace which will fill the whole world, and our life will become peaceful, gentle, and a sweet caress. I believe it, I believe it... [Wipes his eyes with a handkerchief.] Poor, Uncle Vanya, you're crying... [Tearfully.] You've had no joy in your life, but wait, Uncle Vanya, wait... We shall rest... [Embraces him.] We shall rest! We shall rest!' (pp. 244-5)

And finally, from Primo Levi:

The Kitchens remained open, the corvées for cleaning worked as usual, and even the teachers of the little school gave lessons until the evening, as on other days. But that evening the children were given no homework.

All took leave from life in the manner which most suited them. Some praying, some deliberately drunk, others lustfully intoxicated for the last time. But the mothers stayed up to prepare the food for the journey with tender care, and washed their children and packed the luggage; and at dawn the barbed wire was full of children's washing hung out in the wind to dry. Nor did they forget the diapers, the toys, the cushions and the hundred other small things which mothers remember and which children always need. Would you not do the same? If you and your child were going to be killed tomorrow, would you not give him to eat today? (1979, p. 21)

To my mind, the question for psychoanalysis, in the light of the death drive theory, is precisely how to be a witness (Masud-Khan), how to keep faith (Bion) with this *excess and abundance* of suffering, over and beyond representation, which indeed is denied by representation and all the therapies for self-improvement.

7. BAUDRILLARD: FREUD AGAINST FREUD

Here we will conclude our brief review of the death drive by reference, at some length, to the work of Jean Baudrillard. He is included here, even though he is not an analyst, because his work is preoccupied with death, suffering and disappearance and he is representative of those continental philosophers who have mounted a powerful critique of classical psychoanalysis. As he says himself, the only genuine function of the intellectual is: 'To embrace contradictions, to exercise irony, to take the opposite tack, to exploit rifts and reversibility - even to fly in the face of the lawful and the factual. If intellectuals of today seem to have run out of things to say, this is because they have failed to assume this ironic function, confining themselves within the limits of the moral, political and philosophical consciousness despite the fact that the rules have changed.' (1990, p. 39)

In order to try and capture this occluded remainder with which psychoanalysis must keep faith, a very different approach may be required, an approach like Baudrillard's, which is aphoristic, contradictory, reversible, violent, impressionistic and chaotic. As Rojek and Turner imply in their introduction to a collection of articles, *Forget Baudrillard* (1993), he presents himself as a symptom as much as a solution to the labyrinth of postmodernity. He writes in the style that he is at the same time denying. However Baudrillard's courage and sympathy are crucial. We could make the same assertion about Baudrillard that Michael Tanner makes about Nietzsche: 'At every stage in his career Nietzsche was more concerned with what to do about the omnipresence of pain than about any other issue.' (1992, p. xxii)

Baudrillard emerged, in the English speaking world, only in the 1980s, as a leading yet controversial theorist of postmodernity, when a flood of his works began to appear in English. According to Gane's (1993) brief historical review, Baudrillard became a university teacher of sociology in 1966 at Nanterre (University of Paris X) at the relatively late age of 37. Baudrillard was politically radicalized as a result of the influence of Sartre and the Algerian war of independence in the 1950s. His first publications were in Sartre's journal *Les Temps Modernes* in 1962-3. Not only Sartre, but Nietzsche and Dostoyevsky were central to his line of exposition in what was the new form of cultural analysis influenced by structuralism and an application of Freud and Marx to the analysis of consumerism. However, Baudrillard's importation of Mauss and Bataille introduced a new problematic and a critique of the concept of rational 'need' as an explanatory notion and its replacement by the notion of consumption as the major form of class domination. Baudrillard was to take up a position against Marxism by his juxtaposing of Mauss's idea of the gift as forming part of a system of exchange radically different from modern capitalist commodity exchange. For Baudrillard, it was not use-value that should be contrasted with exchange value, but *symbolic exchange* that should be contrasted with commodity exchange[1]. Baudrillard believed that Marxists were trapped in a theoretical collusion with capitalism by assuming that needs and uses were *outside* the capitalist order: whereas he was to argue that it is only from the position of the symbolic order, or symbolic exchange, that the most radical critique of the contemporary can be made. Commodity exchange for Baudrillard became broadened into just one aspect of a larger (semiotic) code system in modernity, the expansion of which is correlated with the progressive marginalisation of older (symbolic) cultures by rationalization and bureaucratization.

Thus Baudrillard was to set the symbol against the reductive order of the sign (signifier/signified), the symbolic order against the structural law of exchange, including what he called the 'phallic exchange standard'. Baudrillard envisaged a whole progressive consensus that has evolved into our modern conception of reality, and, he was to set against this, a hidden order of *fatal* reversibility, which has the ironic and ultimate power of sacrifice, inversion and death.

As psychoanalysis has played a central part in this modernising, rationalising evolution towards a better way of life, we will limit ourselves mainly to Baudrillard's critique of Freud and psychoanalysis within contemporary culture. If Lacan's project was claimed as the well known, 'return to Freud', Baudrillard's might be 'setting Freud against Freud'.

Symbolic reversibility

Baudrillard informs us that what he calls the symbolic, haunts modernity. The symbolic here is the domain of the fatal, and in *post*modernity it takes its revenge on all that is scientifically programmed and dialectical. The symbolic exacts revenge on human omnipotence and it acts, above all secretly, to evade all controls. Beyond rational communication and equilibrium, there is for Baudrillard a mode of challenge, of seduction, of play, a destabilization that makes new things appear. Baudrillard says: 'All my ideas on symbolic exchange, on seduction, have to do with this idea of reversibility. From the moment the two terms are no longer governed by a single given supersession, it is obvious that they can be attracted into another logic. The dialectic was perhaps a specific form. Reversibility is another.' (1993, in Gane, p. 184)

The symbolic order is superior to the semiotic order, or the obligation of gift is superior to the cash economy and commodity exchange. These former terms are being destroyed by the latter. However, the position is more complex and ironic that this evolution implies. For the semiotic by its sheer proliferation and promiscuity is liquefying from within. We will return to this at length later on.

In one of his more systematic works, *Symbolic Exchange and Death* (1976), Baudrillard sets forward his argument about symbolic exchange and Freud's notion of the death drive. We will follow his theorizing in some detail. He speaks of the modern *extradition* of death. Under the sign of universal rationality in modernity, humanity is split from inhumanity.[2] Inhumanity is humanity's structural double. At the core of our culture 'is an exclusion that precedes every other, more radical than the exclusion of madmen, children or inferior races, an exclusion preceding all these and serving as their model: the exclusion of the dead and of death' (1976, p. 126) This exclusion is paradoxical, because madmen, delinquents and misfits are welcome in our cities, only because what Baudrillard calls their 'death function' cannot be assimilated. Thus excluded, death *pervades* modernity. 'It is correct to say that the dead, hounded and separated from the living condemn us to an *equivalent death.*' (ibid. p. 127) This is the inexorable and ineluctable logic, indeed power, of the symbolic, where such separations are only apparent, and exchange must be exacted in a hidden and fatal way. Thus survival itself becomes the equivalent of death, and life has been lost in advance.

Through science, we have made death autonomous, individualistic and natural. For the primitive, death is a *social* relation. Death is not conjured away or overcome but, as we noted in the last chapter, articulated through initiation. The young initiates die symbolically in order to be reborn. Instead of a line separating the living from the dead, there is an *exchange* between the ancestors and the living, a circulation of gifts, where death can no longer establish itself apart, as an end or agency in itself. Instead the young initiates commune with the ancestors who will instruct them and initiate them culturally. Here, birth and death are no longer separate but reversible.

However, Baudrillard emphasizes this is no 'staging a second birth to eclipse death' (ibid. p. 132) He is anxious, as is the present author, that his thesis does not slip into an idealisation of the primitive, playing life off *against* death, by a more subtle overcoming or transcending of death - the danger that humanistic psychotherapies ultimately fall into. Baudrillard's point is reversibility, but not redemption. He notes that birth is a death as is registered in, for instance, the Christian sacrament of baptism. He notes that psychoanalysis has clarified this reversible relation also. Without mentioning Oedipus specifically, he notes that the survival of life, unilaterally, is a sort of crime against the symbolic insofar as life survives without its reciprocal exchanges with death. Initiations erase this sense of criminality by (re)establishing the social.

Baudrillard's notion of the symbolic is, as he says, 'neither a concept, an agency, a category, nor a 'structure', but an act of exchange and *a social relation that puts an end to the real*, which resolves the real, and, at the same time puts an end to the opposition between the real and the imaginary.' (ibid. p. 133) Whereas Lacan seems to emphasize the *structure* of the symbolic and its differentiating function, Baudrillard asserts its *social action*. It is beyond any operational use or functionality, and is therefore it seems closer to, but not precisely, the Lacanian real. Apparently reversing the Lacanian symbolic, Baudrillard's symbolic puts an end to all the disjunctive codes whereby life is separated from death, man from nature, male from female, conscious from the unconscious, and so on. Baudrillard's symbolic is circulation, exchange and solubility. It dissolves human categories that in their establishment create symbolic *dis*order. Initiation *re*-establishes circulation and makes everything available for exchange.

In this context must be seen the fundamental prohibition against incest. This law against incest *frees* the child to circulate amongst the living. Initiation, goes further, freeing the initiates to circulate amongst the living *and the dead*. Baudrillard insists: 'This is an absolute law: obligation and reciprocity are insurmountable. None can withdraw from it, for whom- or whatever's sake, on pain of death.' (ibid, p. 134) This Law and the Debt that follows from it are unchanging and unceasing. The modern unconscious in this sense represents all that from which we have been cut. From this standpoint the Oedipus of psychoanalytic theory is the *negative* Oedipus, which institutes the symbolic agency of the law and saves us from fatal fusion with the mother. It is this agency, mediated by the so-called Name-of-the-Father, that mediates the exchanges possible *after* repression. Without the (phallic) mediation, without this access to the symbolic (in Lacan's sense), the subject is to remain unbarred and destined for psychosis.

Does this mean, asks Baudrillard, that primitive cultures, without repression, are psychotic? Only, of course from our restricted vantage point behind the bar of the law. In primitive societies, access to the symbolic is not via the agency of the law, but the symbolic here is the cycle of exchanges, of giving, returning and exchanging. Baudrillard cites the ritual sacrifice of the King, for instance, as having nothing to do with the acting out of repressed patricidal wishes. The King gives his death as part of the great symbolic cycle of exchange. There is no seizure of power on the one hand or guilt on the other. Similarly, the double of the primitive is not the alienated shadow self of the modern subject, but a partner with whom the primitive has a *living* relationship, good or bad, an exchange through gesture and ritual. The modern subject becomes confined in the 17th century, just as the mad as described by Foucault were to be confined. At this time the double as continuity, partner and exchange is lost and returns as a haunting other (in the Imaginary register), as *unheimliche* - the frighteningly unfamiliar in the familiar. The divided subject, the barred subject, can only dream of a lost continuity and a lost object (the objet *a*).

With the turn of the 16th century, the iconography of death was still joyous, collective, theatrical and folkloric, before it was to become lonely, anguished and interiorized. Then death was to be abolished, at the beginning of the modern period, by accumulation and deferral, by the growth of capital. Here accumulation and growth precisely oppose symbolic exchange. Hoarding is the opposite of gift exchange. This seeming impossibility of symbolic exchange is death. Baudrillard says: 'The elimination of death is our phantasm, and ramifies in every direction: for religion, the afterlife and immortality; for science, truth; and for economics, productivity and accumulation.' (ibid. p. 147) If we try to accumulate life as *value*, then death also accumulates, on the other side, as the symbolic equivalent, and becomes (perversely) the object of desire. And this, according to Baudrillard, is the only way we can make sense of the death drive itself. 'It's just as if death, *liberated from the subject*, at last gained its status as an *objective* finality.' (ibid. p. 148)

Freud develops the theory of the death drive at the same point as the general system of production changes into reproduction. Baudrillard asks the question as to whether or not the death drive is simply a discovery of universal application and importance, or is it theorized *at a given moment* in the development of the system? In either case (and this book has taken the death drive in *both* senses), Freud overturns quite profoundly Christian and Western metaphysics in general, in his insistence on death as an indestructible principle beyond Eros, indeed beyond the subject, class and history. Ultimately, it is not possible to *integrate* the death drive, or to sublimate it. This is a radical break with Western thought, in which death is traditionally either denied, sublimated or dialecticised in some form of constructive aggression or pursuit of the Good, or the pursuit of creative well-being under the rubric of humanistic psychotherapy and progressive rationality generally.

Eros is nothing but a detour taken by life and taken by culture towards death. This, as we have seen, is Freud's position. The binding function of Eros is undermined by the fragmenting function of the death drive and the devolution towards the prior inorganic state, by repetitions or 'the tendency to reproduce the non-event... that is to say, death.' (ibid. pp. 149-150) However, this position comes close to a biological determinism, as if the death drive is programmed in advance into the genetic code. Freud was moving in this direction, as has been shown, and modern biological research backs this up (see chapter five). However, such positivism is itself put into question by Freud, when he indicates that: 'The theory of the instincts [drives] is so to say our mythology.' (1933a, p. 95) Baudrillard prefers to see the death drive as a myth, not as a fundamental pulsion, but as a fable, a story of *our* culture. He summarises his position in terms that are close to those of Lacan (see chapter four), as well as, for instance, Marcuse. Baudrillard asserts:

> The death drive nourishing repressive violence and presiding over culture like a ferocious superego [Lacan's symbolic], the forces of life inscribed in the compulsion to repeat; all this is true, but true of our culture. Death undertakes to abolish death, and, for this very purpose erects death above death and is haunted by it at its own end. The term 'pulsion' or 'drive' is stated metaphorically, designating the contemporary phase of the political-economic system... where the law of value, in its most terroristic structural form, reaches completion in the pure and simple compulsive reproduction of the code, where the law of value appears to be a finality as irreversible as a pulsion, so that it takes on the figure of a destiny for our culture. (Baudrillard, 1976, p. 152)

However, if Freud situates the death drive in biology, then it is caught in a science that *arbitrarily* separates the living from the dead, and studies living things as dead specimens! Biology already produces the dead, therefore, all the death drive can do is contribute to this process. Remove this separation of living and dead, as in primitive cultures, and the death *drive* dissolves too. Similarly, Baudrillard argues, the psychical separated from the body killed off, in the domain of the repressed unconscious, all that was to be put out of symbolic circulation, and then inevitably found the death drive at the heart of its functioning.

Baudrillard wants to understand the death drive as an autonomous principle acting against the scientific positivity of psychoanalysis itself. 'Death', he says, 'merely meanders through successive topologies and energetic calculi, ultimately forming the economics of the unconscious itself, denouncing all that *as well* as Eros' positive machinery, ... the positive interpreting machine that it disrupts and dismantles like any other... It must be wrested from psychoanalysis and turned against it.' (ibid. p. 154)

Beyond, or instead of the entropy of the Freudian death drive and its tendency to reduce life to zero, Baudrillard cites Bataille's introduction of the opposite sense - death as excess, as superabundance and prodigality to the point of unbearable anguish. Life only exists in bursts and in exchanges with death, in continuity, in opposition to the discontinuous economies of individual existences. But here, Baudrillard is even critical of Bataille because he feels that Bataille falls into the trap of an 'aesthetics of transgression' along with all those who espouse libertarian ideologies of festival and celebration. They do so only under the bar of repression of which liberty is only its mirror. Baudrillard wants us to imagine something other than the bar and its interruption. Not transgression versus prohibition, but another order of reversal and fluid excess that puts an end to the bar, and sees life and death as inextricably mixed and indefinable. From this position there is no end to death and no end in death.[3] Only from the position of the modern subject's 'infinitesimal consciousness' death becomes final and irreversible. Even here, our own death is a myth, a fabrication of our own end, because in reality the subject is never there. Death is everywhere, but *in our minds* it has to be localised, pinned down and controlled. Thenceforth, the body becomes the site of sex, anguish and death.

In primitive cultures there is no such thing as 'natural' meaningless death. Every death is social, public and collective. It is the result of another evil adversarial will (no biology here), which the group must expiate or absorb, by various rites and feasting. For us, without the symbolic and initiatory order in which death or sacrifice is given and received, death is 'indifferent negativity', a residue, a remainder, a waste. The dead did once have a symbolic status, as did madmen, bandits, children and animals when the social was articulated on their radical *difference*. Now there is progressive absolution, reform and therapy via 'the social logic of equivalence' - killing with therapeutic kindness and mediated inferiorization. Now, the fundamental objective is: 'to snatch death away from radical difference in order to submit it to the [deadly] law of equivalence.' (ibid. p. 172)

Consequently, every death and violence that escapes the system of control becomes dangerous and subversive. The fascination with great criminals and murderers is that they reincarnate the useless brutality of the symbolic cycle. Carnage is everywhere, but this is fine if it can be brought within statistical equivalence. However, sex, death, madness and violence tend always to escape this general equivalence, and have to be repressed, and therefore become fascinating.

In his next major work, *Seduction* (1979), Baudrillard describes the return of symbolic exchange within pervasive consumerism and the masculine principle of production. Here however, we must first understand Baudrillard's orders of artifice or simulacra. Reality, as a given essence, does not exist. There can only ever be *simulations* of reality or signs which represent or stand in for reality. 'The principle fundamentally and from the very beginning is that there is *no* objectivity to the world.' (Baudrillard, in Gane, 1993, p. 140) Baudrillard quotes *Ecclesiastes:* 'The simulacrum is never that which conceals the truth - it is the truth which conceals that there is none. The simulacrum is true.' (In Poster, 1988, p. 166)

Simulations

Here, Baudrillard cites in approximate historical sequence, a number of simulations of human reality. These will be briefly outlined, before special focus is given to the final phase of simulation, that of the order of the universal code as it exists in late and global capitalism.

(1) The feudal order: Here the system, the caste system is static and brutal. Assignation is complete and there is no class mobility. The few signs that there were are clear and fixed, their circulation is restricted. Each sign carries with it prohibition and mutual obligation between

persons. People are bonded together in fixed systems of mutual reciprocity.

(2) The counterfeit is the dominant system in the classical period from the Renaissance to the Industrial Revolution. Here, signs become emancipated, when the prohibition on their production is removed. Signs appear according to demand, counterfeiting the obligatory signs and removing the clarity of the earlier system. However, these signs still appear and, as Baudrillard says, would dearly love still to be bound signs incurring mutual obligation, but this (artificial, ceremonial) reality has gone to be replaced by so-called *natural* referents. This is the era of the Baroque, the theatrical and fashionable, revealing the great potential of the new bourgeois class and the end of the sign's exclusivity. This is the truly counterfeit world of churches and palaces with magnificent ornamentations in all materials, and, 'the demiurgic ambition to exorcise the natural substance of things in order to replace it with a synthetic substance.' (Baudrillard, 1976, p. 52) There was felt to be the need to create efficient simulacra to reunify the world split by the Reformation. This, according to Baudrillard, was the Jesuitical mission to universalise the world.

(3) From pure theatre to the machine: this simulacrum no longer plays on the difference between appearance and the real, but merely absorbs the difference in a new universe of technical operativity. No more theatrical illusion, no more pretence, no more counterfeits, but the *production* of signs with no caste tradition, with no restriction on their status or freedom or reproducibility. Baudrillard warns us not to fall into the trap of believing that this is *the original* process, but rather a phase in the order of signs, an episode in the order of simulacra. This simulation is a definite challenge to the real which begins with production and quickly moves, by its very nature, into *serial re*-production in a rational attempt to master the world. The signs of the productive order are without illusion (no more masks no more appearances). They therefore are crude, dull, functional, repetitive and efficient signs. This becomes a system of the infinite reproducibility of potential identical objects. Thus with men themselves, who at the beginning of the industrial revolution begin to increase their own reproduction, growing 'increasingly similar to the system of production of which they were nothing more than the miniaturized equivalent. The simulacrum's revenge...' (1976, p. 54) But there is still a further move in a new order, which is to subsume all others.

(4) The simulation of the code. As soon as 'dead labour' gains the upper hand over 'living labour' (the period of primitive necessary accumulation), serial production gives way to generation through models *without end*. No more counterfeits of the original, no more production of pure series, but now, *pure* generativity as part of a cybernetic global order. This is the order of *in*determinacy and the semiotic code as the extermination of referents and finalities. Here, Baudrillard believes, the system takes off from any last connection with the real. Fashion, the media, advertising, information, communication endlessly, means the generation of an entirely new principle of meaning that is no longer based on reason or use value, but on equivalence and exchange value.

Baudrillard draws on the work of Thomas Sebeok who understands the genetic code to parallel the semiotic code. DNA is the most fundamental semiotic network and the prototype for all others. The base sequence of the DNA can be seen as the play of infinitesimal signifiers in which any former transcendental illusions are replaced by the digital. Encoded and inscribed biologically and culturally there is no longer any possibility of escape. Baudrillard says: 'God, Man, Progress and even History have successively passed away to the advantage of the code ...' (1976, p. 60) This puts an end to any revolutionary possibility: 'With the revolution you could still make out the outline of a victorious and human generic reference, the original potential of man. But what if capital wiped generic man himself off the map (in favour of genetic man)? ...the only threat that capital has ever faced historically came from this mythical demand for rationality which pervaded it from the start...[but] once it became its own myth, or rather an indeterminate aleatory machine, something like a *social genetic code* - capital no longer left the slightest opportunity for a deterministic reversal. This is the real violence of capital.' (ibid. p. 60)

In all former orders of simulacra, in all religions, culture and ancient mythologies, there was preserved the power of illusion in opposition to the real. 'Symbolic culture has always been lived as a denegation of the real, something like a radical distrust: the idea that the essential happens elsewhere than in the real.' (Gane, 1993, p. 62) This is what has now gone. We have made 'every effort to materialise this world, realize it, in order to escape from this total illusion. And the 'realizing' of the world, through science and technology, is precisely what simulation is - the exorcism of the terror of illusion by the most sophisticated means of 'the realization of the world'. And so it's illusion against *simulacre*, the only system of defence that men have found to avoid confronting this illusion.' (ibid. p. 184) In other words, this final radically disenchanting realization is nothing more than another (conventional, rational) illusion, but an illusion which demonically has no sense of itself as such. This is the illusion that continues to *believe* it has the power to kill off all former illusions. Here enters Baudrillard's symbolic reversibility now in the name of the primordial dynamic of seduction.

Phallic power

For Baudrillard, the world is seduced *in advance*. Seduction *precedes* production. If this is so, the whole modern order of production is doomed. But we will step back a little, for Baudrillard, in part at least, is with Freud and Lacan, 'Freud was right: there is but one sexuality, one libido - and it is masculine. Sexuality has a strong discriminatory structure centred on the phallus, castration, the Name-of-the-Father, and repression.' (Baudrillard, 1979, p. 6) Power and production is phallic power whether wielded by men or women. The feminine, on the other hand, has always been elsewhere, and is not what opposes the masculine but what *seduces* the masculine. The masculine is based on the law, repression and the unconscious, whereas the feminine is based on the challenge, on play on the seductive reversibility of appearances that forever remain outside manipulative control[4]. Baudrillard states that the women's movement is ashamed of seduction: 'They do not understand *that seduction represents mastery over the symbolic universe, while power represents only mastery over the real universe.*' (ibid. 1979, p. 8)

Let us look more closely at the psychoanalytic notion of (phallic) power before taking up Baudrillard's challenge again. Children have many and multifarious demands and needs some of which can be met and satisfied, but others, as we have seen, *that are always left over*. This remainder, as has been emphasized all along, constitutes desire as such. There is always this reaching after more. Male children obtain intense sexual pleasure from the penis. According to Freud, it is the penis for both sexes that has come to represent the high point of desire itself. Symbolically, the penis becomes abstracted from the body to become the phallus. For Lacan, the phallus is the signifier of signifiers. The phallus 'is the signifier destined to designate as a whole the effects of the signified.' (1977 [1955], p. 285) Lacan is speaking about the symbol which harks back to the erected, painted, sculpted *Phallos* of the ancient 'mysteries', which must always remain hidden. For Lacan, the phallus has a special capacity to create meaning thereby uniting sexuality on the one hand and logic on the other. Lacan states, that 'The phallus is the privileged signifier of that mark in which the role of the logos is joined with the advent of desire... it is the most tangible element in the real of sexual copulation... It might also be said that, by virtue of its turgidity, it is the image of the vital flow as it is transmitted in generation.' (ibid. p. 287) It has a number of properties that support the claim of its privileged position in the psychical economy. Apart from the capacity to ejaculate (the vital flow), and to link in copulation (as Bion emphasizes), it can be rigid or flaccid, it may discharge too soon or too late, it may be too short or too long, it may be displayed or concealed, it maybe attached or detached, and so on. These properties make it mean more than just childhood infatuation and idealization of an organ, but as Bowie (1991) says, the phallus is the 'dialectician *par excellence*'. At the very least it can symbolize presence and absence - the first symbolisations of the child in relation to the coming and going of its mother that Freud observed in his grandson. Because of its unique capacity to represent possession and non-possession, presence and absence, it is the basis for the whole articulation of a *structure*. Ultimately, only trivially and initially part of the human body, and thereby able to signify sexual difference, the penis cum phallus is to become elevated to a universal system of meaning.

Lacan's theory is phallocentric, but the pursuit of phallic power is highly paradoxical. This is a highly vulnerable power that can be cut down or cut off. Post-Oedipally, never quite being or having this (phallic) power, being forced to identify with a loss or a lack, we are destined to search for it again to attempt to fill in the gap in our lives, that gap of meaning and satisfaction. What Bowie calls 'desire-space' is not just 'unknowable and unmappable by the subject: it is the place of permanent catastrophe'. This has been emphasized throughout this book and brought into sharpest relief by reference to suffering and the death drive. Bowie goes on to say, 'Psychoanalysis, alone among other intellectual disciplines of the modern age, has the concepts [notably the death drive] with which to theorize that catastrophe, but has for the most part, in defiance of its own discoveries, chosen to cultivate a stable Euclidean garden instead.' (Bowie, 1991, p. 138) The reality of the Euclidean phallic moment is far from stable.

But why does it have to be the phallus (derived ultimately from the penis) that is the pivotal signifier of the symbolic? Why not, as others have emphasized, the breast, the womb, the vagina or the clitoris? There are a number of answers that could be given. Firstly, the desire of the mother *is* the phallus. The little child, boy or girl, desires above all the one thing the mother does not give in all her complex caretaking activities. But this begs the question as to why she wants the phallus that she cannot have. The answer is that she has been forbidden the phallus by the Law of the father (during her own Oedipus), and this is indeed further confounded by the fact the father doesn't have the phallus either. He himself has had to mourn the loss of the phallus. Another answer coming from Lévi-Strauss, in *The Elementary Structures of Kinship,* is androcentric in that it is men who give/exchange the phallus through the mediation of women and children. But Lacan emphasizes that the father does not possess the phallus, *by nature*. He 'has it' only insofar as he has given it up through symbolic castration. The phallus may well represent masculine power, but only *symbolically*, not naturally and not sexually. It is not a man's by right, and it is therefore open to both men and women equally. However, this still does not get us beyond the question as to why it has to be the phallus that obsesses both sexes.

Borch-Jacobsen reminds us that we will be helped in our explanation by Lacan's register of the Imaginary. It is the *image* of the body that in turn privileges the phallus long before there is any realization of sexual difference. At the mirror stage the *erect form* is emphasized, also in the power of the standing stone in ancient cultures. Borch-Jacobsen summarizes Lacan, 'The erection of the phallic statue therefore properly belongs to man, as *homo erectus*. And what predisposes the phallus to the function as the 'signifier of power' (as 'master signifier') is first of all the fact that it is erected, raised upright, like the human body or the statue of stone. This is not surprising, since erection is power and height, the ability to stand upright, on one's own legs, that fascinates the infant, the 'being grown up' that polarizes his rivalry.' (1991, p. 216) The emphasis is on seeing, and on the link that Freud made between upright posture and the dominance of the visual functions. And it is the phallus's very visibility that favours its central role in symbolization over and against the female organs which cannot be seen although they may be felt. Lacan is quoted: 'The feminine sexual organ has the character of an absence, a void, a hole, which causes it to be less desirable than the masculine sexual organ in terms of provocativeness.' (ibid. p. 217)

We have come full circle, because the phallus, although undoubtedly connected to the visibility of the penis is really not, in the end, gender specific. Borch-Jacobsen concludes: 'Thus it is not surprising that the phallus, actually penile and masculine, is simultaneously so asexual in Lacan. It is nothing but the object in which the subject, before any sexual characterization, represents himself to himself, in his fixed, permanent, substantial identity.' (ibid. p. 218) So although the subject ultimately wants to be this phallus, he has to only desire it, from a distance as it were, and its symbolic power after Oedipus.

This line of argument equates masculinity with activity, visibility, differentiation, separation, the Law and so on, while leaving femininity outside and elsewhere. The symbolic is clearly masculine, as it is based on differentiation, articulation and *mastery* in language. Can women only imitate men by entering into rivalry with those who 'possess' the phallus? This argument misses an essential point, namely, that the feminine is sovereign, uncastrated and complete pleasure in itself. In this sense the feminine is desire itself - *jouissance* - although no subject, male or female, can be it. Woman, as a subject within the symbolic, on the other hand, according to Lacan in his controversial seminar XX, *Encore,* is 'not all' (*Pas toute*), or 'not-one' (*pas une*). From the point of view of the symbolic, she is castrated, and condemned like the man to search in myriad ways for phallic pleasures in power and mastery. This is only a partial and limited pleasure forever separated from that little bit more, the absolute of enjoyment. This loss causes man to search for *it* in the woman, who comes to represent this objet a for the man - that trace of a lost desire that he is forever in search of, and which Lacan reminds us is a phantom. But this surplus of enjoyment, this encore, is barred by the Law. Woman, by not fearing castration, is less restricted by the Law and may illusively hold the secret of enjoyment, indeed a mystical ecstasy without *knowing*, as Lacan emphasizes, anything about it.

Lacan is not simply being provocatively and offensively sexist here. Much of the time he is writing about the formation of the subject rather than about specific gender and sexual differences. Ways of being a man or a woman are already there in language and discourse (the Lacanian symbolic), into which the subject is obliged to insert him/herself and reinvent anew for himself. To *speak* about sexual difference, or one's experience as a man or a woman, is already to be in the imaginary and symbolic, or, more simply the social. Speaking in whatever way we like, as man or woman, involves us, at least to a degree, in phallic mastery.

The upright phallus delineating difference from sameness, order from chaos, culture from nature, leads the phallic child away from the pre-symbolic maternal real, that is the mother who may catastrophically love us to death. Thus, as Joseph Smith argues, 'Everyone is implicated in phallocentrism. Phallocentrism is comforting. Deconstructing or fighting against phallocentrism is a denial that one has already secretly adopted it as a defence... a way of defending against knowing that the phallus and all the fighting about it represses the chora.'[5] (1991, pp. 120-121)

Returning to Baudrillard, 'the Phallus... [becomes] the absolute signifier around which all erogenous possibilities come to be measured, arranged, abstracted, and become equivalent. The *Phallus exchange standard* governs contemporary sexuality in its entirety, including its "revolution".' (1976, p. 116) Baudrillard provides us with examples of the interplay of the phallus and castration in fashion. He says, 'The playscript of erection and castration is everywhere.' (ibid. p. 101) The tight fitting bracelet, the belt, the necklace, the ring, the line of the stocking on the thigh, the line of the glove on the arm or the shawl partly covering the eye, all serve to erect and phallicize parts of the body as a play with and denial of castration. Any part of the body can be used as a phallic equivalent and serve fetishistically to deny castration. Baudrillard makes it clear that it is not the sex organs themselves that are of erotic interest in the sexual economy so much as the phallus as the general equivalent. Just as in the political economy it is not the commodity itself that is important, but rather the form of exchange. In the 'political economy of desire', each party exchanges phallic values, 'indexed on a general phallic equivalent... in accordance with a contract and converts its own enjoyment into cash in terms of a phallic accumulation...' (ibid. p. 103)

Any part of the body can be caught in this phallic erotic signification, or the whole body itself, especially the female body - the fetish object, the 'phallic simulation' *par excellence,* lending itself to phallic equivalence because it is *without* the penis. The male body will not do because it does not carry the exciting reminder of castration and the thrill of overcoming it. The female body is smooth and phallic in form, lacking nothing, cool, perfect and worshipped as such. From this point of view strip-tease is an erotic celebration and the unveiling of rapturous self-perfection and closure, within an aura of gestures that designates the female form as the phallus. This could not be more different than simply undressing. In the strip there is a transformation from natural to *sacred* nudity.

The overvaluation and fetishism of the female form serves only to obscure the analysis of power itself, whereby, in the broader context Baudrillard suggests, 'all signifying material of the erotic order is made up of nothing but the outfits of slaves (chains, collars, whips, etc.), savages (negritude, bronzed skin, nudity, tattooing) and all signs of the dominated classes and races. This is how it is for the woman in her body, annexed to a phallic order which, when expressed in political terms, condemns her to non-existence.' (ibid. p. 104)

Towards cool seduction

Opposing this phallic confident and definite masculinity, there has always been seduction. Seduction is the play with signs, with artifice, with simulation, with reversibility. Strip-tease is a seduction, a slow moving narcissistic autoerotic ceremonial, when it works well. When it works badly, the seductive effect loses its charm and degenerates into sexual realism and pornography which is of no interest. But in the last order of simulacra, Baudrillard will posit a universalization of seductive strategies, a staged and planned narcissism now placed under the sign of *value*. This is cool seduction in which every subject is obliged to enter into a 'fierce discipline' of erotic self management in accordance with mass marketed signs and a *closed and totalized* simulation.

Baudrillard cites this new order, no longer under the Name-of-the-Father, but, via incestuous regression to the Desire-of-the-Mother. Here, instead of the Law, repression, the acceptance of castration and the lack, we have the *assumption* of a phallic identity, obsessed with itself and its narcissistic plenitude, undivided, consoled and gratified by a permissive tolerance awash with all the manipulated signs of mass consumer culture. Along with this evolution come new anxieties: no longer the fear of the Law and traditional puritan repression, but the greater fear of lacking even one's own lack and the concomitant obsessive manipulation of signs, lest the excluded symbolic returns in the shape of total narcissistic mortification. This return to the mother and her plenitude brings with it the *original manipulation* of the subject by the mother from which there is no longer any escape.

In his later writing, Baudrillard makes a crucial distinction between 'hot' and 'cool' seduction and 'black' and 'white' obscenity. 'In the beginning was the secret, and this was the rule of the game of appearance. Then there was the repressed, and this was the rule of the game of depth...

For something to be meaningful, there has to be a scene, and for there to be a scene, there has to be an illusion, a minimum of illusion, of imaginary movement, of defiance to the real, which carries you off, seduces or revolts you... *this minimal illusion has disappeared for us.*' (1983, p. 65, my italics) This was hot seduction. Similarly, black obscenity was off stage, in the shadows in the dark. This was traditional obscenity, which had its paradoxical place as excluded and unrepresented. From this position it possessed a subversive energy, a seductive power and therefore a symbolic reversibility. Seduction here was the inverse side of the Law, Reason and meaning and it always represented a challenge, a game, a lure, a temptation.

However, Baudrillard warns: 'Everything that forgets this scene and this mastery of illusion and veers towards the simple hypothesis and mastery of the real falls into the obscene.' (1983, p. 50) This is our situation now, where everything is made real and true. White obscenity for Baudrillard is what is *totally revealed* - 'everywhere a loss of the secret, of distance, and of the mastery of illusion.' (ibid. p. 50) Further, 'Everything that is imposed by its objective presence, that is, by abjection, everything that no longer possesses either the secret or the lightness of absence, everything that, like the rotting body, is given over solely to the material operation of its decomposition, everything which, with no illusion possible, is surrendered to the sole operation of the real, everything which, without mask, makeup or face, is given over to the pure operation of sex and death - all this can be called obscene and pornographic.' (ibid. p. 57)

Baudrillard will continue to refer to this excess of reality as banal, as equivalent, as indifferent, as meaningless (via an excess of meaning and information), as cancerous - as a reproduction of sameness towards death. Here is the symbolic reversal that haunts modernity - the repudiation of the 'death function', that returns in the midst of the teeming aleatory life of postmodernity. 'The real is growing ever larger, some day the entire universe will be real, and when the real is universal, there will be death.' (Baudrillard, 1979, p. 32)

Baudrillard envisages this cool seduction coming from the *feminine* figure of unlimited sexual demand in the now decoded and liberated sexual universe. Ultimately her sexuality is to be 'gaping' and 'devouring', which puts the marked masculine erection into a terminal condition of fragility and threatened impotence. 'By contrast, the female sex remains equal to itself in its availability, in its chasm, its degree zero.' (ibid. p. 26) The generalised feminisation of culture cannot tolerate any scarcity or goods or sex. Thus everything will be feminised, all good and services, available and open to all. The Phallus, as the marked term is no longer interesting or significant, as we move to a more neutral or indeterminate position characterized by the diffusion of the feminine. And the masculine that once informed, as we have seen, all that was to do with the productivity, growth and power, 'is at present lost in the obsessive simulation of all these themes... Today, behind the mechanical objectification of the signs of sex, is the masculine as fragile, and the feminine as degree zero that has the upper hand.' (ibid. p. 27)

Sadie Plant criticizes what she calls Baudrillard's fear of cool seduction, or, as she says: 'seduction at an extreme [is] untenable for man, the feminine extended beyond the object of man's desire to an unfamiliar, hostile zone outside the comforts of mystery and enigma... which refuses to play.' (In Rojek and Turner, 1993, p. 102) Referring to Irigaray, she says 'what if this strange and indeterminate fluidity begins to speak, become real, becomes something that is neither the masculine order of production nor the seductive on which it depends?'. (ibid. p. 103) Plant has missed the point by counter-posing male productivity with female seduction, with the latter at long last getting the upper hand. Baudrillard's point is that seduction has always had the upper hand, only up until now the subject (both male and female) has been saved by the strong illusion (the last illusion) that repression works. Cool seduction collapses this last frontier. Repression and its enigma is ending in cybernetic control. This is a final seduction that indeed refuses to play by *totally playing with us to death:* no longer seduction by the secret and disappearance, but seduction by openness, transparency and boundless positivity.

While posing as the absolute opposite, this is violation and violence, because it removes the critical distance essential to subjectivity. Baudrillard links this cold seduction with the ubiquity of the media image: 'The violence of old was both more enthusiastic and more sacrificial than ours. Today's violence, the violence produced by hypermodernity, is terror. A simulacrum of violence, emerging less from passion than from the screen: a violence in the nature of the image. Violence exists potentially in the emptiness of the screen, in the hole the screen opens up in the mental universe.' (1990, p. 75) Or, 'Television is the event's true "final solution".' (1979, p. 160)

The image and the code remove radical Otherness. We are therefore condemned to the 'hell of the same'. This vast neutralization is really the loss of Otherness by the spread and universalization of the code. Our belief in pluralism and diversity is really only a subdivision of the Same with the radical foreignness subtracted from it, or recast and re-imagined to make it acceptable and assimilable. 'Crude otherness, hard otherness - the othernesses of race, of madness, of poverty - are done with. Otherness like everything else has fallen under the law of the market, the law of supply and demand.' (1990, p. 124) Baudrillard will paraphrase Freud: 'Where Other was, there has the Same come to be'. So if Otherness or the 'Other scene' was the domain of psychoanalysis, it too has disappeared.

The disappearance of psychoanalysis?

In the absence of illusion, postmodern theory suggests that all depth models have ended or simply disappeared with the end of Modernity itself (see, for instance, Jencks, 1991, Jameson, 1991, Eco 1973, Young 1989, Frosh 1991). With everything potentially exposed, a number of traditionally paired terms have collapsed - manifest and latent, appearance and essence, or the existential notion of authenticity versus inauthenticity and alienation, the opposition between signifier and signified. It has transpired that there is *no* depth and *no* truth to uncover. In postmodernity, there are now only surfaces, plays of light, reflections, refractions, diffractions and the autonomy of language. Also, this will be the end of psychoanalysis. If there is no longer any solid real upon which to call, there must instead be endless reproductions of scenes, retrospections, scenarios, interminable streams of circulating imagery and discourse (interminable therapy) as a cover for the horror (at one time the secret) that nothing is real. Up until very recently, this horror was kept from us by illusion, but now even this is gone.

Against Baudrillard, analysts would argue that the unconscious (as depth, or as Other) still exists. Then it would be necessary to recall the slippage of the unconscious from the Kleinian vocabulary where splitting is the dominant defence not repression. Similarly Bion's conception of alpha-function, Winnicott's concept of the true and false self, none of these is exclusively unconscious or conscious. And for Lacanians, there is definitely no such thing as the 'inner life', or 'interiority', or 'depth'. The unconscious is not considered as 'within', or somehow 'underneath' the conscious/preconscious system. Borch-Jacobsen states the position clearly: 'For Lacan, disciple of Kojève, the desire of man is not a drive, not a "pressure" arising from within the biological body, not an immediate affect or feeling of self... the human subject has *no interiority,* no interior in which to store or save for himself the so-called unconscious representations' (Borch-Jacobsen, 1991, p. 149, my italics) The unconscious becomes a property of language and the speaking-being. Baudrillard says that the unconscious was our last great adventure, and the last attempt to establish secrecy in a world with no secrets, but in the end it's become reduced to psychology. Finally, when we come to psychopathology, so-called narcissistic and borderline personalities dominate the picture with their lack of depth and cool hard surfaces. Thus, the problematizing of the unconscious is the death (drive) that haunts psychoanalysis.

Baudrillard has referred to psychoanalysis as the 'most admirable edifice, the most beautiful hallucination of the back world.' (1979, p. 41) With all the psychoanalytic theories taken together, we have 'the most beautiful construction of meaning and interpretation ever erected', which now, 'collapses under the weight of its own signs, which were once terms heavy with meaning.' (ibid. p. 58) Too much meaning in a sudden reversal becomes toxic and aleatory. Meaning has gone the same way as depth, which has gone the same way as affect.

The founding moment for psychoanalysis was the abandonment of the seduction theory and consequently the *final* moment of psychoanalysis will be the vengeful return of cool seduction, the inhuman (*Das Es*), and the transparency of the unconscious, man *without a shadow*. The abandonment of seduction was of course down to Freud. Between 1893 and 1897 infantile seduction was Freud's main assumption for the causation of later neurosis. The childhood scenes of passive seductions were to hold the key to both hysteria and obsessional neurosis, that is until the famous letter to Fliess on September 9th, 1897 in which he states that he no longer believes in this theory. It was to be replaced by such notions as unconscious phantasy, psychical reality and infantile sexuality, and a definitive loss of innocence for the child (an innocence currently being revived and asserted in the heated debate about sexual abuse, as if Freud and psychoanalysis indeed never existed).

However, the notion of infantile seduction as formative and pathogenic lies in the background in Freud's later thinking also. This was always only ever a partial abandonment. In various ways, Freud continues to posit something *extra* that lies behind the sexual phantasies, something that we have already commented upon, that is the enigmatic signifying focus for *primal* repression (see chapter four). There is, for instance, the primal scene in the Wolf Man where the seduction of the infant by its mother, including her activities over the child's bodily hygiene inevitably stimulated, and perhaps even aroused for the first time, pleasurable sensations in her genitals. Finally and most fundamentally, some *inherited* 'primal phantasies' can be conceptualised as a phylogenetic encounter with sexuality. What Freud and psychoanalysis never really abandon is the possibility of a fundamental explosive real of sexual trauma, by insisting that this can be observed in unconscious sexual phantasies.

However, it is at least this partial abandonment that Baudrillard is exposing. In truth, seduction never went away. For the primal repressed, as we have already mentioned, has *no* signifier and so it cannot be kept at bay in the unconscious and therefore is free to roam anywhere and everywhere, resisting any attempts to pin it down and master it. Seduction is everywhere whatever strategies are erected to ignore it or indeed to repress the phantasies that proliferate from it.

According to Juliet Mitchell and echoing what we have in part explained, there is in both men and women a fundamental repudiation of the feminine - 'a repudiation which, for Freud, was the bedrock of psychoanalysis both as theory and therapy.' (Mitchell, 1984, p. 386) 'femininity *does* come to represent this point where meaning and consciousness vanish. Since this point is chaos, that which has been made to stand in for it - made to indicate the gap - is unbearable and will be repudiated. In the loss of balance [via seduction], something to fill the gap will be hallucinated, a breast; produced as fetish, envied - a penis. The clinical experience of splitting and of castration is horror - penis envy, hallucination, fetishism are quick relief.' (ibid. p. 392) One cannot contemplate a gap or an absence, so instead we will say, in relief as it were, that something has been taken away. Castration, this absence, is then a cover for nothing. The focus is on *de*privation, rather than an original privation.

Classical psychoanalysis rests on repudiation of seduction. Seduction is this deadly pull towards the feminine. Psychoanalysis has pulled the other way, towards production, of meaning, truth, interpretation and sexual repression and the phallic economy. All this provides a kind of security - a balance of forces within the economy of the subject and his relations with the world. The subject or better still the self was invented precisely to defend against the real. This was a protected domain, the unconscious included, of truth to be established.

'Against all of this [real], psychoanalysis has hoisted its desiring subject, its Robinson Crusoe of the unconscious, sworn to an insular economy and to the exorcism of all external aggression... the only destiny of the subject should be to discharge its tensions, to purge itself of it internal excitations... that continually threaten the psychological fortress with disintegration.' (Baudrillard, 1983, p. 140) Seduction, thus excluded, has become the virus of the death drive.

Baudrillard sees psychoanalysis as an extension on the psychical front of the notion of private property and capital to be accumulated, managed and exploited. Your unconscious is your capital or your potential, to be invested to be capitalized upon. Indeed Freud referred to the unconscious wish as the capital of the dream that seizes the entrepreneur of the day residue to get itself expressed in a disguised form. He wasn't to know that we might seize it. Seduction is denied, excised and replaced by its visible phallic form, namely 'sexuality': 'Wherever sex has been erected into a function, an autonomous instance, it has liquidated seduction.' (Baudrillard, 1979, pp. 39-40) Sex becomes a management issue, a cool matter of choice, entertainment and life-style. However, seduction has its revenge in all manner of failures of the sexual relation.

For classical psychoanalysis, the manifest discourse is only 'material' from which latent *insights* will be extracted *producing* truth enabling the ego to become the *master* of its own truth. The latent discourse is the only valuable one. The accumulation of meaning via interpretation will put the analysand in touch with his unconscious. He will then be able to manage his own liberation. This whole process is referred to by both analysts and analysands as 'work'. They will speak of the 'working alliance'. Resistance is what opposes the work of the analysis. Psychoanalysis is the sad science as it requires work - of mourning, of all the various losses and lacks that the subject as subject is heir to. Baudrillard points out that, 'Psychoanalysis tells us to assume our fragility and passivity, but in almost religious terms, turns them into a form of resignation and acceptance in order to promote a well tempered psychic equilibrium.' (ibid. p. 83) At the beginning, psychoanalysis engaged in the discovery, the seduction, of the unconscious and the 'Other scene'. Later, in a subtle reversal, psychoanalysis becomes the taming and management of the unconscious, the unconscious, not as Other, but more of the Same. In the context of the postmodern celebration of the *hyper*-real, all this labour may be done for anyway, or simply overtaken, as the unconscious (the last private domain) is wrested from its seclusion and offered for sale.

Baudrillard comments that, 'it is not an inconsiderable source of entertainment to see seduction sweep across psychoanalysis with Lacan, in the wild-eyed form of a play of signifiers from which psychoanalysis - in the rigour of its demands and in its form, in the form Freud wanted - is dying just as certainly, nay even more certainly, as from its institutional banalization.'[6] (ibid. p. 57) Thus, perhaps Lacan avenges both his own exclusion from the International Psychoanalytic Association and the original foreclosure (of seduction) by Freud. Lacan's seductive effects are immense: the sheer breadth of his scholarship; the unpredictability of the 'short sessions'; the gratuitous difficulty of the texts; his principled incoherence (Roustang, 1986); the slow translation into English of the seminars; the relentless attack on the ego; the short iconic phrases; the legendary silence of the Lacanian analyst; the proliferations of models; all to counter the pervasive domestication of the subject and the imaginary elevation of the ego.

Only those who lie completely outside seduction are ill. Psychoanalysis believes that it treats disorders of the sexual drives, when the real disenchantment comes from the disappearance of seduction. What else can castration mean, asks Baudrillard? 'To be deprived of seduction is the only true form of castration.' (Baudrillard, 1979, p. 121)

Classical psychoanalysis, while privileging the extension of reason and meaning in all its seriousness and religiosity, has missed the effects of seduction and initiation which make of us not a subject but an object in the 'play of the world'. Psychoanalysis begins with an inaugural exorcism which bars the mother's primordial power with that of the dead Law of the Father. From this perspective, the mother's power is wholly negative and diabolical. Baudrillard tells us that seduction is something more. Seduction returns us to the sovereignty of the world, the play of appearances and disappearance, to the domain of the Rule not the Law. Here the stakes are higher, in the order of cruelty, tragedy, ritual and sacrifice, the challenge, the duel, 'something necessary and rigorous... Death remains the ultimate risk in every symbolic pact.' (ibid. p. 124)

Whereas the law is clear, the rule must remain veiled. 'We should never touch upon the enigma, under pain of falling into obscenity, and Oedipus will have no other resort but to become blind in order to escape this obscenity.' (Baudrillard, 1983, p. 144)

Lacan, in his Seminar on Anxiety (1962-3), speaks of Oedipus:

He who possessed the object of desire and of the law, he who enjoyed his mother, Oedipus to give him his name, takes this further step, he *sees* what he has done... The fact that he sees what he has done has a consequence that he sees - this is the word before which I stumble - the moment afterwards, his own eyes swollen with their vitreous humours on the ground, a confused pile of filth - since how can we put it? - because since he had torn his eyes from their sockets he had quite obviously lost his sight. And nevertheless it is not that he does not see them as such, as cause-object [objet a] finally unveiled of the final, the ultimate, no longer guilty, but *beyond the limits, concupiscence, that of having wanted to know.* (6.3.63, pp. 5-6 my italics).

Baudrillard's writing is criss-crossed with every possible contradiction. True to its style and form, it contains its own delirium and reversibility, its own symbolic exchange. It virulently resists exposition and explanation. It is alternately light and ephemeral, and searing and intense. In a serious moment he talks about his only interest is in 'the inhumanity of things'. This inhumanity is linked with the *pure* event which happens in our absence, but which becomes obscene to the extent that it is made transparent in its too realistic multi-media simulation.

The play of catastrophe

Seduction, in its hypermodern form, becomes smooth, cool, digital and indifferent. The shift is from the play of seduction versus the law, to the total technology of fascination. Games, once dangerous, competitive and combative, are now coolly elevated to the electronic and atomistic. Baudrillard claims that this change is part of a general process of cooling with systems of dissuasion and extermination. Communication becomes the functioning of the social within a closed circuit bounded by the media. The empty form of contact for contact's sake, promiscuous yet useless. Baudrillard suggests that the 'digital narcissus is going to slide along the trajectory of a death drive and sink in his or her own image.' (1979, p. 166) Ultimately, this is cold narcissism without even the minimalist experience of oneself as illusion. Biotechnology and genetic engineering make new cold forms of artificial propagation possible, bypassing the erotic, as if 'there is a death drive that pushes sexed beings towards a form of reproduction anteri-

or to their acquisition of sexual identities.' (ibid. p. 168) Back to the dead immortality of the protista.

It is part of the logic of late capitalism that we can no longer begin to figure where we are. The subject has become caught in the glare of the lights of a system so total, so cold and unmindful, that the only danger left is that he may yet feel the pain of this paralysis. Jameson says:

> Postmodern theory is... the effort to take the temperature of the age *without instruments* (my italics) and in a situation in which we are not even sure there is so coherent a thing as an "age", or zeitgeist or "system" or "current situation" any longer. Postmodern theory is then dialectical at least insofar as it has the wit to seize on that very uncertainty as its first clue and to hold to its Ariadne's thread on its way through what may not turn out to be a labyrinth at all, but a gulag or perhaps a shopping mall... We went out one morning and the thermometer was gone. (1991, p. xi)

There are no longer any instruments to take the temperature. The illusion, the tenuous illusion is of electronic totality, *one* world *whole* world, against the Real. It is the beautiful world that *creates* the catastrophe. Baudrillard's notion of indestructible symbolic power, around which we have centred the discussion, has returned to make everything circulate in what he terms a slow-moving catastrophe. He says:

> Beneath the transparency of the consensus lies the opacity of evil - the tenacity, obsessiveness and irreducibility of the evil whose contrary energy is at work everywhere... The principle of Evil is not a moral principle but rather a principle of instability and vertigo, a principle of complexity and foreignness, a principle of seduction, a principle of incompatibility, antagonism and irreducibility... Trying to redeem the accursed share or the principle of Evil can result only in the establishment of new artificial paradises, those of the consensus, which for their part do indeed embody a true death principle [death drive].(1990 pp. 106-107)

The attempt to force what he calls an uninterrupted production of positivity and antisepsis results in ever more virulent forms of symbolic disorder. Any statement in support of this principle, this 'fundamental rule', is likely to be met with incomprehension. Baudrillard says: 'At this rate every last negative sentiment will soon be forced into a clandestine existence.' (ibid. p. 108) What has been maliciously misunderstood by rational consensus liberalism is that every strategy of liberation affects good and evil equally. The liberation of morals and minds entails crimes and catastrophes. The liberation of law and pleasure leads to a 'catastrophic surplus value', which the media immediately cannibalise and circulate endlessly in a permanent 'catastrophe management'. 'Frozen out for so long, crimes and catastrophes make their joyous and official entrance... the true signs of freedom and the natural disorder of the world.' (ibid. p. 109) At one time Evil was held at a distance, it was obscene and opaque, limited and constricted, but once liberated, it enters on a phase of uninterrupted dissemination, circulating 'in the same arterial system as the Good and feeds of it, in all innocence, and all perversity.' (Baudrillard, 1992, p. 47)

As a result of symbolic disorder, the world is held together by catastrophe and the news flash. 'Creating ultra-rapid communication networks immediately means transforming human exchange into a residue.' (ibid. p. 78) Here subjectivity is reduced to surfing and overdosing on suffering. Baudrillard suggests an almost permanent *jouissance:* 'We are the consumers of the ever delightful spectacle of poverty and catastrophe, and of the moving spectacle of our own efforts to alleviate it.' (ibid. p. 67) There is no longer any time or (transitional) space for the subjective work of mourning or the resolution of the past. Meaning, voided by incessant news, approaches radical indeterminacy and ultimately, glacial indifference. With the continuous flow of imagery and information, it now becomes impossible to think and to symbolize. Thinking puts a brake on ideas, and without this capacity ideas proliferate to occupy the whole of mental space, and worse still, overflow as pollutants, as so much waste.

Baudrillard's writing, more than any other perhaps, depicts the autonomy of what we have termed the death drive now liberated from its unconscious haunt, free at last to circulate without restraint amongst the abject survivors of a devastated electronic planet. The progressive thought that this haunting presence of symbolic disorder might at some point succumb to the soft technologies of Eros, of therapy, dialogue and mediation, must now be completely dispelled by Baudrillard's celebratory depiction of a viral universe of hidden forces that seek revenge on a culture that fatefully and uniquely believes itself to be free of the Debt.

CONCLUSION: CLINICAL IMPERATIVES

With the foregoing consideration of analytic theory and in particular the theory of the death drive, what now must be the work of a psychoanalyst or psychoanalytic psychotherapist? Indeed can we use a word like 'work' any longer, since psychoanalysis cannot lay claim to be primarily a productive activity in any ordinary sense of the word? There is, after all, no telling what way things will go in the analytic encounter. Indeterminacy lies at the heart of things. There are now many varieties of that species analytic encounter. One great change since Freud's time, under the demise of the illusion of productivity, has been the end of the notion of analyst as expert, at least amongst analysts themselves. Even those ego-psychologists attuned to social adaptation, so parodied by Lacan, would hardly consider themselves as experts, 'the subject supposed to know'. While *academic* expertise and literature has grown and proliferated in psychoanalysis as elsewhere, practitioners as practitioners know little - they are simply there, in place as analyst, attempting to remain in and guardian of the so-called analytic position.

Analysands come to the analytic situation because of personal suffering, and they come looking for an expert who knows the answer to their question. The question of the analysand's (suffering) being-in-the-world is addressed to the analyst who is in the place of the Other - the whole enchanting panoply of meanings that are in the humanly constituted world. The analysand will gradually and painfully come to the realisation that there is no *one* definitive answer (there is no Other of the Other), but there is only a lack (castration), or a transitional or potential space, and aspects of the analyst's technique and personality (see Bollas, 1989), which the analysand herself may be able to *use* (Winnicott, 1971). The position of the analyst is to maintain that empty space as humanly as possible, so that no thought can come to rest at fullness or completion. This distance that is created and maintained by the analyst and symbolized by his position behind the couch, is a feature, by and large as I understand it, of *all* psychoanalytic approaches. This analytic space properly maintained can be used by the analysand to create representations of himself, mainly but not exclusively through words and feelings.

But a sense of lack, disappointment and suffering pervades the analytic scene which reveals itself in a persistent, insistent demand for closure, for gratification of infantile cravings and yearnings for love. This is the transference which is created, maintained and intensified by the artificiality of the psychoanalytic situation itself, which imposes a strain on analyst and analysand alike - analysis carried out in a state of deprivation. This is the overriding clinical imperative, not to collapse this space into what can become a closed, dual, imaginary relationship, with the loss of a sense of strangeness, the sense of the challenge, the sense of Otherness. Here, the danger is that analyst (and the analytic situation) becomes just an other (with a small 'o'), who has allowed herself to become too transparent, too present, too visible. To engage in fulfilling or gratifying the other's desire is paradoxically to deprive the other of his strangeness to himself, his own unthought thoughts. In Bion's terms, the analytic container will have become saturated making new linkages impossible. The analytic space will become deadened with sameness in what will now be a *simulation* of exploration, with the element of challenge, strangeness and drama drained from it.

However, analysts cannot simply refuse to have anything to do with the desire of the analysand. This is a denial of encounter, and would simply be a repetition in the countertransference of a cold childhood austerity, leading to another parody of the analytic encounter whereby the analysand quickly learns to be collusive or, better still, leaves the failed encounter amidst some confusion and despair. The analyst is called upon to respond, to say something, and put into words what has hitherto been in some way unspeakable and unsymbolizable. This is the interpretation of transference resistance, another clinical imperative.

This speech of the analyst does not of necessity, or does not automatically, proceed from the analyst as expert, as producer, as provider of psychoanalytic insights and diachronic reconstructions which serve only to objectify the analysand and leave him with only an image of himself refracted through a psychoanalytic prism. This process, so the argument goes, will lead him further and further away from himself into alienating identifications with the benevolent analyst, along the lines of the model proposed by Strachey (1934). The analyst speaks, but only to enable the process to have some life, or to come to life again. Strachey is not to be misunderstood as offering a too immediate reassurance against a hostile superego.

However, the substance of this book turns around the fact that our greatest problems exist when the whole analytic encounter is deadened, not so much by any errors that the analyst might make, but by the splitting, deadening attacks made on it by derivatives of the death drive, the 'internal Mafia gang' of narcissism allied with the death drive, negative narcissism (Rosenfeld 1987). These attacks threaten to engulf the *whole* analytic enterprise, or to surround it with an obscene knowing, a rigid determinism, or thought confusion, born of the analysand's omnipotence. Here there is a concerted attempt to destroy all containers of meaning. As Klein says, an analysis that does not encounter primary envy, is an analysis not worth the name. The analytic situation can play host to a parasitic relationship, which corrodes it from within.

Here, then is the third clinical imperative which will involve us in a perilous engagement with deadness and the capacity to endure splitting processes which are not so much spoken in words, but communicated via violent projections which the analyst is required to contain and metabolize, over long periods, without retaliation. Here the 'patient' analyst has to be especially sensitive to her own persecutory and paranoid anxieties as they arise in her own countertransference reactions (see chapter three, also Racker, 1968), which might impel her to feel intimidated by and rejecting of her analysand. This is the psychoanalysis of primitive split-off affects, which can be gross, homogenizing, immediate and infinite (Matte-Blanco, 1976, Rayner 1995).

These malignant, silent, splitting attacks can continue unabated with the result that the analysand and the analyst feel totally controlled by potentially infinite unconscious affects. Here, the fourth clinical imperative is called for, a controversial area indeed, which involves some militant 'act of freedom' (Symington 1983), some way of encountering, speaking about, or bringing to a stop a totally controlled situation. Nina Coltart gives the example of a patient who 'fell violently silent, exuding ever-stronger black waves of hatred and despair... The change in him from late mid-life crisis neurosis to something which breathed psychosis was heavy in the atmosphere...Very close attention to these things is the essence when faced with such massive Beyond Words challenge... His gaze when he glanced at me was shifty, evil and terrified. He was as if possessed. When I spoke about what I saw and felt [use and expression of the countertransference], he glowered, grunted and sank further into an ungainly heap.' (Coltart 1986, p. 194) Finally, 'I simply and suddenly became furious and bawled him out for his prolonged lethal attack on me and on the analysis... This outburst of mine changed the course of the analysis.'(ibid. pp. 194-195) Winnicott had something of this in mind when he spoke of 'the analyst's need to be able to hate the patient objectively.' (1947, p. 196) The analyst's expression of strong affects is a controversial aspect of technique. At best, it should be used rarely, and may appear to be the only option when finally death takes hold and digs in. Someone has to verbalise and give voice to the violence that is deadening everything.

There is another type of patient discussed by Balint (1968), of whom Margaret Little also speaks, 'who cannot in any circumstances take life for granted', whose fear of annihilation is extreme and all pervasive, and who may during treatment develop a delusional transference of *unity*. Little believes that it is necessary for the analyst, in certain circumstances, to recognize 'the truth *for the analysand* of his delusion of absolute identity between them, his entering into it, and demonstrating its psychic truth and its objective untruth.' (1981, p. 144) This allowance for regression, and a temporary *closing* of the analytic space requires some modification of classical psychoanalytic technique. It comes, as Little reminds us, as a natural *extension* of that technique to enable, 'the 'stillness at the centre' which allows of movement and perception, it is the *sine qua non* for living continuously in one's body, for having an identity, and for being identical with, and being able to make assertion or statement of, oneself.' (ibid. p. 153) This commitment to engagement in the analytic encounter, emphasized by the British Independent tradition, may bring problems (the danger, minimized by Little, of malignant regression) and may represent an extreme of clinical imperative, but it is done with the purpose of bringing the analysand into life.

Phillips critically summarizes these, what he calls, revised roles of the analyst as *playing mother*. He says:

> Psychic progress along developmental lines (Anna Freud); the secure internalisation of the good object (Klein); achievement, however precarious, of the Depressive Position (Klein and Bion); a virtual True Self destiny (Winnicott). There is, I think, an inevitable connection between the analyst already in position as the mother - and especially the pre-Oedipal mother - and psychoanalysis as the coercion or simulation of normality... '[Thus beginning to] foreclose the transference turns psychoanalysis into perversion, perversion in the only meaningful sense of the term: knowing too exactly what one wants, the disavowal of contingency, omniscience as the cheating of time; the mother who because she knows what's best for us, has nothing to offer.' (1993 p. 115-116)

The Lacanian position, as I understand it, privileges desire, allows freedom for desire to emerge, as best it can in its limited way, *only* through speech and the formations of the unconscious. The subject should come to recognize and name his desire, (that is the efficacious action of analysis) and, 'In order to free the subject's speech, we introduce him into the language of his desire, that is to say, into the *primary language* in which, beyond what he tells us of himself, he is already talking to us unknown to himself, and, in the first place, in the symbols of the symptom.' (Lacan, (1953)[1977] p. 81)

However, there is a very problematic issue here. And one in which there has been *no* meeting of minds. That is, the connection between the essential beyondness of desire, jouissance and the death drive. What Lacan calls (in the seminar on Ethics, 1959-60), the law beyond the law: or, in a more Kleinian formulation the equation between desire and envy. Ultimately desire, as Freud made very clear and we have been emphasizing throughout, is desire for death. Clinically, this manifests itself in self-destructiveness, self-mutilation, masochism, repetitious acting-out, and so on. In Bion's terms, an anti-learning, a minus-K, becomes a continuous destruction of the apparatus for thinking thoughts. Here, contra Lacan, is the crucial clinical question: Is the analyst not minimally obliged to intervene and *name* this malignancy in desire, that can, often enough, *pre-empt* the long and open wait for desire to emerge *through language*. The fact that such interventions on the part of the analyst may make him into 'the one who knows' - the one who knows *better,* or makes him into a paternalistic or maternalistic figure, even a pedagogue or moralist and so on, who invites retaliation, doesn't gainsay a crucial clinical reality - namely the subject, the Zetzel (1968) category 4 hysterical subject, for example, locked into being too much in the Real pitting himself *against* language and the emergence of any creative desire via language. Not to mention the less disturbed patient, who is also prone, as the Kleinians have emphasized so well, to proceed from a split-off envy.

The Kleinians have pointed up clearly the dominance of a primitive murderous superego - what Bion refers to as a meaning, destroying object. Kleinian psychoanalysis has therefore very much to do with revealing and making conscious this insane and *inhuman* aspect of the self that *is* desire, which holds desire in thrall, or seems to monopolise or *become* desire itself. Psychoanalysis, in this paradigm shift, is then seen as a *prophylactic* measure - an attempt to release desire from a ravenously greedy life crippling double, a violent imaginary, that *prevents speech* - comes long before speech - and indeed operates by way of a continuous destruction of the linkages that makes language possible.

The point here is that it is not the analyst herself who turns the analytic encounter into a so-called normalising process, restricting freedom, via a mother-analyst who knows best and becomes obscene in knowing *too much*. This can and does happen, but this criticism can be made of any analyst of any persuasion when they act out of an omnipotent position or ideology. My point is that there are moments when the analyst must *know* and *act* to enable the analytic process to begin, to continue or - indeed - to end. These moments occur when the *analysand* in terror or in pleasure feels compelled to act omnipotently and freezes the process into an obscene parody of an encounter.

There is one more related criticism which must be countered. Namely that the analyst intervenes in these types of situations referred to above, out of her own *fear* of the radical desire, the inalienable freedom of the analysand. This is the so-called resistance of the analyst. This could be true, but the position envisaged for the analyst is *not* resistant but, on the contrary, is open to and prepared to tolerate extreme anxieties. However, the clinical imperatives referred to arise out of the very practical need for containment, the maintenance of the analytic structure, to minimize acting out, and above all, to bring violent affects, from oblivion, *into the domain of speech*.

To be sure, the analyst is making a moral judgement about the analysand's situation. To my mind it is a judgement that occasionally needs to be made. More than pure analytic neutrality and *laisser faire* is called for in extreme situations. For instance, is violence justified - against the violent husband, the corrupt political regime, or the self? In the first two cases, perhaps, yes, as the death drive is directed outwards against a greater evil? Against the self, as in suicide? Perhaps no. What constitutes freedom for the subject in these critical instances? When does freedom become pathology - an infantile rage, for instance, which takes no heed of the adult? Is not the analyst in some degree bound to bring (seduce) the analysand into the wide circuit of life (even if this is only a deferred death)? The analyst cannot simply shirk these encounters and avoid speaking about them.

Having made this digression and considered these clinical imperatives and dilemmas that arise directly out of the operation of the death drive and its derivatives, we may now return to the theme of the open ended exploration and encounter at the heart of the analytic tie. At this point we will take up the Baudrillardian theme of the originary and elementary nature of seduction (chapter seven). At the heart of the transference is not so much the emergence of love and hate from the unconscious, but seduction. A seduction which has never been repressed and never been left behind, but returns as the essence of Being and life. Whenever analysis is entered into, whether as analysand or analyst, there is a scene of seduction, however minimal. Seduction happens to the participants. To undergo it means to endure it, to be affected by it. It strikes, it exceeds us. Everything seduces. In this sense, psychoanalysis is *submitted* to, by both the analysand and the analyst. Both submit themselves to the mystery that surrounds them. There is not one person in charge as analyst, treating another who is the patient. *Both* enter a structure, which is the psychoanalytic situation. The analyst's function is to maintain the structure; the analysand is there to use the structure. There is a mutuality of influence based on unknowing. Both participate in seductive indeterminacy.

The entire symbolic universe is founded upon its potential for seductiveness. Language seduces itself, in the joke, the flash of wit, the pun. To a large extent this is what analysis is - letting seduction happen. But, most of the time both participants are entirely unaware of this seductive effect. This is all to the good, for were either participant to become aware of it, there would be a temptation to *use* and exploit it, with the danger of the acting out of the erotic transference and countertransference becoming a real possibility. Seduction acts outside of awareness. It operates via the riddle, the ellipse, the barely decipherable, the challenge, the chance, the risk. It energizes the whole process and gives the sense of what Winnicott refers to as the spontaneous unforced gesture, the sense of aliveness and reality at the heart of infancy and the true self throughout life. Baudrillard says, only those who lie outside seduction are ill.

Against Phillips above, it seems that the British Independent tradition, criticized for emphasizing the fateful role of bad early environment provision, comes closest to the recognition and sense of that enjoyment, the 'news from within', that ceaselessly pulsates at the heart of Being. Seduction occurs quite naturally, and it is fundamentally something that cannot be taught or be part of any *technique*. Technique has to do with *production* which attempts to over-rule seduction via the law. However, seduction goes on in secret and in silence. Any technique without it is dead. Any analysis without it is dead.

The psychotic is acutely aware and in terror of the fluidity and aleatory nature of the seductive universe. In so far as the subject is not psychotic, there is little or no awareness of this underworld of seduction. The psychotic, on the other hand, omnipotently tries to stop seduction and establish absolute Truth. Hence the common delusion of being Christ crucified in the struggle to restore this truth. The psychotic tries to stitch up and weave the thread of signifiers over the gaping hole that appears in the symbolic universe (see chapter four), or conversely to fatally disperse all the signifiers to eliminate any awareness of what would arise were they to come together and mean something.

Seduction operates in disregard for truth and meaning. Instead it prefers the secret, the enigma, the opacity and deviation of appearance and surface. Seduction is the unknown circulation in the analytic process standing guard over subjectivity while continuously displacing it. But this secrecy is not deliberate. Nothing is being consciously withheld. The relative silence of the analyst is not a deliberate withholding, but instead fosters the play of the imagination, the freedom in free association. Free association is seduction - the seduction of one word idea by another, the seduction of ideas by each other, the free play of no sense. The last clinical imperative is to stand guard over free association as seduction, to enable the liveliness of the analytic encounter to continue.

But what about the *latent* discourse, interpretation, the production of meaning and truth, making the unconscious conscious, with which classical psychoanalysis, in particular, has always been involved? Analysis will always be involved with the production of meanings, with some element of *holding*. Interpretation has its place, but only in so far as it contributes to the unfolding narrative, the ceaseless *movement* of meaning, without trying to finally break open the secret. Baudrillard tells us that interpretation never seduced anyone. Classical theory points out that premature interpretation increases resistance. Interpretation is appropriate providing it serves the purpose of illusion, providing it retains a certain charm, lightness, drama, subtlety and otherness. Otherwise it contributes to the myth of the fully analysed person, the person who bores us with too much insight.

Winnicott was aware of this paradox at the heart of the process. We will quote him at length:

> I suggest that in health there is a core to the personality that corresponds to the true self of the split personality; I suggest that this core never communicates with the world of perceived

objects, and that the individual person knows that it must never be communicated with or be influenced by external reality. This is my main point, the point of thought which is the centre of an intellectual world and of my paper. Although healthy persons communicate and enjoy communicating, the other fact is equally true, that *each individual is an isolate, permanently non-communicating, permanently unknown, in fact unfound...*

At the centre of each person is an incommunicado element, and this is sacred and most worthy of preservation... Rape, and being eaten by cannibals, these are mere bagatelles as compared with the violation of the self's core, the alteration of the self's central elements by communication seeping through the defences. For me this would be the sin against the self. We can understand the hatred people have of psycho-analysis which has penetrated a long way into the human personality ... [with its] need to be secretly isolated. (1963b, p. 187)

The death drive may only be the *death* drive from the vantage point of the ego, the law (of the dead father) and productive reason. Forgo these temporarily, as in the analytic encounter, and it is the death drive that animates and propels the beautiful symbolic exchange, transformation and enjoyment of analyst and analysand. Surely this is life! Michel Henry (1985) constantly emphasizes *life* in his excellent book on the genealogy of psychoanalysis. By life, Henry means what subsists *outside of representation*, a *primary* affectivity, constitutive of being itself, that 'is forgetful by nature, as immanence, which insurmountably expels ek-stasis and thus all possible forms of thought.' (1985, p. 211) Life is being sufficient *to itself*, the 'original joy of existence, as the experience of life's superabundance and power.' (ibid. p. 207), outside of any human representation of it, outside human knowing. Repression, as Freud (1915c) emphasized, bears down on affectivity, causing the human subject to become divided within. But Life itself, in itself alone, is *one*. For Henry, the unconscious is representation's other; *'the unconscious is the name of life.'* (ibid. p. 286) He goes on to say that the representational unconscious (Freud, Lacan) 'has nothing to do with the unconscious that secretly refers to life's essence... in which being reveals itself to itself outside and independent of ek-stasis, in the radical immanence of its self-affection as life.' (ibid. p. 287)

According to Henry, 'Freud grasped only life's obscure basis, that locus of the first anxieties where, driven into itself, it thinks foremost of fleeing from itself. He followed the path of self-liquidation to the end, recognizing only its atrocious aspect, the death drive...' (ibid. p. 315) The death drive may be masquerading as life and in fact be the very essence of life itself. Freud did not see, according to Henry, 'that pain belongs to and constitutes the inner edification of being, that *birth is a transcendental birth,* that the insupportable is inseparable from and leads to intoxication.' (ibid. p. 315) However, this intoxication is in love with itself, as it endlessly seduces itself in the domain beyond representation, that is beyond us - life's 'auto-affirmation'. On *this* side, situated within the Symbolic, the subject is cut off from life and, to that degree, afraid of it.

Analysis, as we have been stating, should make us, to some degree less afraid and more able to enjoy. Henry comments: 'Does not the cure itself demonstrate that the representation of one's situation, its conflicts and their history, by analysis is useless so long as the precondition of that consciousness, a modification of life, does not occur?'. (ibid. p. 316) Modification, yes, but to aspire to an infinite, mystical, absolute (undivided) subjectivity, while still bound finitely in servitude to *this* life (deferred death), no. Henry states: 'Freud stands before the abyss where all power dissimulates its essence - namely, the original impossibility of its being objected as an object.' (ibid. p. 322) This originary power, Henry calls Life's hyperpower, which has no need of us as subjects, yet is the source of every drive, affect, representation. He says: 'To catch the secret of our being, psychoanalysis was in complete agreement: drives manifest themselves only in their 'acts', in the exploded whole of the subject's unperceived behaviour - its representations, its affects - and all these indications are sacrificed to a hermeneutic reading. We must therefore hack through a forest of symbols to find the great paths along which drives have tried to discharge themselves and by which life has tried to be rid of itself. To regrasp that being, exploded and dispersed across the ek-stasis of time ... to blaze a trail through the labyrinth of those screens.' (ibid. p. 325-26) That is, to joy, celebration, forgetfulness, seduction, being itself.

However, at a certain imperceptible point, a point of distance and knowledge, all can go into sudden and catastrophic reversal when the illusory scene of seduction opens onto the unillusioned obscene truth of suffering, which ceases to be a game, an intoxication, a *play* with disappearance. Losing our footing, we topple off the stage, falling forever.

The last clinical imperative might be just this: *silent* keeping faith with the possibility of the prefiguring of death, the universal presence of suffering and brutality in the universe, and the impossibility, in the end, of avoiding this formal rigour of the real, as excessively prodigious life-death drive. The beauty of seduction, and the 'sacred horizon of appearances', only makes sense from *this* point of view. Seduction is only ever trivial and banal unless it occurs as a challenge to and in ecstatic defiance of this *zero real*. Baudrillard says and exemplifies in his writing that theory, speech, creativity are a perpetual *challenge to the real*. 'The real... is the insurmountable limit of theory. The real is not an objective status of things, it is the point at which theory can do nothing. That does not necessarily make of theory a failure. The real is actually a challenge to the theoretical edifice. But in my opinion theory can have no other status other than that of challenging the real.' (in Gane, 1993, pp. 122-123) Nietzsche suggests that, what he calls the 'light image manifestations', we get after staring too long at the sun, 'are the inevitable products of a glance into the terrible depths of nature: light patches, we might say, to heal the gaze seared by the terrible night.' (1872, p. 46)

NOTES

Chapter 1

1. There is an immediate problem here with the translation of the German word *Trieb*. Normally, as is well known, this term is translated by Strachey as 'instinct'. Yet for many theorists, the notion of instinct is too biological implying a more or less fixed patterns of behaviour familiar to zoologists. However, psychoanalysis, concerned as it is with *human* reality, prefers to speak of *drives*, that imply variability of object, aim and satisfaction more in keeping with human desire. Drives imply a pressure without a definite aim and *with no ultimate satisfaction.* Although, the present author favours the translation of *Trieb* as drive and *Todestrieb* as death-drive, the term 'instinct' will continue to be used particularly in connection with Freudian ideas and quotations. This will minimize textual disruption.

2. This notion of a single instinct or libido may seem close to Jung's idea of 'psychic energy'. However, libido always implies the *sexual* drives, even if, in the case of narcissism, these have been secondarily de-sexualized. Jung disputed the specifically sexual character that Freud attributed to libido, preferring the more general idea of life energy, that can flow in biological, psychological, spiritual or moral channels in order to maintain what Jung believed was a natural tendency of the psyche towards equilibrium, and *contra* Freud towards a pattern of meaning (teleology). Also, for Jung the drives are structured by being bound up with archetypes in the collective unconscious. These archetypes wait to be realized in the subject's life. Although Freud had an ongoing interest in phylogenesis, he was much more interested in the *personal* history of his analysands (ontogenesis), and refuted the idea of a collective unconscious.

3. The emphasis on neutrality *within* the consulting room has led to a parallel quiescence on the wider political and cultural scene, as if tolerance and a benign optimism was the greatest good. The crisis created by this moral vacuum within liberal democracies may now be becoming apparent.

Chapter 2

1. The formation of the ego is therefore based on a radical misunderstanding of the world. For Lacanian psychoanalysis, this is equivalent to the *méconnaissance* of the 'mirror-phase' which inaugurates the infantile ego and which leaves it mark on all ego activities thereafter. For Kleinians, the distortion and misperception is brought about by the extreme *affectivity* of the infant, which at the beginning is rooted in biology. For the Lacanians, the distortion arises as a result of the *mental* tendency to find unities and syntheses (the first being the infant's jubilant sight of itself in the mirror). These unities exist only in the imagination and are always seen by Lacanians as narcissistically self-serving and alienating. (see chapter 4)

2. Melanie Klein did not consider the countertransference to be of any use in the analytic setting. However, Kleinians in general and the Independents, pay great

attention to their own affective states as well as their patients' during the session. However, the countertransference remains a controversial tool. In this instance, however, where there is real danger, the malignancy will be discernible to the analyst trained in this school. Affects do not deceive.

3. To understand the working through of the depressive position as leading to emotional growth and integration towards maturity, a leaving behind of archaic violent phantasies, is perhaps too simplistic and optimistic, although it is a position that seems to be held sometimes by Klein herself. In the next section of this chapter, it will be shown how this position is ultimately untenable.

4. There are at least two very different conceptions of the unconscious posited here. For Lacan, the unconscious consists of abandoned signifiers (emotionally charged archaic 'ideas' [*Vorstellungen*]), which cannot become conscious directly, but only indirectly though the mechanisms of condensation, displacement, etc., that Freud described in *The Interpretation of Dreams*. This unconscious is radically other to the self - a stranger within. Later, with the advent of the second topography in 1923, Freud developed a more *affective* view of the unconscious, driven by a chaotic cauldron of drives. This is closer to the Kleinian unconscious, altogether more diffuse, descriptive and potentially *able to become conscious directly*, especially in the transference. The main thrust of the British school has been that, from the beginning (in infancy) these affects are linked to and indistinguishable from objects. Marjorie Brierley (1937) says that in the infant affect and object are indistinguishable. Therefore affects should be regarded less as simply discharge phenomena, but as potentially adaptive complex ego activities. Hence the British school, especially the Independent tradition, places its emphasis on object *relations*. While, the death drive, as we have been stressing all along, points in the other direction, towards an unavoidable outsideness of the drive, an excess of affectivity.

5. This emotional intensity was repeated with her own family and her analysis of her own children. Two of Klein's key 'cases' were Fritz and Felix (Erich and Hans). Also, according to Grosskurth, the case of a seventeen-year-old girl, Lisa, is her daughter Melitta. Now, we would be horrified by the thought that an analyst would analyze their own children. The loss of privacy, the risk of incestuous intrusion, and the potential for manipulation is enormous. However, Freud analyzed Anna, but at least he never published the case.

Chapter 3

1. As Meltzer says, 'Bion has constructed a quasi-philosophical system where thought sits amazed in Plato's cave straining itself to apprehend the noumena of the world.' (1978, part 3, p. 2) Bion developed a theory of thinking that he hoped would be verified by psychoanalytic investigation. He was both a logical posivitist (adhering to the theory and practice of science) and empiricist (adhering to experience). As Bleandonu (1994) says, 'Bionian epistemology, Janus-like, looks both ways: to experience and to pure mind.' (p. 190) Bion bases his epistemology on Kant's 'thing-in-itself', and the distinction between phenomenon (what we can

sense) and noumenon (beyond the limit of our perception). This latter is represented by 'O' - Ultimate Reality, which can only be known by *transformations* (Bion, 1965) by the patient or analyst. 'O' for Bion, the infinite, largely replaces the unconscious of the classical point of view. The distinction between infinite and finite seems more important that the distinction between conscious and unconscious. Similarly, while Freud was concerned with reconstructing the past, Bion, and Kleinian analysis generally, as we have noted, is concerned mainly with the 'here and now'.

Bion was interested in the discoveries made in geometry about the nature of space. Mental space for Bion is unknowable, but can be represented in thought. Not in the psychotic, though, who destroys space only to be tormented by the enormity of it. The question of (psychoanalytic) knowledge is linked to 'vertices' - a multiplicity of different points of view, converging on the same object from different perspectives. For instance, the paranoid-schizoid position is conceptualized geometrically as just two vertices in reversible perspective. The analytic space requires *more* depth. Bion draws on the Plato's theory of Forms or Ideas - essences that have always existed (as thing-in-themselves) beyond the real of sensuous experience, that await discovery by the soul. In this sense thoughts *precede* the mental apparatus to think them. It is not thinking that produces thoughts, as we normally understand things, but essences that wait for a mind to think them. Bion also draws on the mystics (see note 6 below) and develops his radical view of psychoanalytic asceticism.

Bion's speculations form a bricolage as he takes from many different sources, as well as appearing to 'present himself as being in isolation, generating his ideas *de novo* in a process of spontaneous generation; a guru linked in with 'truth' in a way that ordinary mortals are not.' (Hinshelwood, in the foreword to Bleaudonu 1994, p. xi) Further on, Hinshelwood suggests that, 'Most people take parts of Bion and develop their own views; then work clinically or philosophically, with what they have produced from the bit they have taken away.' (p. xi) This is all I can claim to have done, in what follows, where I have focussed on the death drive, its power to disrupt thinking, and the analyst's developing capacity to tolerate fragmentation without closure or psychosis.

2. The symbolism referred to here has a wider reference than the classical view of symbolism (Jones 1916). The classical view is that only what is repressed is symbolized, or only what is repressed needs to be symbolized. The meaning of the symbol is unknown to and resisted by the subject. The sense in which the term is being used here includes the notion of sublimation. Here the meaning of the symbol can become conscious with the associated affects. Symbolism in this much wider sense used by the British school partakes of both the primary and secondary processes. Lacan's use of the term symbolic is different again as will be noted in the next chapter.

3. Language and thinking deceive. Gone here is any simple equivalence between words and reality, or words simply describing (containing) reality. This is similar (although conceptualized differently) from Lacan's (1953) notion of 'empty speech', and the alienated dimension of speech in general. These issues will be taken up in full in the next chapter.

4. The moments of persecution or loss of coherence are always painful for the analyst and particularly dangerous for trainee analysts. There is a risk of complete loss of self-esteem and the collapse of the analytic position. Here, I have found, reassurance from the trainee's supervisor is essential. More often than not the trainee feels herself to be doing something wrong, inadequate, or not to be suited to the work, and so on. When in fact, the trainee, unbeknownst to herself, is being denuded by the analysand, and is feeling the effects of this denudation. Seeing this can enable the trainee to survive and bear the destructive projections. The trainee's technique may also be in error, but this is more likely to have been caused by the strain imposed by the projections.

5. Analysands from very so-called dysfunctional families have not been sufficiently shielded from catastrophic anxiety. For example, they have been repeatedly exposed to parental violence and/or sexual abuse and family break-up. They find themselves incapable of telling an ordered life history that is stretched out over time. They live *with* the catastrophe which is ever-present which may present in hysterical or psychosomatic symptoms (McDougall 1989), or, the absence of affect, or with attempts a self-injury - 'signals' of the ongoing distress that have never been symbolized.

6. Chief amongst these 'security systems' is of course religion. Bion's notion of Faith is wider than the conventional religious term. However, as David Black has pointed out, contra Freud's celebrated view that religion is 'the universal obsessional neurosis of humanity' (1927, p. 43), 'Religion... turns the universe from It to Thou (in Buber's profound and simple insight).' (Black, 1993, p. 624) From a Kleinian perspective, Black continues, 'It [religion] is a socially constructed and maintained system of internal objects, analogous to those spoken of in psychoanalysis... Unlike analytic objects, they are derived from a definite cultural tradition and are elaborated over time to meet the experience of practitioners.' (ibid. p. 624) For Bion there can be an excess of 'morality', a 'Super' ego as Bion calls it which is in omniscient opposition to learning from experience, an 'envious assertion of moral superiority without any morals' (Bion, 1962a, p. 97) - a psychotic defence, a means of controlling the world. However, against this Bion's mysticism is informed by Meister Eckhart, who used the term God (*Gott*) to describe the God of creation, and Godhead (*Gottheit*) as divine power. God is related to activity and knowing 'K', whereas the Godhead is 'O' (see Bleandonu, 1990, p. 211) I imagine, like Tillich's (1952) God beyond God.

7. I have mainly concentrated on those aspects of Bion's work to do with linking and unlinking, the life and death drives, and catastrophe in 'O'.

Chapter 4

1. At this point I must make my position clear. This chapter is written from a committed Lacanian position, and while what follows is primarily but not exclusively for non-Lacanians, it does involve simplifications and omissions, but hopefully no *dilution* of the Lacanian position.

2. Lacan's importation of terms such as *alienation* into psychoanalysis gives weight and political authority to this notion of an irredeemable estrangement. The term has a long and varied history. Originally having to do with progressive insanity or the transfer of property, more recently, of course, it has been used to describe modern conditions of powerlessness and reification in mass technological culture. The main influence here has been the discovery of Marx's *Economic and Philosophical Manuscripts* of 1844, following on Hegel and Max Weber.

3. *Jouissance* - literally enjoyment of a sexual nature, which is forbidden under the Law and the pleasure/reality principle. However, the English word enjoyment is insufficient. *Jouissance* implies more abandon and intensity. Transgressing the Law involves intense pleasure or pain since there is only so much pleasure that the subject can bear. *Jouissance* is *beyond* the pleasure principle and is therefore closely identified with the death drive itself, and according to Macey's reading of Lacan, 'the pleasure principle is a barrier or an obstacle to *jouissance*.' (1988, p. 203) The problem with linking jouissance with the death drive is the equation of the death drive with the zero of the Nirvana principle (see chapter one), because Macey indicates that '*jouissance* refers to an *almost* intolerable level of excitation rather than to its reduction or extinction.' (ibid. p. 203)

4. The use of the word 'Symbolic' requires explanation. It is the central theme of Lacanian psychoanalysis. The Symbolic is one of Lacan's three registers, together with the Imaginary and the Real. The development of this concept owes much to anthropology, and the work of Lévi-Strauss who developed the notion that the social world is structured by laws that regulate kinship relations, and Mauss's concept of gift exchange. Since what is most commonly exchanged between people is the gift of speech, the symbolic register is closely associated with language. It is the realm of culture, the social, and most importantly of the law that regulates desire in the Oedipus complex. Because it is not natural in any sense, it is therefore an *arbitrary* code composed of differential signifiers, each of which refers only to other signifiers (making signifying chains), and so on forever. Hence Freud's emphasis on free association which in Lacanian terms is the free wheeling following of these chains of signifiers. The symbolic is an *autonomous* register entirely separate from the natural world. The Symbolic is also the realm of the unconscious, designated by Lacan as the big Other to emphasize the radical alterity and the multiple meanings inherent in language, with which psychoanalysis is deeply involved. Hence, the well known aphorism: the unconscious is structured like a language. This also means that the unconscious is not somehow 'inside' the subject, as all other psychoanalysts have assumed. There is no inside anyone. The unconscious is neither inside or outside, it is merely otherness. The symbolic is thus a Kafkaesque universe, at once familiar (because we know nothing else, or can formulate nothing that went before or is outside it), and yet concealing a mystery that sustains desire.

Lacan's concept of the symbolic contrasts strongly with classical psychoanalytic notions of symbolism, where the symbol and the symbolized are relatively fixed and at least potentially meaningful. Lacan wanted to emphasize the cruel and meaningless nature of the signifier and its lack of any simple relation to the signified (the referent). Lacanian analysis, uniquely basing itself in the symbolic, focuses on the analysand's signifiers - the words, phrases, part of words, speech which *represent* the analysand idiosyncratically, unbeknownst to himself. It follows from this that there is *no* possibility of a coming to know, or coming to terms with the Symbolic, or finding ultimate resolution with the Other. What can be hoped for is that the subject will assume *his place* as subject to the symbolic, which will involve him in 'symbolic castration'.

All other schools of psychoanalysis are criticized by Lacan for largely ignoring the symbolic register, preferring to understand phantasy, defence mechanisms, psychological processes in general, all of which Lacan downgrades to the Imaginary register. In this connection too, he is critical of the interest taken by object relations theorists in primitive affects, which we have elaborated in the previous two chapters. Lacan has designated that these are of no interest for psychoanalysts, as analysts should be concerned wholly with the symbolic function. For Lacanians, there is nothing in the unconscious but signifiers. Likewise, the Oedipus complex is not so much a formative event in childhood that happens at a particular time (the precise timing disputed between the Freudians and Kleinians), but for Lacan, it has a *structuring* function that inaugurates or inscribes the symbolic in the subject. It must happen, but the timing is irrelevant.

5. 'Barred', here refers to the Saussurian bar between the signifier and signified, which Lacan wants to emphasize as a bar to meaning and closure. There is always an 'other' meaning. The bar represents the resistance to knowing of the unconscious. It is also the bar (the rule) of the arbitrary nature of the Law, the bar that castrates or cuts through the subject, the bar on the completion of meaning, and the bar that makes a simple fulfilled life and relationships impossible.

6. All modern discussion on sexual abuse is non-psychoanalytic in the sense that it ignores the unavoidable encounter of the infant with primal and precocious seduction (prior to any capacity to symbolize it), establishing the enigma of sexuality in the child/adult, which subsequently the pervert can readily exploit. This issue is taken up again in chapter seven.

7. Lacanian theory is often contrasted with Object Relations theory. In the former there is no adequate relationship between the lost object and the desire it evokes. In the latter, according to Lacanians, there is 'the possibility of a complete and perfectly satisfying relation between the subject and object' (Evans 1996, p. 124), which is biologically based upon need and its satisfaction. Clearly, any serious reading of Klein, Fairbairn, Winnicott and others will find this view is incorrect. Clearly, the good object can mitigate distress to some degree, but the analysis of envy in chapter two points to a *permanent* attack on the object. Similarly for Winnicott (1971) the 'use of an object' involves its ruthless destruction. At root, the object is never adequate.

8. The ethics of psychoanalysis as a treatment is central to Lacan. The analyst, while being supposedly neutral, cannot avoid moral and ethical questions. The question of ethics in psychoanalysis is intimately bound up with the death drive.

In this sense this book, without being too pretentious about it, attempts to be ethical. For Lacanians, what is unethical is the implicit or explicit offer of a cure to the analysand. In his Seminar on Anxiety (1962-63), Lacan states that: 'It is quite certain that our justification as well as our duty is to ameliorate the position of the subject. And I claim that nothing is more uncertain in the field that we are in than the concept of cure.' (12.12.62. p. 2) However, he says that the cure may come 'as a bonus'. But clearly to *aim* for a cure is false and part of a normative ethic of adaptation. From the Lacanian point of view, the analysis does not aim to soften the analysand's severe superego, to reduce his sense of guilt, neither is it libertine giving free rein to the id. Nothing new here, Anna Freud said as much in 1936. What is emphasized is the *absolute* freedom of the subject to *speak and act* in accordance with his desire and to resist any form of domination or objectification however benevolent (even if: 'It's for your own good'). However, this speech and action is *not* 'acting out' whereby the subject evades responsibility for what he (unconsciously) does and says. This freedom is *tragic*. *Oedipus Rex* is the tragedy at the heart of psychoanalysis. Speaking of Antigone, Lacan says, 'tragedy is in the forefront of our experiences as analysts.' (1959-60, p. 243) Yet this pure Lacanian ethic raises all kinds of problems, some of which I attempt to address in the concluding chapter of this book. Let us say for the moment, that what is demonstrated as tragic, other analysts see as pathology. This may lead to ridiculous statements like: if only Oedipus, Macbeth, Lear, etc. had been analyzed!

9. The Lacanian emphasis on the father is unique in post-Freudian psychoanalysis and psychotherapy. Lacan emphasized that the question of 'What is a father?' runs throughout Freud's work. As early as 1938 Lacan calls attention to the role of the father. 'I do think that a great many psychological consequences follow from the social decline of the paternal imago.' (1938, p. 45) He links the failure of father with a failure of sublimation in the child. Hence Lacan's sustained critique of object-relations theorists who have emphasized the role of the mother, and turned psychoanalysis into what Adam Phillips has called 'emotional nurturance'. However, it is the *symbolic* father (not necessarily the real father) who intervenes, in his *position* or *function* within a structure. His role is crucial in the formation of the symbolic. Ultimately, his function is derived from the *dead* father of the 'primal horde' who has been murdered by his own sons (Freud 1912-13), and accounts for the fact that the Law is dead. The symbolic is impregnated with the death of the father.

Chapter 5

1. Clearly this formulation of the death drive, contingent only upon environmental failure, makes its emergence wholly pathological.

2. This is not a reductionist argument, i.e. that the death drive causes these conflagrations. This would be too simplistic and banal a conclusion. It is far more complex. It has to do with the *effect* of the largely unacknowledged precariousness of human subjectivity. The death drive is our metaphor that registers both the catastrophic excitement and enclosure of this real of suffering. More of this in chapter seven.

3. The only exception to this rule, that isolated cells die, is the individual blastomere, the first cells generated by the fertilized egg. Clearly these cells must survive without external signalling.

4. At the level of cellular and biochemical processes, it is a biological truism to say that all organisms are similar in spite of great *external* diversity.

5. The p53 gene, so-called because it codes for a protein that has a molecular weight of 53,000 atomic mass units.

6. It would be stretching the analogy too far perhaps to suggest that this accidental finding of cell biology underpins at a cellular level the accidental 'finding' by psychoanalysis of the death drive on the level of the individual human subject.

7. This is too large and important an area of cultural theory to be developed here. The reader is referred to Frosh (1991), Kennard and Small (1997), Kristeva (1993), Postman (1995), Weatherill (1994, 1995).

Chapter 6

1. We could speculate about how adolescents initiate themselves into the meaning of life, death and sexuality: drug addiction; crime; peer groups and gangs; anorexia; sport; new religions; excesses of all kinds. Adolescence as a new and modern social 'invention' acts as a spreading out of the transition from childhood to adulthood, as if it might smooth the path. In reality, it increases the pain, as there is now no explicit public marking of this rite of passage to signify the loss (the death) of the innocence and safety of childhood.

2. The use of the word 'unconscious' in this chapter refers to a descriptive unconscious, not the unconscious as outlined by Freud (1900). This is the unconscious that is also unrepressed. This is not an unconscious that Lacan would recognize or believe to be relevant to psychoanalysis.

3. To a greater or lesser degree, the displacement of the ego is an objective of many different psychotherapies. Not so for the later Freud, as he wanted the ego to reach down into the id, in his famous phrase: '*Wo es war, soll Ich werden*' (where Id was, there shall Ego be)(Freud 1933a, p. 80) Lacan, as we have seen, favoured the enigmatic split subject, and reverses the emphasis in Freud's statement, by stressing the word *soll*. *There*, in the unconscious is where the ego should be, now *subject* to the unconscious. For Jung, the ego must be enlarged in relation to the shadow which is to be recognized and integrated. Jungians envisage an ego-Self axis, where, 'the ego stands to the self as the moved to the mover, or as object to subject.' (CW 11, para. 39) For Lacan, as we have seen, the subject all but disappears in the signifying chain. Whereas for Jung, the Self, far from being split and fading, is the *ordering* principle of the whole personality.

4. The gamble here is that the Other is God, ultimately guaranteeing meaning,

admittedly at a remote point. Lacanians, on the other hand, make it clear that the Other is *not* God. Post-castration, the subject discovers that the Other lacks, there is *no* transcendental meaning, *no* meaning beyond meaning. The Lacanian position is atheistic, while appearing oracular, timeless, ahistorical.

5. A very broad generalization has been made here. What is being suggested is that a whole range of psychotherapies and counselling, including the British tradition in psychoanalysis at least, all subscribe, and this is perhaps the only common denominator amongst them all, to the notion of psychic *growth*.

Chapter 7

1. Marxist theory has it that capitalist economies do not produce things for their 'use value' directly, their natural value as it were, but for their 'exchange value' with other commodities. It is the cost of the labour that will determine their exchange value on the principle of a general equivalence of commodities.

2. The notion of growth in humanistic psychotherapies (set out in the previous chapter) is just one instance of this universal rationalizing process that emphasizes our humanity and absorbs inhumanity and death.

3. Here Baudrillard's symbolic exchange looks more and more like *jouissance*. It is therefore the inverse of the Lacanian symbolic which enjoins the subject to enjoy as little as possible. By contrast, *jouissance*, according to Leclaire, denotes the 'immediacy of access to that 'pure difference' which the erotic seeks to find at the extreme point where it borders on death, and sometimes even in the annulment of the border itself ... the assurance *of reversibility into the oscillating and cyclical economy of desire in the strict sense .'* (quoted in Macey, 1985, p. 204)

4. In keeping with Baudrillard's thesis so far, it will be clear that the reversible form secretly prevails over the dominant form. Hence the feminine prevails over the masculine, which is soluble in it. He comments: 'one think[s] of the innumerable rites for the exorcism of female powers which can be found throughout primitive societies (Bettelheim). To cast out women's power of fertility, to encircle and circumscribe that power, and eventually simulate and appropriate it, is the purpose of the couvades, the artificial invaginations, excoriations and scarrings - all the innumerable symbolic wounds (up to an including the initiation and institution of a new power: political power) for suppressing the females' incomparable "natural"advantage.' (1979, p. 101) If seduction involves something of the secret return of the excluded, it must therefore involve some element of sacrifice in return, as it were, the risk of violence and death for the seduced.

5. The 'chora' is a matrix-like space coming from the mother that is nourishing and unnameable, that Kristeva takes from Plato's *Timaeus*. For Kristeva, the chora is the receptacle of narcissism. She says: 'Let us enter for a moment, into that Freudian aporia called primal repression. Curious primacy, where what is repressed cannot really be held down, and where what represses always already

borrows its strength and authority from what is apparently very secondary: language. Let us therefore not speak of primacy but of the instability of the symbolic function in its most significant aspect - the prohibition placed on the maternal body (as defence against autoerotism and incest taboo).' (1980, pp. 13-14) Kristeva links the chora with the narcissistic crisis of the subject and his abjection, that is, 'the violence of mourning for an 'object' that has always already been lost... [taking] the ego back to its source on the abominable limits from which, in order to be, the ego has broken away.' (ibid. p. 15)

6. More recently psychotherapists across Europe have been organising themselves professionally, creating trainings and professional standards. While appearing to be impeccably productive, this process has a seductive effect, luring more and more people into the artificial culture of trainings and therapy. One of the reasons for the recent professionalization of psychotherapy, one suspects, has been the felt need to close down this seductive and chaotic dispersal of not just psychoanalysis, but all the adaptively radiating and explosive forms of psychotherapy and counselling on offer. There is, on the one hand, a great move towards reconciliation and the minimization of differences within psychotherapy for political purposes, but also, on the other, a desire to situate psychotherapy as a productive credible force over and against seductive diffusion and the death drive. Properly licensed professional practitioners will minimize risks to patients (now called 'clients'), and to establish 'boundaries' on all fronts - between therapist and client, between psychotherapy and other professions, and most importantly between psychotherapy and the real - all to make things clear, accountable and democratic.

BIBLIOGRAPHY

Abraham, K. [1924](1988), 'The influence of oral erotism on character-formation', in *Selected Papers on Psychoanalysis,* pp. 393-406, London: Hogarth.
Anouilh, J. (1954), *Antigone,* (ed.) Landers, W., London: Harrop.
Balint, M. 1952), *Primary Love and Psycho-analytic Technique,* London: Tavistock.
Balint, M. (1968), *The Basic Fault,* London: Tavistock.
Baudrillard, J. (1976)[1993], *Symbolic Exchange and Death,* Paris: Editions Gallimard, Trans. Hamilton Grant, I., London: Sage.
Baudrillard, J. (1979)[1990], *Seduction,* Paris: Editions Galilee, Trans. Singer, B., London: Culture Texts.
Baudrillard, J. (1983), *Fatal Strategies,* Paris: Editions Grasset, Trans. Beitchman, P. and Niesluchowski, W., London: Semiotexte/Pluto Press.
Baudrillard (1980-1985)[1990], *Cool Memories,* Paris: Editions Galilee, Trans. Turner, C., London: Verso.
Baudrillard, J. (1990)[1993], *The Transparency of Evil,* Paris: Editions Galilee, London, Trans. Benedict. J., London: Verso.
Baudrillard, J. (1992)[1994], *The Illusion of the End,* Paris: Editions Galilee, Trans. Turner, C., London: Polity Press.
Bion, F. (ed.) (1992), *W.R. Bion Cogitations,* London: Karnac.
Bion, W. (1967) [1984], *Second Thoughts: Selected Papers on Psycho-Analysis,* London: Heinemann, reprinted 1984 London: Karnac.
Bion, W. (1953)[1967], 'Notes on the theory of schizophrenia', pp. 23-35, in *Second Thoughts: Selected Papers on Psycho-Analysis,* London: Heinemann, reprinted 1984 London: Karnac.
Bion, W. (1956)[1967], 'Development of schizophrenic thought', pp. 36-42, in *Second Thoughts: Selected Papers on Psycho-Analysis,* London: Heinemann, reprinted 1984 London: Karnac.
Bion, W. (1957a)[1967], 'Differentiation of the psychotic from the non-psychotic personalities', pp. 43-64, in *Second Thoughts: Selected Papers on Psycho-Analysis,* London: Heinemann, reprinted 1984 London: Karnac.
Bion, W. (1957b)[1967], 'On Arrogance', pp. 86-92, in *Second Thoughts: Selected Papers on Psycho-Analysis,* London: Heinemann, reprinted 1984 London: Karnac.
Bion, W. (1958)[1967], 'On Hallucination', pp. 65-85, in *Second Thoughts: Selected Papers on Psycho-Analysis,* London: Heinemann, reprinted 1984 London: Karnac.

Bion. W. (1959)[1967], 'Attacks on Linking', pp. 93-109, in *Second Thoughts: Selected Papers on Psycho-Analysis*, London: Heinemann, reprinted 1984 London: Karnac.

Bion, W. (1962a), *Learning from Experience*, London: Heinemann, reprinted 1984 London: Karnac.

Bion, W. (1962b), 'A Theory of Thinking', pp. 110-19, in *Second Thoughts: Selected Papers on Psycho-Analysis*, London: Heinemann, reprinted 1984 London: Karnac.

Bion, W. (1963), *Elements of Psychoanalysis*, London: Heinemann, reprinted 1984 London: Karnac.

Bion, W. (1965), *Transformations*, London: Heinemann, reprinted 1984 London: Karnac.

Bion, W. (1970), *Attention and Interpretation*, London: Tavistock, reprinted 1984 London: Karnac.

Black, D. (1993), 'What sort of a thing is a religion? A view from object-relations theory', Int. J. Psycho.-Anal. 74, pp. 613-624.

Bleandonu, G. (1994), *Wilfred Bion his life and his works 1897-1979*, Trans. Pajaczkowska, C., London: Free Association Books.

Blomfield, H. (1987), 'Human destructiveness: an essay on instinct, foetal existence and infancy', Int. Rev. Psycho-Anal. 14, pp. 21-32.

Borch-Jacobsen, M. (1991), *Lacan The Absolute Master*, California: Stanford University Press. Trans. Brick, D.

Bollas, C. (1987), *The Shadow of the Object*, London: Free Association Books.

Bowie, M. (1991), *Lacan*, London: Fontana Press.

Chasseguet-Smirgel, J. (1985), 'Perversion and the Law' in *Creativity and Perversion*, London: Free Association Books.

Coltart, N. (1986), 'Slouching towards Bethlehem... or thinking the unthinkable in psychoanalysis in Kohon G. (ed.) *The British School of Psychoanalysis - The Independent Tradition*, London: Free Association Books.

Conrad, J. (1983), *Heart of Darkness*, introduction by Paul O'Prey, London: Penguin.

Cuddon, J. (1982), *A Dictionary of Literary Terms and Literary Theory*, London: Deutsch.

Czermak, M. (1977)[1994], 'The onset of psychosis', in Schneiderman, S.(ed.) *How Lacan's Ideas are used in Clinical Practice* New Jersey: Aronson.

Eco, U. (1973)[1990], *Travels in Hyperreality*, Gruppo Editoriale Fabbri-Bompani, Sonzono, Etas. S.p.A. Picador, , Trans. Weaver, W. New York: Harcourt Brace.

Eco, U. (1980)[1983], *The Name of the Rose*, Gruppo Editoriale Fabbri-Bompani, Sonzono, Etas. S.p.A. Picador, Trans. Weaver, W., New York: Harcourt Brace.

Eigen, M. (1985), 'Towards Bion's starting point: between catastrophe and faith'. Int. J. Psycho-Anal. 66, pp. 321-32.

Eliade, M. (1957)[1968], *Myths, Dreams and Mysteries*, Trans. Mairet, P., Harvill Press, 1960. London: Fontana.

Eliot, T. S. (1963), *Collected Poems 1909-1963*, London: Faber and Faber.

Fisher, D. (1991), *Cultural Theory and Psychoanalytic Tradition*, New Brunswick and London: Transaction Publishers.

Freud, S. (1891), *On Aphasia, A Critical Study*, New York: International University Press.

Freud, S. (1893-5), *Studies on Hysteria*, S.E. Vol. II, London: Hogarth.

Freud, S. (1894), 'The Neuro-Psychoses of Defence', S.E. Vol. III, London: Hogarth.

Freud, S. (1895), 'The Project for a Scientific Psychology' S.E. Vol. I, London: Hogarth.

Freud, S. (1905a), *Jokes and their Relation to the Unconscious*. S.E. Vol. VIII, London: Hogarth.

Freud, S. (1905b), 'Fragment of an Analysis of a Case of Hysteria' S.E. Vol. VII, London: Hogarth.

Freud, S. (1910), 'Five Lectures on Psycho-Analysis' S.E. Vol. XI, London: Hogarth.

Freud, S. (1911a), 'Psycho-Analytic Notes on an Autobiographical Account of a Case of Paranoia', S.E. VII, London: Hogarth.

Freud, S. (1911b), 'Formulations on the Two Principles of Mental functioning', S. E. Vol. VIII, London: Hogarth.

Freud, S. (1914a), 'On Narcissism: an Introduction', S.E. Vol. XIV, London: Hogarth.

Freud, S. (1914b), 'Remembering, Repeating and Working-through (Further Recommendations on the Technique of Psycho-Analysis)', S.E. Vol. VII, London: Hogarth.

Freud, S. (1915a), 'The Unconscious', S. E. Vol. XIV, London: Hogarth.

Freud, S. (1915b), 'Instincts and their Vicissitudes', S.E. Vol. XIV, London: Hogarth.

Freud, S. (1915c), 'On Repression', S.E. Vol. XIV, London: Hogarth.

Freud, S. (1916), 'Some Character Types met with in Psycho-analytic work', S.E. Vol. XIV, London: Hogarth.

Freud, S. (1916-7), *Introductory Lectures on Psycho-Analysis*, S.E. Vol. XV, London: Hogarth.

Freud, S. (1920), 'Beyond the Pleasure Principle', S.E. Vol. XVIII, London: Hogarth.
Freud, S. (1923), 'The Ego and The Id', S.E. Vol. XIX, London: Hogarth.
Freud, S. (1924a), 'The Loss of Reality in Neurosis and Psychosis', S.E. Vol. XIX, London: Hogarth.
Freud, S. (1924b), 'The Economic Problem of Masochism', S.E. Vol. XIX, London: Hogarth.
Freud, S. (1925), 'Negation', S.E. Vol. XIX, London: Hogarth.
Freud, S. (1926 [1925]), 'Inhibitions, Symptoms and Anxiety', S.E. Vol. XX, London: Hogarth.
Freud, S. (1927), 'The Future of an Illusion' S.E. Vol. XXI, London: Hogarth.
Freud, S. (1930), 'Civilization and its Discontents', S.E. Vol. XXI, London: Hogarth.
Freud, S. (1933a), *The New Introductory Lectures,* S.E. Vol. XXII, London: Hogarth.
Freud, S. (1933b), 'Why War?', S.E. Vol. XXII, London: Hogarth.
Freud, S. (1937), 'Analysis Terminable and Interminable', S.E. Vol. XXIII, London: Hogarth.
Freud, S. (1940 [1938]), 'An Outline of Psycho-Analysis', S.E. Vol. XXIII, London: Hogarth.
Freud, S., (1953-73), *The Standard Edition of the Complete Psychological Works of Sigmund Freud,* 24 Vols. London: Hogarth.
Frankl, V. (1946), *Man's Search for Meaning,* London: Hodder and Stoughton.
Fromm, E. (1974), *The Anatomy of Human Destructiveness,* London: Penguin.
Frosh, S. (1991), *Identity Crisis: Modernity, Psychoanalysis and the Self,* London: Macmillan.
Frost, R. (1968) 'Home Burial' pp/100-1 in *Voices* ed. Summerfield G. London: Penguin.
Gane, M. (ed.) (1993), *Baudrillard Live: Selected Interviews,* London: Routledge.
Gordon, R. (1978), *Dying and Creating: a Search for Meaning,* London: Society of Analytical Psychology.
Gleik, J. (1987), *Chaos,* London: Sphere Books.
Golan. G, Rosenheim. E, Jaffe. Y (1988), 'Humour in Psychotherapy', Brit. J. Psychotherapy, Vol 4, No. 4, pp 393-400.
Grosskurth, P. (1985), *Melanie Klein,* London: Maresfield Library.
Grotstein, J. (1979)[1981][1983], 'Who is the Dreamer Who Dreams the Dream and Who is the Dreamer Who Understands It?',

Contemporary Psycho-Analysis, 15: 110-169. Revised in Grotstein J., ed. *Do I Dare Disturb the Universe?* Beverly Hills: Caesura, reprinted London: Karnac.

Grotstein, J. (1992), 'Reflections on a Century of Freud: Some Paths Not Chosen'. Brit. J. Psychotherapy, Vol 9. No 2., pp. 181-187.

Guntrip, H. (1968), *Schizoid Phenomena, Object Relations and the Self,* London: Hogarth.

Happold, F. (1971), *Prayer and Meditation,* London: Penguin.

Heaney, S. (1988), *The Government of the Tongue,* London: Faber and Faber.

Hebdige, D. (1988), *Hiding in the Light,* London: Routledge.

Heimann, P. (1952), 'Notes on the Theory of the Life and Death Instincts', in Klein, M., Heimann, P., Isaacs, S. and Riviere, J., *Developments in Psycho-Analysis,* London: Hogarth.

Henry, M. (1985)[1993], *The Genealogy of Psychoanalysis,* Published as *Genealogie de la psychanalyse: Le commencement perdu,* Paris: Presses Universitaires de France. Trans. Brick, D., California: Stanford University Press.

Hinshelwood, R. (1989), *A Dictionary of Kleinian Thought,* London: Free Association Books.

Hinshelwood, R. (1994), *Clinical Klein,* London: Free Association Books.

Isaacs, S. (1948)[1952], 'On the Nature and Function of Phantasy', Int. J. Psycho-Analysis 29: 73-97; republished (in Klein, M., Heimann, P., and Riviere, J., *Developments in Psycho-Analysis,* London: Hogarth.

Jameson, F. (1991), *Postmodernism, or, the Cultural Logic of Late Capitalism,* London: Verso.

Jencks, C. (1991)[1992], *The Post-Modern Reader,* New York: St. Martin's Press, London: Academy Editions.

Jones, R. (1970), *The New Psychology of Dreaming,* London: Penguin.

Jung, C. (1960), 'Structure and Dynamics of the Psyche', Vol. 8, para. 797-800, in *The Collected Works of C.G. Jung,* London: Routledge.

Jung, C. (1958), Psychology and Religion: West and East, Vol. 11 para. 842, in *The Collected Works of C. G. Jung,* London: Routledge.

Jung, C. (1953), Two Essays on Analytical Psychology. Vol. 7 para 269, in *The Collected Works of C. G. Jung,* London: Routledge.

Kennard, D and Small, N. (1996), (eds.) *Living Together,* London: Quartet.

Klein, M. (1927)[1975], 'Symposium on child analysis', pp. 139-169, in *Love, Guilt and Reparation and Other Works 1921-45,* London: Hogarth.

Klein, M. (1928)[1975], 'Early stages of the Oedipus conflict', pp. 186-198, in *Love, Guilt and Reparation and Other Works 1921-45*, London: Hogarth.

Klein, M. (1929)[1975], 'Infantile anxiety-situations reflected in a work of art and in the creative impulse', pp. 210-218, in *Love, Guilt and Reparation and Other Works 1921-45*, London: Hogarth.

Klein, M. (1932)[1975], *The Psycho-Analysis of Children*, London: Hogarth.

Klein, M. (1933)[1975], 'The early development of conscience in the child', pp. 248-257. in *Love, Guilt and Reparation and Other Works 1921-45*, London: Hogarth.

Klein, M. (1935)[1975], 'A Contribution to the Psychogenesis of Manic-Depressive States', pp. 262-289, in *Love, Guilt and Reparation and Other Works 1921-45*, London: Hogarth.

Klein, M. (1937)[1975], 'Love Guilt and Reparation', pp. 306-343, in *Love, Guilt and Reparation and Other Works 1921-45*, London: Hogarth.

Klein, M. (1940)[1975], 'Mourning and its Relation to Manic-Depressive States', pp. 344-369, in *Love, Guilt and Reparation and Other Works 1921-45*, London: Hogarth.

Klein, M. (1945)[1975], 'The Oedipus complex in the light of early anxieties', pp. 370-419, in *Love, Guilt and Reparation and Other Works 1921-45*, London: Hogarth.

Klein, M. (1946)[1975], 'Notes on some Schizoid Mechanisms', pp. 1-24, in *Envy and Gratitude and other works 1921-1945*, London: Hogarth.

Klein, M. (1952)[1975], 'Some Theoretical Conclusions Regarding the Emotional Life of the Infant', pp. 61-93, in *Envy and Gratitude and other works 1921-1945*, London: Hogarth.

Klein, M. (1957)[1975], 'Envy and Gratitude', pp. 176-235, in *Envy and Gratitude and other works 1921-1945*, London: Hogarth.

Klein, M. (1958)[1975], 'On the development of mental functioning', pp. 236-246, in *Envy and Gratitude and other works 1921-1945*, London: Hogarth.

Klein, M. (1963)[1975], 'On the sense of loneliness', pp. 300-313, in *Envy and Gratitude and other works 1921-1945*, London: Hogarth.

Kohon, G. (ed.) (1986), *The British School of Psychoanalysis: The Independent Tradition*, London: Free Association Books.

Kristeva, J. (1980)[1982], *Powers of Horror*, Paris: Editions du Seuil, trans. Roudiez, L., New York: Columbia University Press.

Kristeva, J. (1993)[1995], *New Maladies of the Soul*, Paris: Librairie Artheme Fayard, trans. Guberman, R., New York: Columbia University Press.

Lacan, J. (1938), 'La famille: le complexe, facteur concret de la pathologie familiale et les complexes familiaux en pathologie' in *Encyclopédie Française*, Paris: Larousse, Vol. 8, pp. 3-16. Or Dublin, trans. Gallagher, C. School of Psychotherapy, St. Vincent's Hospital. (unpublished).

Lacan, J. (1948)[1977], 'Aggressivity in psychoanalysis', In *Ecrits: A Selection*, pp. 8-29, trans. Sheridan, A., London: Routledge.

Lacan, J. (1949)[1977], 'The Mirror Stage as Formative of the Function of the 'I' as revealed in Psychoanalytic Experience', in *Ecrits: A Selection*, pp. 1-7, trans. Sheridan, A., London: Routledge.

Lacan, J. (1953)[1968], *Speech and Language in Psychoanalysis*, trans. Wilden, A., with notes and commentary, Baltimore: John Hopkins University Press.

Lacan, J. (1953)[1977], 'Function and Field of Speech and Language in Psychoanalysis', pp. 30-113, in *Ecrits: A Selection*, trans. Sheridan, A., London: Routledge.

Lacan, J. (1953-54)[1988], *The Seminar of Jacques Lacan: Book 1, Freud's Papers on Technique*, trans. Forrester, J., New York: Norton.

Lacan, J. (1954-55)[1988], *The Seminar of Jacques Lacan: Book II, The Ego in Freud's Theory and in the Technique of Psychoanalysis*, trans. Tomaselli, S., Cambridge: Cambridge University Press.

Lacan, J. (1955-56), 'On a question preliminary to any possible treatment of psychosis', in *Ecrits: A Selection*, pp. 179-225, trans. Sheridan, A., London: Routledge.

Lacan, J. (1957-58), The Seminar of Jacques Lacan: Book V, 'Les formations de l'inconscient'. trans. Gallagher, C. (unpublished).

Lacan, J. (1958)[1977], 'The signification of the phallus', in *Ecrits: A Selection*, pp. 281-291, London: Routledge.

Lacan, J. (1959-60)[1986][1992], *The Ethics of Psychoanalysis, The Seminar of Jacques Lacan, Book VII*, Paris, Editions du Seuil, trans. Potter, D., London: Routledge

Lacan, J. (1960)[1977], 'The subversion of the subject and the dialectic of desire in the Freudian unconscious', in *Ecrits: A Selection*, pp. 292-325, trans. Sheridan, A., London: Routledge.

Lacan, J. (1962-3), *The Seminar of Jacques Lacan: On Anxiety Book X*, trans. Gallagher C. (unpublished).

Lacan, J. (1964)[1977], *The Seminar of Jacques Lacan: Book XI, The Four Fundamental Concepts of Psychoanalysis*, trans. Sheridan, A., London: Penguin.

Lacan, J. (1966)[1977], *Ecrits: A Selection* Paris: Editions du Seuil, trans. Sheridan, A., London: Routledge.

Lacan, J. (1974)[1990], *Television,* Paris: Seuil, trans. Hollier, D., Krauss, R., and Michelson, A., London: Norton.

Laplanche, J. (1981), 'A metapsychology put to the test of anxiety', Int. J. Psycho-Anal. 62, pp. 81-89.

Laplanche, J. (1987)[1989], *New Foundations for Psychoanalysis,* Paris: Presses Universitaires de France, trans. Macey, D., Oxford: Blackwell.

Laplanche, J. and Pontalis, J-B. (1973), *The Language of Psychoanalysis,* London: Hogarth.

Lemaire, A. (1970)[1977], *Jacques Lacan,* Belgium: Charles Denart. trans. Macey, D., London: Routledge & Kegan Paul.

Lewin, B. (1950), *The Psychoanalysis of Elation,* New York: Norton.

Levi, P. (1958)[1987], *If This is a Man: The Truce,* Giulio Einaudi editore S.p.A., trans. Woolf, S., London: Vintage.

Little, M. (1981)[1986], 'On basic unity (primary total undifferentiatedness)', pp.136-153, in Kohon, G., *The British School of Psychoanalysis: The Independent Tradition,* London: Free Association Books.

Macey, D. (1988), *Lacan in Contexts,* London: Verso.

McDougall, J. (1989), *Theatres of the Body: A Psychoanalytical Approach to Psychosomatic Illness,* London: Free Association Books.

Matte-Blanco, I. (1975), *The Unconscious as Infinite Sets: An Essay in Bi-Logic,* London: Duckworth.

McEwan, I. (1992), *Black Dogs* London: Jonathan Cape.

Malcolm, J. (1982), *Psychoanalysis: the Impossible Profession,* London: MacMillan.

May, R. (1975), *The Courage to Create,* London: Collins.

Meltzer, D.(1978), *The Kleinian Development,* London: Clunie Press.

Milner, M. (1952), 'The role of illusion in symbol formation', in *New Directions in Psycho-Analysis,* Klein, M., Heimann P. and Money-Kyrle, R., eds., London: Tavistock, also in Milner (1987) *The Suppressed Madness of Sane Men,* London: Routledge.

Mitchell, J. (1984), 'The question of femininity and the theory of psychoanalysis' in Kohon, G., *The British School of Psychoanalysis: The Independent Tradition,* London: Free Association Books.

Mitchell, J. and Rose, J. (eds.) (1982), *Feminine Sexuality*, London: Macmillan.
Niederland, W. (1984), *The Schreber Case: psychoanalytic profile of a paranoid personality*, New York: Analytic Press.
Nietzsche, F. (1872)[1993], *The Birth of Tragedy*, (ed. Tanner, M.) London: Penguin.
Nietzsche, F. (1883)[1961], *Thus Spake Zarathustra*, trans. Hollingdale, R., London: Penguin.
Phillips, A. (1988), *Winnicott*, London: Fontana.
Phillips, A. (1993), *On Kissing, Tickling and Being Bored*, London: Faber and Faber.
Phillips, A. (1994), *On Flirtation*, London: Faber and Faber.
Plant, S. (1993), 'Baudrillard's woman: the Eve of seduction', pp. 88-106, in *Forget Baudrillard*, (eds.) Rojek, C. and Turner, B., London: Routledge.
Poster, M. (1988), *Jean Baudrillard: Selected Writings*, London: Polity.
Racker, H. (1968), *Transference and Countertransference*, London: Maresfield,
Ragland-Sullivan, E. and Bracher, M. (eds.) (1991), *Lacan and the Subject of Language*, London: Routledge.
Rayner, E. (1991), *The Independent Mind in British Psychoanalysis*, London: Free Association Books.
Rayner, E. (1995), *Unconscious Logic* London: Routledge.
Reiff, P. (1966), *The Triumph of the Therapeutic*, London: Chatto.
Richardson, W. (1994), 'The third generation of desire'. *The Letter*, Summer 1994, pp. 117-135.
Rojek, C. and Turner, B. (eds.) (1993), *Forget Baudrillard*, London: Routledge.
Rosenfeld, H. (1971), 'A Clinical Approach to the Psychoanalytic Theory of the Life and Death Instincts: an Investigation into the Aggressive Aspects of Narcissism', Int. J. Psycho-Anal. 52, pp. 169-178.
Rosenfeld, H., (1987), *Impasse and Interpretation*, London: Routledge.
Roustang, F. (1986)[1990], *The Lacanian Delusion*, Paris: Editions de Minuit, trans. Sims, G., Oxford: Oxford University Press.
Rycroft, C. (1968), *A Critical Dictionary of Psychoanalysis*, London: Penguin.
Samuels, A., Shorter, B. and Plant, F. (1986), *A Critical Dictionary of Jungian Analysis*, London: Routledge.
Schneiderman, S. (1980), *Returning to Freud: Clinical Psychoanalysis in the School of Lacan*, New Haven and London: Yale University Press.

Segal, H. (1973), *Introduction to the Work of Melanie Klein*, London: Hogarth.
Smith, J. (1991), *Arguing With Lacan*, New Haven and London: Yale University Press.
Sophocles [1947], *The Theban Plays* trans. Watling, E. London: Penguin.
Strachey, J. (1934), 'The nature of the therapeutic action of psychoanalysis'. Int. J. Psycho-Anal. 15, pp. 127-159.
Steiner, G. (1989), *Real Presences*, London: Faber and Faber.
Storr, A. (1968), *Human Aggression*, London: Penguin.
Summerfield, G. ed. (1968), *Voices*, London: Penguin.
Symington, N. (1983), 'The analyst's act of freedom as agent of therapeutic change', in Kohon, G., *The British School of Psychoanalysis: The Independent Tradition*, London: Free Association Books.
Tillich, P. (1964), *Theology of Culture*, Oxford: Oxford University Press.
Tillich, P. (1995), *Morality and Beyond (Library of Theological Ethics)*, London: Westminster.
Vaillant, G. (1970), 'Theoretical hierarchy of ego adaptive mechanisms'. Arch. Gen. Psychiat, Vol. 24. pp. 107-111.
Weatherill, R. (1991), 'The psychical realities of modern culture'. Brit. Journ. Psychotherapy, Vol 7. No. 3, pp. 268-274.
Weatherill, R. (1992), 'Are the Kleinians really psychoanalysts at all?' in The Journal of the Irish Forum for Psychoanalytic Psychotherapy, Vol. 2, No. 2, 1-12.
Weatherill, R. (1994), *Cultural Collapse*, London: Free Association Books.
Weatherill, R. (1995), 'Violence and Privacy. What if the container fails?' Free Associations. Vol. 5, Part 2, No. 34.
Weatherill, R. (1996), 'Smooth operators', pp. 50-66, in *Living Together*, (eds.) Kennard D. and Small N., London: Quartet.
Whitmont, E. (1969), *The Symbolic Quest: Basic Concepts of Analytical Psychology*, New Jersey: Princeton University Press.
Williams, H. (1975), *Becoming What I Am*, London: Darton, Longman and Todd.
Winnicott, D. (1945)[1975], 'Primitive emotional development', pp. 145-156, in *Through Paediatrics to Psychoanalysis*, London: Hogarth.
Winnicott, D. (1947)[1975], 'Hate in the countertransference', pp. 194-203, in *Through Paediatrics to Psychoanalysis*, London: Hogarth.
Winnicott, D. (1951)[1975], Transitional Objects and Transitional Phenomena, pp. 229-242, in *Through Paediatrics to Psychoanalysis*, London: Hogarth.

Winnicott, D. (1956)[1975], 'The antisocial tendency', pp. 306-315, in *Through Paediatrics to Psychoanalysis*, London: Hogarth.

Winnicott, D. (1958)[1975], *Through Paediatrics to Psychoanalysis*, London: Hogarth.

Winnicott, D. (1958)[1965a], 'The capacity to be alone', pp. 29-36, *The Maturational Processes and the Facilitating Environment*, London: Hogarth.

Winnicott, D. (1958)[1965a], 'Psychoanalysis and the Sense of Guilt', pp. 15-28, in *The Maturational Processes and the Facilitating Environment*, London: Hogarth.

Winnicott, D. (1959-64)[1965a], 'Classification: Is there a psycho-analytic contribution to psychiatric classification', pp. 124-139, in *The Maturational Processes and the Facilitating Environment*, London: Hogarth.

Winnicott, D. (1963a)[1965a], 'The Development of the Capacity for Concern', pp. 73-82, in *The Maturational Processes and the Facilitating Environment*, London: Hogarth.

Winnicott, D.(1963b)[1965a], 'Communicating and not Communicating Leading to a Study of Certain Opposites', pp. 179-192, in *The Maturational Processes and the Facilitating Environment*, London: Hogarth.

Winnicott, D. (1964), *The Child, the Family and the Outside World*, London: Penguin.

Winnicott, D. (1965), *The Family and Individual Development*, London: Tavistock.

Winnicott, D. (1965a), *The Maturational Processes and the Facilitating Environment*, London: Hogarth.

Winnicott, D. (1967), 'The mirror-role of mother and family in child development', pp. 111-118, in *Playing and Reality*, London: Tavistock.

Winnicott, D. (1968), 'Contemporary Concepts of Adolescent Development and their Implications for Higher Education', pp. 138-150, in *Playing and Reality*, London: Tavistock.

Winnicott, D. (1969), 'The Use of an Object and Relating through Identifications', pp. 86-94, in *Playing and Reality*, London: Tavistock.

Winnicott, D. (1971a), *Playing and Reality*, London: Tavistock.

Winnicott, D. (1971b), *Therapeutic Consultations in Child Psychiatry*, London: Hogarth.

Winnicott, D. (1986), *Home is where we start from*, London: Penguin.

Winnicott, D. (1988), *Human Nature*, London: Free Association Books.

Young, R (1989), 'Post-Modernism and the subject', *Free Associations*, 16, pp. 81-96.

Zetzel, E. (1968)[1987], 'The So-Called Good Hysteric', pp. 229-245, in *The Capacity for Emotional Growth*, London: Maresfield.

Zizek, S. (1992), *Enjoy Your Symptom*, London: Routledge.

Index

Abraham, Karl 32, 50
addiction 74, 85, 92-3
adolescents 121-2, 194
affects 188, 192
    affective processes 47, 65
affective signals 68-9
    affectivity in excess 187, 188
    outside representation 183
    primary 183
agglomerations 61, 62-3
aggression 46, 78
    excessive 25
    external sources 24, 26-7
    and injustice 27
    life-promoting 4
    not biological in Lacan 75
    reactive 24-6
    as sign of life 24, 26
    see also cruelty; death drive; destructiveness; sadism; violence
alienation 78, 79, 85, 124-7, 191
alpha elements 55-6
alpha-function process 55-6, 100-1, 125
    failure 60
analysis/analyst *see* psychoanalysis; psychoanalyst
anarchy
    beyond the law 94-5
annihilation anxiety 29
anorexics 74, 84
Anouilh, Jean 95-6
anticathexis 18-19, 44
Antigone 94-5, 193
antisocial tendency 24
anxiety 10, 16
    attacks 9
    castration 16-17, 47, 97
    catastrophic 190
    Lacan 90, 93
    nightmare 90
    persecutory 25, 107
    primary 44
    primordial 29, 30-1
    projected 54
    seat of 16
    unthinkable 26
    in writing 136-7
apoptosis 5, 112-15, 117
Aristotle 134
arrogance 66

asexuality
    and immortality 83, 116
    and sameness 21-2
astronomy 72, 145-6
attention 83-4
Auden, W. H. 135
Augustine, St. Confessions 75

baby *see* infant
Balint, Michael 25, 128, 178
baptism 152
bar, between signifier and signified 80-1, 192
Bataille, Georges 149, 155
Baudrillard, Jean 149-74
    life 149
    biology 4, 5,103-17
    catastrophe, play of 172-4
    the code 157-8
    conception of the symbolic 150-3
    disappearance of psychoanalysis 167-72
    on evil 173
    on fashion 158, 163-4
    the hyper-real 170-1
    and inhumanity of things 151, 172
    on intellectuals 149
    on Lacan 171
    and the obscene 164-5, 171
    orders of artifice or simulacra 156-9
    phallic exchange standard 160-3
    on the real 185
    reversibility 150-6
    seduction 159, 164-7, 168-71
    style 172
    'the unconscious your capital'170
    Fatal Strategies 165, 170
    Seduction 156, 159, 165-6, 170, 172-3, 195
    Symbolic Exchange and Death 151,154, 155, 158
beta-elements (raw sense data) 56, 60-2, 68, 89, 129
Bion, Wilfred 53-72
    life 53
    alpha function 55-6, 60
    beta elements/bizarre objects 56, 60-3, 68, 89, 129
    caesura of birth 71
    catastrophe 68-9
    container-contained 53-7
    depressive position 68

elaborator of Klein 53, 70-1
epistemology 53, 188-9
faith 67-9, 190
hallucination 62-4
morality 190
paranoid-schizoid position 68
probing 'O' 65-7
process of symbolisation 56
projective identification 54, 57-60
psychotic process and death drive 58, 64
reverie 53-7
schizophrenia 53, 58-62
super-ego 190
theory of thinking 55-7, 188-9
'without memory or desire' injunction 65, 123
Attention and Interpretation 65, 66, 123
birth
  afterbirth 91
  for infants 71, 101
  for mother 92
  still-births 92
  trauma 107-8
  see also rebirth
bizarre objects 60-3
Black, David
  religion as a good object 190
Bléandonu, Gérard 71, 188, 189
Blomfield, H. 107-8
Bollas, Christopher 175
Borch-Jacobsen, Mikkel 161, 162, 167-8
Bowie, Malcolm 78, 85-6, 160
Bowlby, John 25
Brahman 143
breast
  for infants 31, 33-7
  absence 56
  bad 34, 37
  as container 55-6, 66
  envy of 36-8, 41
  good 34, 38, 55
  as more 44-5
  sibling rivalry over 75
  as superabundance 44-5
  weaning 17
Brierley, Marjorie 188
British Independent Tradition 3, 24, 25-6, 128, 181, 188
Buber, Martin 190

cancer 112-16
castration
  fashions 163-4
  and seduction 171
  symbolic 83, 100, 161, 192
castration anxiety 16-17, 47, 97
  and envy 61
  and symbolic chain 92
  and women 162
catastrophe
  free-floating 132
  permanent 160, 190
  play of 172-4
  signalling 68-9
cathexis
  anticathexis 18-19, 44
  binding 10
  counter-cathexis 83
  narcissistic 10
  quiescent 10
  sexual 88
cells 5, 105
  programmed death 112-15, 117-18, 194
  unicellular organisms 21
  protista 21-2, 116, 118
chaos theory 108-9
Chasseguet-Smirgel, Janine 26, 110
Chekhov, Anton 147
child
  criminal tendencies 32
  deprivation 24-5
  emotional world 29-33
  play 8-9, 75
  primordial anxiety 29, 30-1
  unwanted 80
  see also infant
chora 163, 195
church 142
  replaced by clinic 28
  religion
civilization
  saved by repression 12
clinical imperatives 6
closure
  pressure for 108-11, 117
Coltart, Nina 177
concern
  stage of 43
confusion 39
Conrad, Joseph 2, 138
constancy
  principle of 19-20
container
  false 65
  /contained relationship 54-5, 65-7
  destroyed 65-6

in prayer 139-40
Copernicus, Nicolas 1, 81
counterfeit order 157
creativity 61, 119, 120, 127, 128-9
    writing 135-8
cruelty 25-7, 61
    and helplessness 110, 117
    in nature 107
    see also aggression; sadism
Czermak, M. 93, 99-100

damaged object 39-40, 42
Darwin, Charles 1, 21, 104, 146
de Chardin, Teilhard 104
de Sade, Marquis 94
de Saussure, Ferdinand 2
death
    elimination of 153
    enjoyment 119-21, 126
    as excess 84-5, 155
    exorcism 5
    extradition 151
    fear of analagous to castration 17
    as initiation 121-4, 151-2
    in language 86
    no unconscious fear of 16
    present in speech 86
    and rebirth in religion and mythology 119-21
    required for life 104-5, 111, 117
    second 94
    and sex 21-2
    as social relation 151-2
    see also suicide
death drive (instinct)
    as autonomous principle 155
    autonomy 174
    and biological determinism 154-5
    clinically 4, 13-16
    'pure culture of' 95, 107
    deflection outwards 11-12, 26-7
    and erogenous zones 23
    and evil 27-8
    as excessive growth 25, 116
    as extreme of sexuality 17
    as final freedom 94
    as innate 27
    as irreducible datum 20
    location 16-17
    masquerading as life 184
    as mythology 25
    origin 73
    psychoanalyst's apprehension of

    in countertransference 177
    as silent 22, 124, 184-5
    and social conservatism 27
    term 6, 23
    and zero state 15
    see also aggression; cruelty; destructiveness; violence
death drive theory 1-6
    in Baudrillard 151-6
    as biological concept 4, 21-2
    in Bion 58, 64
    critique of 22-8
    in Freud 13-23, 25- 8
    Freud's reasons for developing 8-13
    in Klein 15, 31, 53
    in Lacan 17, 20, 84-6, 94-5
    as myth of our culture 154
    and pessimism 27
    and prayer 140-1
    and radical environmental failure 24-6, 28, 106- 7, 109
de-differentiation (self/object) 128-9
denial
    of envy 40
    manic 84
    of psychic reality 42
depressive position 41-5
    and becoming human 43-4
    Ps<—>D interaction 68, 83
    realisation 62
    and Winnicott 43
    and working through of 188
    see also melancholia
deprivation 24-5, 26-7, 169
desire 45, 87
    beyondness 44
    cause 91-5
    completion 84-5
    in dreams 130
    feminine 162
    Lacan 179
    and laughter 134
    of the mother 164
    of the Other 90-1
    and phallus 159-61
destiny, dark power of 15
destructive regression 124, 126
destructiveness 58
    disrupts thinking 58-60
    and extreme cruelty 25
    innate and reactive 23-8
    ontological status 23-4
    responsibility for 26

see also aggression; death drive
devaluation 39-40
disavowal 96
displacement 39
Dostoevsky, Feodor 2, 149
dreaming/dreams 119
    capacity for 68
    Freud on 7, 130, 170
    Jung's 120-1
    nightmares 9, 90, 129
    psychotic 109
    and the real 32
    regression in 130-2
    'while awake' 68
drives
    determination 92, 102
    or instincts? 187
    lured to capitulation 144, 184
    see also instinct theory
drugs 129
    addiction 74, 85, 92-3

Ecclesiastes 145, 156
Eckhart, Johannes 190
Eco, Umberto 34, 167
ecstatic void 3, 84
ego
    affects 188
    autonomy 125-6, (and illusion of 77)
    displacement in psychotherapy 126
    dissociation 119-20, 194
    doomed 77-9
    and early misunderstanding of the world 34
    as fiction 77, 124
    formation of 187
    in *Lacan* 77-9, 194
    primordial anxiety 30-1
    psychosis 97
    reaches down to id 30, 194
    seat of anxiety 16
    and self in *Jung* 125, 194
    splitting 31-3
ego instinct 7-8
Eigen, Michael 69
Einstein, Albert 2, 3
Eliade, Mercea 122
Eliot, T.S. 2, 138
Empedocles 94-5
entropy 103-17
environmental failure 24-6, 28, 106
envy
    of the breast 36-8, 41, 44-5

and castration 61
cause for excessive splitting 37, 39
constitutionally based 36, 38
defences against 39-41
and degree of malignancy 37
dispersal 39
vs. greed 36
and paranoid violence 37-8
penis 15
and perfection 44-5
primary 36-9, 41
and severe mental disorders 38
spoils the good object 36-9, 44-5
Eros (life instinct) 2, 13, 124-5
    aim of 15-16, 23
    and repression 12
    strengthened by emotional ties 4
eroticism 80
erotomania 93
ethics 94
    and cure 143-4, 192-3
Evans, Dylan 192
evil 2, 4, 27-8, 173-4
evolution 1, 4, 104, 117, 118
    diversity 21-2
exchange
    gift 150, 151, 191
    phallic 163
    symbolic 5, 150-3, 156
exorcism
    of aggression 170
    of death 5
    of female powers 193, 195

Fairbairn, Ronald 25
faith 67-9, 190
falsity 65
families, dysfunctional 190
fashion 158, 163-4
father 193
    law of 85
    murdered 193
    paternal metaphor (Name-of-the-Father) 98-101, 102, 152-3
    phallus 161
    see also Oedipus complex
female body 163-4
femininity 159, 161, 162
    repudiation of 169
Ferenczi, Sándor 88
fetishism 163-4, 169
feudal system 156-7
fight or flight response 29, 105-6, 117

fixation 18
foreclosure 96-101, 102, 111
Forget Baudrillard 149
fort-da (game) 8, 75
Frankl, Victor 135
free association 131-2, 182, 191
   and prayer 140
freedom 180
   psychoanalytic act of 177
   terminal 94-6
   and the tragic 193
Freud, Anna 178, 193
Freud, Sigmund 7-28
   life events 12-13
   castration anxiety 15
   and death drive 11-13, 23, 26, 143, 183-4,
   (clinical manifestations 12, 13-16)
   dissolution of the Oedipus complex 15, 31-2, 73
   'Dora' (Freud's patient) 8
   dreams 7, 130
   ego reaches down to the id 194
   and *Einstein* 3
   Eros 13, 15-16, 20, 23, 154
   hate older than love 15
   hilflosigkeit 142
   homeostasis/principle of constancy 19, 22-3
   instinct theory 7-15
   Nirvana 15, 19-20, 22
   his obsession with death 13
   projection 26-7
   protista 21-2
   on psychosis 96-7
   regression 25
   religion 142-3
   repetition compulsion 8-9, 13, 20
   repression, primary 17-19
   and *Romain Rolland* 142-3
   seduction, infantile 168-9
   sex and death 21-2
   on thought 56, 60
   trauma 9, 17-19
   the unconscious 2, 16-18, 188
   the vesicle and (excessive) stimuli 9
   'Analysis terminable and interminable' 15
   Beyond the Pleasure Principle 9-10, 11, 12, 13, 21, 32, 87-8
   Civilization and its Discontents 13, 142-3
   'The economic problem of masochism' 14-15, 22-3

The Ego and the Id 14
'Five lectures on psychoanalysis' 18
Inhibitions, Symptoms and Anxiety 91
'Instincts and their vicissitudes' 15
Introductory Lectures on Psychoanalysis 1, 18
Jokes and their Relation to the Unconscious 133-4
'Negation' 97
'The Neuro-psychoses of Defence' 96-7
New Introductory Lectures 13, 31, 194
'On narcissism' 7
'On Repression' 18
Outline of Psychoanalysis 14, 20
'The Project for a Scientific Psychology' 61;
'Remembering, Repeating and Working Through' 8
Studies on Hysteria 17
'Why War?' 3, 22-8, 150, 184-5
Fromm, Erich 22, 110
Frosh, Stephen 167, 194
Frost, Robert 144-5
frustration 75
   and aggression 24
   tolerance of and thinking 56-7

games 172
   fort-da 8, 75
   see also play
Gane, M. 149, 158
genetic code 103-4, 113-16, 154, 158
gift exchange 150, 151, 191
Gleick, J. 108
God 143, 190
   as Other 195
   and prayer 140-1
   in the real 133
   see also religion
Golan G, Rosenheim E., and Jaffe, Y. 133
Gordon, Rosemary 120
greed 36, 40, 66
Grosskurth, Phyllis 49-50, 188
Grotstein, James 29, 130-1, 132, 139-40
growth
   cancerous 112-16
   of capital 153
   excessive 25, 116
   mental 71
   psychic 195
growth therapies, and ethics 143-4, 195
Grunberger, Béla 26
guilt

in children 32
  unconscious sense of 14-15
Guntrip, Harry 25

hallucination 62-4, 97
Happold, F. 139
Hartmann, Heinz 24
hate 15, 36, 37, 40
  by analyst 177-8
Heaney, Seamus 135
Hegel, G. W. F. 191
Heimann, Paula 25
Heisenberg, Werner 1
helplessness (*hilflosigkeit*) 44, 88, 106, 107-8, 109
  and cruelty 110, 117
  religion 142
Henry, Michel
  critique of Freud 183-4
  and life in itself 183
Hinshelwood, Robert 43, 48, 51, 70, 189
holistic psychotherapy 3
homeostasis 85, 116, 117
  law of constancy 15, 19-20
  and tension increase 9, 22-3, 64
human nature
  'goodness' of as evil illusion 13
  humanity and inhumanity 151, 195
humanistic psychotherapy 143, 152, 154, 195
humour 133-5
hypochondria 93
hysteria 17

iconography 153
id 16, 30, 81
idealization 39-40
identifications 76-7
  narcissistic and alienating 78, 176
  see also projective identifications
identity
  sense of 77
  dissociation 119
  see also ego
ideographs 61
imaginary register 74, 100-1, 161
  illusionizing the world 79, 157-9, 165
  lack of 80
impingement 25
incest 152, 164, 196
independent tradition 24, 25-6, 46, 128, 137, 181, 188
indeterminacy 1

individuation 119, 125, 131, 141
infant
  and background object 139-40
  fear of dying 29
  as *jouissance* for the mother 92
  nameless dread 55
  original organic incoherence 74-5
  various separations 91
  as unwanted 80
  see also birth; breast; child; mirror stage; mother; Oedipus complex
information flow 174
initiation 121-4
  in adolescence 121-9, 194;
  as brutal 121-2
  death as 121-4, 151-2
  psychoanalysis as 123-4
injustice 26, 27
instinct theory
  conservative trend 11
  for evolution 12
  Freud 7-16
  fusion and defusion 11, 13-14, 16
  for mastery 11
  self-preservative 12
  term, 'instincts' or 'drives' 187
  see also death drive; Eros (life instinct); sexual instinct
instinctual representative 18
integration/integrity 31, 64
intellectuals 149
International Psychoanalytical Association 73, 171
interpretation, deep 46, 47, 182
introjection 31, 38, 42, 54-5, 57
  greedy 36
Irigaray, Luce 166
Isaacs, Susan 47-8, 55

Jameson, Frederic 167
  postmodernity as labyrinth 173
jealousy 75
Jencks, C. 167
Jones, Ernest 189
Jones, R. 130
jouissance 78, 79, 83, 84, 92, 191, 195
  alien 90
  and the feminine 162
  for the mother 92
  permanent 174
Jung, Carl 141-2, 194
  and death drive 120

on dreams 120-1, 130
and psychic energy 13, 187

Kafka, Franz 2, 191
Kant, Emanuel 9
Kennard, David and Small, Neil 194
Kerr, John 112
Kierkegaard, Soren 2
Klein, Arthur 50
Klein, Melanie 4, 15, 29-51
  life and losses 49-51
  annihilation anxiety 29
  combined parent object 41, 88
  and countertransference 187-8
  depressive position 41-4, 47
  envy 36-9, 46, (and death drive 35, 36, 53),
  (defences against 39-41)
  more than breast 44-5
  mourning 42-3
  paranoid-schizoid position 35-9, 41-2
  part objects 33-4
  projection and the talion principle 34-6
  reparation 42
  splitting, primitive 31-2
  superego 32-3
  theology 45
  'Envy and gratitude' 3 7, 39
  'On the development of mental functioning' 30-1
  The Psychoanalysis of Children 29, critique of 45-9, 69-71
Kleinian analysis
  goal 46, 51, 70-1
  critique of 45-9, 69-71
  shift to affects 47
Kojève, A. 86, 168
Kristeva, Julia 194, 195-6

Lacan, Jacques 5, 73-102, 189
  aggression not biological 78
  critique of Klein 47
  death drive 84-6, (as terminal freedom 94-6)
  desire of the other 81-2, 90-1, 179
  divided subject 82-6
  doomed ego 77-9
  emphasis on the father 98-100, 193
  empty/full speech 82
  foreclosure 96-100, 102
  IPA opposition 73, 171
  jouissance 78
  mirror stage 75-7

  objet a 91-3
  Oedipus 80, 86, 192
  passion for the negative 94, 144
  paternal metaphor and alpha function 100-1, 144
  as phallocentric 159- 62
  the real 86-91, 144
  seduction of psychoanalysis 171, 181
  social adaptation 175
  symbolic register 79-81
  the unconscious 188, 194
  on woman 162
  Encore 162
  The Ethics of Psychoanalysis 94, 179
  'La Famille' 74
  The Formations of the Unconscious 79-80
  The Four Fundamental Concepts of Psychoanalysis 87
  On Anxiety 90, 172, 193
  Stade du miroir 76
  Lacanian vs. Object Relations theory 115-16
lack (béance) 74, 85
  in the subject 83, 90
language 2, 79-82
  as afterthought 81
  and the beyond 84
  biochemical 115
  death in 86
  as full of holes 82
  and the law 81, 83
  and meaning 81
  Other 79, 81-2
  as phallic 162
  subject to splitting attacks 58-61
  and the Symbolic 61, 80
Laplanche, Jean 17, 89
  seduction theory 88
  with J.- B. Pontalis,
  The Language of Psychoanalysis 16, 18, 19-20, 20-11, 83
laughter 133-5
Leclaire Serge 84, 97-8, 195
Lemaire, Anika 84, 97-8
Levi, Primo 148
Lévi-Strauss, Claude Elementary Structures of Kinship 161, 191
Lewin, B. 130
libido: 11-12, 13, 187
  ego- 7-8
  as masculine 159
  object- 7-8
life

alone is one 183-4
anti-entropic 103
biologically requires death 104-5
origin 104
returns to death 86
life instinct
see Eros
libido
light, perception of 2
linkage and links 58, 65
broken 58
destroyed 61
impregnated with cruelty 61
mouth-nipple 55-6, 61
penis-vagina 61
Little, Margaret 128, 178
loneliness 45
loss/es / separation/s
irretrievable 85
Klein's personal 49-51
lost object 91-3
realization of 41-5
successive 91
summation 83
love
of God 141
and hate 15
and narcissism 7
stifled 40
wish to 64

Macey, David 191, 195
manic defence 42
Marx, Karl 149-50, 191, 195
masculine
as fragile 165-6, 195
phallic power 159-64
as productivity, growth and power 166
masochism 12, 14-15, 79-80
moral 14
primary 14
and the whip 80
maternal imago 74
Mauss, Marcel 149-50, 191
May, Rollo 135
McDougall, Joyce 190
McEwan, Ian 146-7
méconnaissanc 77, 187
melancholia 14, 16, 43-4
see also depressive position; mourning
Melman, Charles 91-3, 100
Meltzer, Donald 45, 188
menstruation 121-2

Merdin, Paul 145-6
metaphysics 2, 154
metazoa 21
and sexual differentiation 16
metonym 93
Miller, Alice 26
Milner, Marion 128, 136
mirror stage 187
erect (phallic) form 161
and origin of aggression 75-7, 78, 102
and paranoid-schizoid position 78
Mitchell, Juliet 169
modernity 5-6, 150, 151, 167
morality
in analysis 180
evasion of 27-8, 187
excess 190
see also ethics; superego
Moriarty, John 146
mother
chora 165, 195
contains the father's penis 40-1
desire of 164
maternal imago 74
and non-violent suicides 74
power 74, 171
relations with infant 35, 53-4, 92, 100, (*jouissance* 92), (reverie 53-7, 101, 125-6), (and child's desire to sleep and return to non-being 74, 101
see also breast; Oedipus complex
mourning 42-3, 196
mysticism 146
mythology/myths 3, 25, 119

names as signifiers 82
see also father, 'Name-of-the'
narcissism 7, 15
and chora 195-6
cold 172-3
destructive 40, 78
negative 109
necrosis 112
negation/negative 94, 97, 144
negative narcissism 109
Nietzsche, Friedrich 2, 134-5, 149, 185
nightmares 9, 90, 129
Nirvana principle 15, 19-20, 22

'O'
ultimate reality 67-9, 190
ultimate truth 130, 132

objects
    background 139-40
    bad 140
    bizarre 60-3
    damaged 39-40, 42
    dead within oneself 43-4
    de-differentiation 128-9
    of desire 92
    excess 92
    good 31-4, 36-40, 42
    internal and external 42-4
    lost 91-3
    part 33-4
    whole 33
object relations 18, 25, 38, 115-16, 188
object relations theory 115, 192
    and concept of evil 28
    vs. *Lacanian* 115-16, 192
obje*t*a 5, 153
    and addiction 92-3
    and psychosis 92
    and the symbolic 91-2, 93
obscenity 171
    black/white 164-5
    linguistic 36
obsession 93
oceanic feeling 140, 142
Oedipus 171-2
    and tragedy 193
Oedipus at Colonus 80, 86
Oedipus complex 22, 31-2, 40-1, 146-7, 152-3
    dissolution of 15, 31, 73
    guilt in 15
    for *Lacan* 83, 192
Oedipus Rex 193
omnipotence
    analysand's 177
    analyst's 67
    and dreams 131, 132
    of ego 79, 140
    fantasies 71
    forsaking 22
    illusion 110
    narcissistic 140
    religious 143
    and technology 109
organism
    desires its own death 11-12
    and immortality 116, 118
    reproduction 21-2
Other/Otherness 79, 81-2, 83, 132-3, 191
    desire of the 90-1

God as 195
jouissance in 90
language 79, 81-2, 90
no, 195
of the Other 175
Other scene (unconscious) 132-3, 191
removed by the code 166-7

paranoia 37, 42
    gaze and voice unveiled 93
paranoid-schizoid position 35-9, 41-2, 68, 106
    and mirror stage 78
    Ps<—>D interaction 68, 83
part objects 33-4
particles/waves 1-2
paternal metaphor (Name-of-the-father) 98-101, 102, 152-3
    and alpha-function failure 100-1
pathogenic idea 18
patience 67
patriarchy, brutality of 26
penis 159
    envy 15, 41
    see also phallus
perfection
    and envy 44-5
    impulsion towards 12
persecution/persecutors 25, 31, 34-6, 37, 39, 106
perversion 79-80, 110
phallocentrism 143
    as denial of the chora 195
phallus
    in fashions 163-4
    psychoanalytic notion of power of 159-64
phantasy, primacy of 26-7, 169
    unconscious 29, 46, 47-8, 168-9
Phillips, Adam 28, 178, 181, 193
phobia 92
phylogenesis 187
placenta 91
    placental parasite 107-8
Plant, Sadie
    critique of *Baudrillard* 166
Plato 56, 188, 189
play
    child's 8-9, 75
    psychotherapeutic capacity to 128
    see also games
pleasure principle 8, 10-11, 92
    place of 19-21

pluralism 167
pornography 111
postmodernity 150, 165, 167
   as labyrinth 149, 173
power 164
   of choice 95
   female 195
   maternal 74, 171
   originary 184
   phallic 159-64
   of the symbolic 151
prayer 138-41
prayer-couple 141
preconception 56
predator/prey response 29, 105-6, 107
primal/primary repression 83-4, 89, 169, 195-6
   no signifiers 98, 169
primal scene 88
primitive cultures
   death 155-6
   initiation rites 121-2
   and the symbolic 151-3, 195
production/productivity
   in analysis 169-70, 175, 181
   masculine 156, 166
   phallic 6, 159
   system of 153, 157-8, 159
projection 26-7, 31
   destructive 36, 53-4
   origin 10, 88
   and talion principle 34-6
projective identification 36
   abnormal and violent 58-60
   container/contained relationship 54-5, 65-7
   normal 57
projective processes
   and language 36
protista
   and immortality 21-2, 116, 118
proto-mind 69, 71
PS<—>D interaction 68, 83
psychoanalysis 26-7, 190
   abandonment of seduction theory 6, 168-71
   acceptance/tolerance 27-8
   as act of freedom 127
   classical 6, 48, 169, 170, 171
   and countertransference 187- 7
   and cure 192- 3
   and death drive 1, 2-3
   disappearance of 169-72

   disappointment 175
   the encounter with deadness 176-7
   and ethics 94, 192-3
   as failed encounter 90
   as faith 67, 69
   and God 133
   grace 27
   as initiation 123-5
   interpretation 46, 182
   Kleinian 45-9, 51, 69-72, 179
   naming malignancy 179
   neutrality 27-8, 187
   and potential space 141, 175-6, 178, 189
   and prayer 141
   as probe 66-7, 69
   the production of meaning 168, 169-70, 177, 182
   security 67, 169
   short sessions 73, 171
   silence 171
   transference 57, 175-6, 178, 181, (resistance 125, 140, interpretation of 46)
   term 3
   work of 170-1, 175
   see also psychoanalyst; psychotherapy
psychoanalyst 70-1
   attitude 123-4
   as expert who knows 175, 179
   and own family 65-6
   with hallucinatory patient 62-7
   as mother 178, 180
   patience 67, 177
   power 46
   role 65-7
   resistance of 68, 180
   speech 176
   suffering 141
   tolerates Ps anxieties 67-8, 70
   training 73, 190
   'without memory, desire or understanding' 65, 123
   as witness 53, 148
   see also psychoanalysis; psychoanalytic relationship
psychoanalytic relationship
   as commensual 66
   and envy 39-40
   parasitic 66, 177
   psychotic 65
   symbiotic 66
   as symbolic exchange 183
psychosis 92, 96-100

    as anti-life process 64
    onset 99
    post-puerperal 92
    and the unmediated real 100, 102
    see also psychotic
psychotherapy 27-8, 119, 126, 143
    holistic 3
    humanistic 143, 152, 195
    negative reaction 14, 80
    play 128
    professionalization 196
psychotic
    analyst as 67
    core 48, 60, 64, 70, 125-6
    destroys perception 63
    destroys source of pain 69
    destroys thinking 60-2
    and dreaming 132
    mind 60, 189
    patients 61-2, 120, 129, 181-2;
    processes 4-5, 58, 64, 65

Raff, Martin 113
Rank, Otto 107
Rayner, Eric 3, 128, 177
real, the/reality 5, 86-91
    beyond 91, 143
    beyond the dream 89-90
    challenge to 185
    and lost object 91
    principle 62
    as trauma 87
    ultimate ('O')
    probing 66-9, 190
    unassimilable 87, 185
realisation
    depressive 42, 62, 64
    positive/negative 56
    of the world 158-9
rebirth 119-21
redemption 5, 143
registers, three
    see imaginary, real, symbolic
registration in unconscious (*Niederschrift*)
    18-19
regression
    benign 25
    creative 120, 122-8, 131-2
    danger for the psychotic 126, 129
    destructive 124, 126
    in dreams 130-2
    forced 121
    incestuous 164

    in life 120
    and phantasy 47-8
    propensity 13
Reich, Wilhelm 26
Reizes, Moriz 49
religion 4, 119, 190
    and Freud 142-3, 190
    as good object 140
    prayer 138-41
    private 141-2
    psychotherapy as 28, 143
    the sacred 127
remainder, beyond representation 89-90,
    91, 143
reparation 42
repetition compulsion
    Bion 69
    Freud 8-11, 13-14, 20
    Lacan 81, 142-4
repression 125
    failure of 89
    impossible 61-2
    instinctual 12
    primal/primary 17-19, 89
    return of the repressed 18-19
    secondary 18
repudiation 96
resistance 140
responsibility 27
resurrection 119
revenge, symbolic 150
reverie 53-7, 101, 125-6
reversibility
    seductive 159
    symbolic 150-1, 195
Richardson, W. 133
Rieff, Paul 141-2
ritual 127
    baptism 152
    exorcism 195
    initiation 121-3, 194
    sacrifice 153
Rojek, C., and Turner B. 149
Rolland, Romain
    and *Freud* 142-3
Rosenfeld, Herbert 40, 109, 127
Roustang, François 144, 171
Rutherford, Ernest 1
Rycroft, Charles 123

sacred, the 127
sacrifice, ritual 153
sadism 12, 25, 32, 53

anal-sadistic stage 110
Samuels, A., Shorter B. and Plant F. 120
schizophrenia 53
  basic psychopathology 38, 58-62
  see also paranoid-schizoid position
Schmideberg, Melitta 50, 188
Schopenhauer, Artur 21, 145
Schreber case history 18, 93, 96-7
science 151, 158
  progress 1-2, 3
Sebeok, Thomas 158
security, psychoanalytical 67, 169
seduction 159-60
  as challenge to the real 88-91
  cool 6, 164-7
  and cybernetic control 166
  hot 165, 168
  infantile 168-9
  primal 5, 87-9, 192
  of psychoanalysis 171, 181
  repudiation of 169-70
  symbolic 150-1
Segal, Hanna 44-5
self
  and catastrophe 68
  de-differentiation from object 128-9
  and ego 125, 194
  greater 139
  not pre-given 115
  see also ego; identity
self-love
  see narcissism
semiotic code 150, 151, 158
sense organs, expulsion through 63
separation
  see loss
sexual abuse 87, 192
sexual instinct 7-8
  see also libido
sexuality
  and death 17, 21-2
  in evolution 21-2, 83, 118
  genetic difference 116, 118
  and narcissism 7
  union 15-16
  see also femininity; masculine
signifier/s 2
  in analysis 191-2
  archaic ideas 188
  bar 80-1, 192
  broken chain of 80-1
  enigmatic 88
  in genetic code 158

  lack of 83
  law of 82
  phallus the major 159-60, 163
  treasure-house of 81
Smith, Joseph 19, 163
social action 152
social adaptation 77, 175
social conservatism 27
social relations 115, 151-2
  antisocial tendency 24
somatic zones 23
Sophocles
  Antigone 94
  Oedipus at Colonus 80, 86;
  Oedipus Rex 193
space
  analytic 141, 175-6, 178, 189
  astronomy 146
  exchange 191
  prayer 141
  psychic 129
speech
  of analyst 176
  empty or full 82
  exchange 191
  for psychotics 99-100
  splitting 35
  and cancerous growth 112-16
  excessive due to envy 39
  as against foreclosure 96-101
  schizophrenic 58-62
  secondary 64
stammering 66
Steiner, George 2
stimuli 23
  excessive 9-10, 17-19, 27
  internal, projected into outside world 9, 10, 27
  and primal repression 17-19
  protection against 9-10, 87-8
Storr, Anthony 24
Strachey, James 176, 187
subject
  abolition 79-80
  human, and cells in relation to death 115-16
  no interiority 167-8
  lacks in 83, 90
  and language 79- 82, 102
  split or divided 82-6
  as unstrung 93
  see also ego
subjectivity 74, 115, 116-17, 166, 193

creative 82
sublimation 189
suffering
    abundance 148
    alleviation 143-4
    in analysis 141
    attachment to 14-15
    inflicted from without 26-7, 69
    seen as inevitable 27
    see also catastrophe
suicide 50, 64, 78, 80
    adolescent 122
    cellular 116
    non-violent 74, 75
    tragic 94-6, 193
superabundance 44
superego
    as culture of the death instinct 14, 32
    early development 31-3, 190
    heir to Oedipus complex 15, 31-2
    murderous 179
    as 'psychotic enclave' 89
    sadistic 14, 15, 73
suppression 7
    see also repression
symbolic exchange 5, 150-3, 156
    in analysis 98-101
symbolic register 79-81, 102, 191-2
    abolition 79-80
    castration 83, 100, 161, 192
    catastrophe 173-4
    as culture of the death instinct 107
    the dead father 102, 193
    and death drive 85
    as masculine 162
    and *objet a* 91-3
    and seduction 150-1
    and social action 152
    symbolism 191
    in *Jones* 189
    reversibility 150-1, 159
symbolization 88
    requirements for 56, 61-2
Symington, Neville
    and the act of freedom 177

taboo 110, 196
talion principle 34, 47
Tanner, Michael 149
technology 158, 172
    and omnipotence 109
Thanatos
    see death drive

therapy
    see psychotherapy
Thing-in-itself 111, 188
thinking
    and depressive position 62
    developmental history of a thought 56, 189
    embryonic 55
    primary process 56
    theory of 55-6, 188-9
    thoughts without a thinker 89
    unconscious 56, 57, 122
Tillich, Paul 27, 190
time
    fragmentation 108
    historical/primordial 122-3, 127-8, 129
    notion of 9
torus 86
tragedy 94-6, 193
transcendental 120, 142
transference,
    in analysis 57, 175-6, 178
    counter- 38, 68, 177, 187-8
    resistance, interpretation of 46
    and seduction 181
transformations, in 'K' and 'O' 67, 189
traumas 87, 88
    birth 107-8
    sexual 17, 169
    traumatic neuroses 9, 17-19
Trieb 187
truth 71, 123-4
    and laughter 134-5
    food for the mind 124
    universal 130-2
Turkle, Sherry 73

uncertainty
    fear of 109-10
uncertainty principle 1
ultimate reality ('O') 67-9, 190
unconscious, the 167-8, 194
    affective 30, 188
    beginning of creation 122-3, 194
    child's 30
    collective 187
    counsel of 141
    and dreams 130-1
    Freudian 2, 16-18, 170, 188
    Lacan's v Klein's 167-8, 188
    as life itself 183
    location 132-3
    as myriad consciousnesses 130-1

in psychoanalysis 170-1
structured like language 191
and thinking 56, 57, 122
timelessness of 9
as unrepressed 194
unconscious phantasy 29, 46
and instinct 55-6
prior to language 47-8
sexual 168-9
unicellular organisms 21
see also protista
Upanishads, The 143

Vaillant, G. 135
vesicle 9-13, 87-8
violence 25, 26-7, 75, 91
in children 32
justification 180
paranoid 37
of pleasure *see jouissance*
seduction 166
social 156
today 106-7, 166
void 89, 91, 144-8
primitive 84
Vorstellungen 188
fail 143

Wallon 108
war 2, 9, 12, 22, 26, 146-7
Watson, James, and Francis Crick 103
Weatherill, Rob 40, 48, 106, 194
Weber, Max 191
Weismann, August 21
Whitmont, E. 119, 141
whole person 33
wholeness 74-5, 121, 142
Williams, Harry 139
Winnicott, Donald 27, 107, 132, 175, 177, 181, 192
against the death drive 24-5
the capacity to play 128, 182-3
the mother as mirror 75, 77
and non-communication 182-3
on writing 136
'Wolf-Man' (*Freud's* patient) 96, 97, 169
women
and castration 192
female body 163-4
as not one 162
see also femininity; mother
World War I 2, 9, 12
writing

and the turmoil of PS<-->D 135-8

Young, Robert 167

Zarathustra 134-5
zero state 15, 64, 84
Zetzel, E. 179
zones, somatic 23